Huldah

Huldah

The Prophet Who Wrote Hebrew Scripture

PRESTON KAVANAGH

PICKWICK *Publications* · Eugene, Oregon

HULDAH
The Prophet Who Wrote Hebrew Scripture

Pickwick Publications
An Imprint of Wipf and Stock Publishers
199 W. 8th Ave., Suite 3
Eugene, OR 97401

www.wipfandstock.com

ISBN 13: 978-1-61097-195-9

Cataloguing-in-Publication data:

Kavanagh, Preston.

Huldah : the prophet who wrote Hebrew scripture / Preston Kavanagh.

xx + 202 pp. ; 23 cm. Includes bibliographical references and indexes.

ISBN 13: 978-1-61097-195-9

1. Huldah (Biblical prophetess). 2. Bible. O.T.—Authorship. 3. Women prophets. 4. Women in the Bible. 5. Ciphers in the Bible. I. Title.

BS1197 K3951 2012

Manufactured in the U.S.A.

This biography of Scripture's Huldah is dedicated to Marilyn Peterson Hollinshead—family friend, mentor to authors, and granddaughter of Hulda. It was Marilyn who first suggested that I write a book about Huldah the female prophet, who has turned out to be one of the most influential women of antiquity. Thank you, Marilyn.

Contents

Figures and Tables

FIGURES

TABLES

Figures and Tables

Acknowledgments

I AM GRATEFUL TO K. C. Hanson, editor-in-chief at Wipf and Stock, for his wisdom and for his advice on how best to introduce new ideas to others who work in biblical studies. I appreciate the exacting care of Barbara Oldroyd in chasing error and inconsistency from the *Huldah* text. And I thank John Page, president of Multimedia Communications International, for his global comprehension of the digital techniques required first to find and then to record those who wrote Hebrew Scripture.

Abbreviations

ABD	*Anchor Bible Dictionary.* 6 vols. Edited by David Noel Freedman. New York: Doubleday, 1992
ANE	Ancient Near East
Ant	Josephus *Antiquities*
AOAT	Alter Orient und Altes Testament
BAR	*Biblical Archaeology Review*
BASOR	*Bulletin of the American Schools of Oriental Research*
BCE	Before Common Era
BDB	*The New Brown-Driver-Briggs-Gesenius Hebrew and English Lexicon.* Francis Brown et al. Peabody, MA: Hendrickson, 1979
Bib	*Biblica*
c	circa
DH	Deuteronomistic History
Dtr	Deuteronomistic Historian, seventh century
E	English
EncJud	*Encyclopaedia Judaica.* Corrected edition. 17 vols. Edited by Cecil Roth and Geoffrey Wigoder. Jerusalem: Keter, 1972
H	Hebrew
HS	Hebrew Scripture

IDB	*Interpreter's Dictionary of the Bible.* 4 vols. Edited by George A. Buttrick. Nashville: Abingdon, 1962
J Source	Yahwist Source
JBL	*Journal of Biblical Literature*
JSB	*Jewish Study Bible.* Edited by Adele Berlin and Marc Zvi Brettler. Oxford: Oxford University Press, 2004
Meg	*Megillah* tractate of Babylonian Talmud
MT	Masoretic Text
NCBC	New Century Bible Commentary
NRSV	New Revised Standard Version of the Bible
OT	Old Testament
P Source	Priestly Source
RSV	Revised Standard Version of the Bible
WBC	*Women's Bible Commentary.* Expanded ed. Edited by Carol A. Newsom and Sharon H. Ringe. Louisville: Westminster John Knox, 1998

Glossary

Anagrams—Anagrams used some or all the letters within Hebrew text words to spell hidden names. Letter sequence was ignored and athbash variations of names were regularly employed. For example, "whoring," as frequently used by Ezekiel, contains an anagram of "Huldah." See Kavanagh, *The Exilic Code*, 21–27.

Athbash—Athbash generates twenty-one other ways to spell any Hebrew word. It divides the Hebrew alphabet in half to form facing rows of letters. Eleven letters run right-to-left; the other eleven run left-to-right. Next, tractor-tread rotation changes the interfaces, allowing the parallel rows of letters (with one adjustment) to generate twenty-one new ways to spell a name. Athbash is discussed more fully in Kavanagh, *Secrets of the Jewish Exile*, 198–205.

Chi-squares—A frequently used statistical calculation that this book employs to test how well groups of anagrams or coded spellings in a passage (usually a chapter) match their frequency in the remainder of Scripture. The answer is given in probability of occurrence. See *Statistically Significant*.

Coded Spelling—Encoded spellings use one—and only one—letter from consecutive text words to spell a name. A five-letter name would borrow a letter from five Hebrew text words in a row. Letters chosen could fall in any sequence. Kavanagh, *The Exilic Code*, 6–13, discusses this further.

Deuteronomistic Historian, Dtr—A person or group that, in 1943, Martin Noth said wrote and/or rewrote the Former Prophets, from Deuteronomy 5 through Second Kings. Scholars have been unable to identify the authors, but chapter 7 does so. The Dtr group includes Micaiah, Daniel, Huldah, Jacob, and Ezra.

Glossary

Deuteronomistic History—DH includes Deuteronomy 5–28, Joshua, Judges, First Samuel, Second Samuel, First Kings, and Second Kings.

Diaspora—Refers to Jews living outside of Israel during and after the sixth century BCE.

Exile—Refers to the 597–539 BCE period, when the Babylonians exiled the members of the upper levels of Judean society.

Ezra, Priestly Source—Kavanagh, *The Shaphan Group*, pages 23–44, uses anagrams to establish that Ezra the scribe and priest was author of the Priestly Source (P Source). He worked during the late monarchy and early Exile rather than during the Restoration period, and he consistently supported Huldah.

Group of Coded Spellings—Group is defined as a statistically significant concentration of the same coded spelling within a single chapter. Spellings within a group range from one to close to one hundred. Counting groups is a handy way to compare the coding strength of different names within a chapter or book. The completed calibration of Jewish personal names against Scripture produces 1.7 million groups.

J Source—The J Source was a person or group who worked during the ninth century BCE and was among the first to write Hebrew Scripture. Some of the coded spellings mentioned in this book may help identify that source. Several of David's sons, including Shephatiah and Solomon, are suspects.

Jacob, Second Isaiah—Second Isaiah is thought to have written Isaiah 40–55. His true name was Jacob (see Kavanagh, *The Exilic Code*, 62–84) and his father's name was probably Isaac. Jacob worked closely with Huldah and defended her in the book of Proverbs.

Micaiah—Micaiah the scribe was the son of Gemariah and the grandson of Shaphan. Micaiah served in the court of King Jehoiakim and was presumably exiled to Babylon in 597 BCE. Encoded spellings of Micaiah's name in the DH outnumber all others, making him the best candidate for leader of the Dtr group.

Shaphan, Shaphan Group—Shaphan was secretary to King Josiah and leader of a group of scholars (including Huldah) who, during the late monarchy and early Exile, wrote much of Scripture.

Statistically Significant—Statistical significance addresses the probability of occurrence, with above .001 being the point of exclusion. Significance grows with rarity. Groups of encodings or anagrams are generally the things so measured.

Word Links—A Word Link connects two passages that have in their texts the same unique batch of words. That particular batch will appear nowhere else in Scripture except in those two passages. (See Kavanagh, *The Exilic Code*, 62–84.) *Huldah* mentions Word Links but does not apply them.

Zoar—Moabite city on the southeastern edge of the Dead Sea where Huldah sought refuge about 573 BCE, after the defeat at Jerusalem.

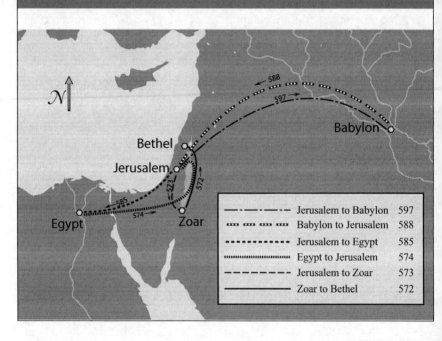

Huldah's Travels
597 – 572 BCE

N

Babylon

Bethel

Jerusalem

Egypt

Zoar

— · — · — · —	Jerusalem to Babylon	597
▬▬ ▬▬ ▬▬ ▬▬	Babylon to Jerusalem	588
▪▪▪▪▪▪▪▪▪▪▪▪	Jerusalem to Egypt	585
▬▬▬▬▬▬▬▬▬▬	Egypt to Jerusalem	574
– – – – – –	Jerusalem to Zoar	573
────────	Zoar to Bethel	572

Huldah's Life
640 – 564 BCE

Huldah in:	BCE	Events
	640	**640** – Born in Jerusalem
	639	
	638	
	637	
	636	
	635	
	634	
	633	
	632	
	631	
	630	
	629	
	628	
	627	
	626	
	625	
	624	
	623	
Judah	622	**622** – As prophet, interprets temple scroll
	621	
	620	
	619	
	618	
	617	
	616	
	615	**615** – Marries Jehoiakim, bears Jehoiachin
	614	
	613	
	612	
	611	
	610	
	609	**609** – Becomes queen
	608	
	607	
	606	
	605	
	604	**604** – Sees king burn Jeremiah's text
	603	
	602	
	601	
	600	
	599	
	598	
	597	**597** – As queen mother, exiled to Babylon
	596	
	595	
	594	
	593	
Babylon	592	**592** – As elder, calls on prophet Ezekiel
	591	
	590	
	589	
	588	
	587	
Judah	586	**586** – To Jerusalem, siege, to Mizpah, then Egypt
	585	
	584	
	583	
	582	
Egypt	581	
	580	
	579	
	578	
	577	
Wilderness	576	**576** – Hires Cyrus
	575	
Judah	574	
Zoar	573	**573** – Campaign fails, to Zoar
	572	**572** – Flees to Bethel
	571	
	570	
	569	
Bethel	568	
	567	
	566	
	565	
	564	**564** – Dies at Bethel

1

New Techniques Highlight Huldah

THIS BOOK SEEKS TO measure—for the first time ever—the extraordinary impact of Huldah the prophetess upon Hebrew Scripture. The book will cite entire chapters of Scripture that Huldah wrote. In difficult times, she overcame high barriers to women. She helped shape Israel's history and was a principle author of Hebrew Scripture. As such, she added to God's Word a feminine aspect that has inspired numberless believers—men and women alike. After reading these pages, many readers will be able to affirm that Huldah is among the most influential women in human history.

This text will rely upon athbash, anagrams, probabilities, and coded spellings to reason that Huldah first became the wife of Judah's King Jehoiakim and then queen mother to Jehoiachin, her son, who succeeded his father, Jehoiakim, on the throne. After 597 BCE, when the Babylonians exiled her and young Jehoiachin, Huldah served as elder, author, advisor, merchant, prophet, priestess, and commanding general. As queen mother—even in exile—Huldah became head of the Asherah cult, something that deeply offended former colleagues who were exclusively monotheistic (twenty years before, Huldah's prophesies had helped accomplish the Josiah-era reforms. These centralized Yahweh's worship at Jerusalem, excluded other deities from Solomon's temple, and destroyed older worship sites).

Huldah's Asherah relationship, and particularly her leadership in a disastrous military adventure drew savage criticism. Anagrams and coding were basic tools employed by those who wrote Scripture. Using these, her more extreme opponents equated her with Jezebel and the "loose woman" of Proverbs. In the books of Kings alone, they fashioned twenty-one demeaning Huldah anagrams from "caused to sin." Ezekiel matched that total of Huldah insults with variants of "whoring" in just *two* of his chapters (16 and 23). In Judges 9, critics reached the depths when they attached the name Huldah to the raping of the Levite's concubine and the grisly dismembering of her body. Given the tenor of this criticism, one must conclude that another of Huldah's faults was that her gender was female. Understanding the totality of this animus helps us to grasp the life setting of the scores of OT chapters that conceal significant numbers of Huldah signatures.[1]

Huldah was an extraordinary writer—arguably she ranks with Second Isaiah as the best in Hebrew Scripture. For example, she probably penned: "How the mighty have fallen!," "I have escaped by the skin of my teeth," and "Let us make humankind in our image."[2] Other verses by her that kindle the spirit are: "Your people shall be my people, and your God my God"; "As soon as the people heard the sound of the trumpets, they raised a great shout, and the wall fell down flat"; and "After the earthquake a fire, but the LORD was not in the fire; and after the fire a sound of sheer silence."[3] Also, Huldah is both the personified Wisdom and the Good Wife of the book of Proverbs.[4] Further, what appear to be her own writings about Deborah, Abigail, Bathsheba, Tamar, and Rebecca almost certainly conceal autobiographical elements.[5] Later chapters will consider these.

Scripture-wide computer searches indicate that Huldah had astounding versatility. She is represented in the Pentateuch, Prophets, and Writings. Numbers, Joshua, Ezekiel, Daniel, Psalms, and Proverbs each contain unusual (i.e., statistically significant) masses of coded names like Huldah-the-prophetess and Huldah-the-queen-mother. Still, coding does not guarantee authorship. Others could and did write about or against her. We know already, for example, that Ezekiel filled several of his own chapters with Huldah anagrams simply to target his attacks. Those chapters were not written *by* Huldah but rather *about* her. Also, a book like Proverbs, which is favorable to Huldah, might not have been written during

1. See appendix 1 for a list of 1,773 Huldah anagrams.

2. 2 Sam 1:19; Job 19:20; Gen 1:26.

3. Ruth 1:16; Josh 6:20; 1 Kgs 19:24.

4. The references for Wisdom are Prov 1:20–33 and Proverbs 8; the reference for the Good Wife is Prov 31:10–31.

5. The reference for Deborah is Judges 5. References for Abigail are 1 Sam 25:14, 18; 27:3; 30:15; 2 Sam 2:2; and 1 Chr 2:16 and 17. The reference for Bathsheba is 1 Kings 1. For Tamar, it is Genesis 38, and for Rebecca, Genesis 24.

her lifetime. Instead, it might have consisted of remembrances by Huldah's followers or word-of-mouth traditions passed between generations.[6] A further word of caution: a previous study of coded names shows that Huldah worked with a group of fourteen others. They were led by Shaphan, King Josiah's Secretary.[7] A majority of Shaphan-group members seem to have collaborated on composing much of the Psaltery, though psalm-by-psalm coding shows that Huldah frequently participated. The same pattern appears in the books of Joshua and Proverbs and, to a lesser extent, in Numbers and Daniel. Though biblical authors apparently worked in teams, we still shall be able to link Huldah herself to specific words, verses, passages, and often whole chapters of Scripture. This book devotes itself to chronicling those achievements.

And what can this mean to feminist scholars? They need a champion and Huldah provides a superb one. Moreover, in years ahead scholars quite possibly will place Huldah the Hebrew prophet alongside the very greatest women of antiquity.

NEW TIMES, NEW DISCOVERIES, ACTUAL FACTS

Readers may wonder why the accomplishments of this extraordinary woman are, after twenty-five centuries, suddenly coming to light. The answers lie in the fields of archaeology, biblical studies, computers, and probability. The Dead Sea Scrolls prove that one can rely, in good measure, upon the wording of the MT. Cumulative scholarly advances now lead biblical students to ask better-informed questions of that text. Computers prodigiously collect answers to those questions. And modern probabilities allow one to wade through the answers.

Here is how this writer, for one, has benefitted from these advances. Though seminary-trained, I had worked for years at a large utility company, and in 1985 happened upon the likely identity of Second Isaiah. Deciding to switch careers, I arranged early retirement, bought a computer, brushed up on Hebrew, and commissioned a search program. For the past quarter century, working almost every day, I have sought to identify the authors of Scripture. Mostly, I did the tedious labor that seems always and everywhere to consume the scholar's day. But as the years passed, I did find things. In rough sequence of discovery, they are:

6. However, massive coding of Shaphan-group names proves that Proverbs was written during Huldah's lifetime. See Kavanagh, *The Shaphan Group*, 120–21.

7. Ibid., 111.

- Second Isaiah's name was Jacob.
- Scripture teems with coded spellings.
- Athbash generates added ways to spell an encoded name.
- Ezra's proper era is the Exile rather than the Restoration.
- Word Links is a simplified word association technique.
- Babylon executed Judah's leaders as substitute kings.
- Ezekiel, who was the Suffering Servant, perished as a substitute king.
- The synoptic gospels portray Jesus as a substitute king.
- King Jehoiachin died in Babylon as a substitute king.
- The Priestly Benediction is about Jehoiachin.
- Daniel was a real biblical person, not a mythical figure.
- Biblical writers extensively used anagrams.
- A catastrophic Cyrus-led revolt marked the nadir of the Exile.
- Asaiah helped to lead that revolt.
- The rebels took Jerusalem and held it for a time.
- The author of the P Source was Ezra.
- The brothers Ezra and Jozadak contended for the chief priesthood.
- The Shaphan group authored hundreds of chapters of Scripture.
- Huldah was a dominant figure during the late monarchy and early Exile.
- Daniel, Jacob, Asaiah, Micaiah, Azariah, and Huldah led the Dtr group.

Among all these discoveries, the most significant findings may be how Scripture's authors identified themselves. They used two methods. The first is the anagram. To form anagrams, biblical writers used some or all the letters within a single text word to spell a hidden name. Letter sequence was ignored.[8] An example in English is carthorse, which is an anagram of "orchestra." In Hebrew, an anagram of חלדה, Huldah, is contained within החלד, "weasel" (Lev 11:29), which could not have been a compliment. Any literate teenager in ancient Israel could have quickly mastered anagram composition.

8. For more on anagrams, see Kavanagh, *Secrets of the Jewish Exile*, 207; *The Exilic Code*, 21–27; and *The Shaphan Group*, 23–26.

The second method of identification, while also simple, required more of both art and training. This is termed "coded spellings." Coded spellings require one—and only one—letter from consecutive text words to spell a name. A five-letter name would draw upon five Hebrew text words in a row. Again, letters could fall in any sequence.[9]

Finally, the ancients applied a letter-exchange system called athbash, which generated twenty-two ways to spell each name.[10] This greatly expanded the vocabulary available to biblical authors when they encoded spellings and anagrams. Take Huldah anagrams, for example. Without athbash, Hebrew Scripture produces only nineteen Huldah anagrams. But after applying athbash, the total jumps to 1,773. As we shall see, Huldah, her allies, and her enemies frequently used anagrams to convey information. Readers can use a standard commercial search program to locate anagrams within Scripture.[11] The process, while simple, requires perseverance.

Now to coded spellings. Over the years, consultants have written and revised for this writer a computer program that searches Scripture for coded spellings. Using probabilities to sort the data, the program is calibrated to retain only the strongest one-half percent of coded spellings—a level that surely excludes most coincidental findings. For comparison, a five-percent retention level is common in both the social sciences and large-scale medical studies. Readers can assume that conservative applications of probabilities underlie the whole effort set forth in this book.[12]

9. Coded spellings are more fully explained in Kavanagh, *Secrets*, 207–8; *The Exilic Code*, 6–13; and *The Shaphan Group*, 1–5.

10. Athbash is discussed more fully in Kavanagh, *Secrets*, 198–205; *The Exilic Code*, 27–31; and *The Shaphan Group*, 12–17. Jeremiah 51:41 revealed the key to the athbash code when it used Babylon (בבל) and Sheshach (ששך) interchangeably. Huldah herself probably wrote the words that enabled us to break the athbash code. Coded spellings of her name run through vv 39–40 and 42–43 of Jeremiah 51, which flank v 41, the key verse. Athbash first divides the Hebrew alphabet in half to form facing rows of letters. Eleven of the letters run right-to-left; the other eleven run left-to-right (Babylon thus becomes Sheshach). Then tractor-tread rotation changes the interfaces, allowing the parallel rows of letters eventually to generate twenty-one other ways to spell the chosen name. Since a final adjustment is not described here, those who wish to duplicate this should first consult one of the references for a fuller explanation.

11. Kavanagh, *The Exilic Code*, 22 n. 1, describes how to use BibleWorks to search for anagrams. It might take two days of work to locate all anagrams for a single name.

12. Here are two other safeguards. The probability of coincidence of any spellings result cannot be higher than .001, or one in a thousand. A second conservative measure involves a large, randomly picked set of dummy words. The assumption is that the results from running these dummy words against Scripture established the norm for

Fortunately, anagrams and—to a slightly lesser extent—coded spellings resist alterations in the biblical text.

Biblical scholars have repeatedly expressed to this writer that coding could not have survived the centuries of textual changes that the Masoretic Text has undergone. This study, like those of most other scholars of Hebrew Scripture, relies upon the Leningrad Codex of the Masoretic Text. The MT has a better than 95 percent letter-for-letter congruence with the Qumran Isaiah scrolls, which date to about 150 BCE. This sort of fidelity in copying bodes well for what might have happened prior to 150 BCE. In that period, ideological battles could have pushed coding losses higher—while, at the same time, posting coding gains. The reason for positing gain is that those who edited earlier writings also knew coding. They would have substituted or added their own encodings to whatever text they amended.

This happens often. For example, vv. 2–3 and 6–7 of Isaiah chapter 9, which is the Wonderful Counselor / Prince of Peace passage, teem with Huldah encodings. These suggest that Huldah was either the mother or the grandmother of the new child. Well and good, but there is more. Editors have doctored the passage, adding verses 8 through 11. These are also densely coded with Huldah, but the language is hostile to her. In all, Isa 9:2–11 (H1–10) conceals 26 Huldah spellings within 125 text words. The entire balance of Scripture has 2,657 such spellings in 305,371 text words. The chi-squared probability of coincidence within Isaiah 9 is zero. The Huldah coding—hostile and friendly mixed together—cannot be coincidental. This is an example of a change in the MT that actually added text words and coding. Also, of course, the editors may have subtracted an unknown number of text words with coded spellings.

Scholarly opinion is that the original Hebrew texts have been edited and modified so that the surviving Masoretic Text is just one of several versions.[13] Certainly, the MT is not wholly the original text. It is, however, the text we have—a text that still contains *several million encodings*. And these can help students of the Bible immensely. Consider this result. The Society of Biblical Literature has convened the best minds in biblical studies to find the identity of Dtr—the person or persons who wrote the book of Deuteronomy and framed the books of Joshua, Judges, Samuel,

what might happen coincidentally. We subtracted coded spelling results on the wrong side of this norm, which reduced findings by an additional 20 percent. Kavanagh, *The Shaphan Group*, 85–86, discusses this adjustment.

13. Email dated September 1, 2011, from professor Juha Pakkala, University of Helsinki, to the author.

and Kings. This is the Holy Grail of biblical scholarship. Within the SBL, an organized search has been going on for years, but still no luck. Yet this writer, with four months of labor, has been able to locate the Dtr members within Deuteronomy and calibrate their influence on the book (a later chapter discusses Dtr's identity). Probabilities, fast computers, and this new technique of finding encoded spellings made this possible. Without even considering the Dtr find, surely several million newly discovered lines of encodings justify a look.

Is the coding that remains after Scripture's editors finished their work coincidental? No, little of it is coincidental. The social sciences commonly use a .05 probability breakpoint (1 in 20) to determine whether or not something occurs by chance. By contrast, this author has incorporated .001 in the computer search program, 1 in 1,000, which is fifty times more selective.[14] Those several million lines of encodings are no coincidence. All this engenders confidence that this book's findings are truly the work of Scripture's original authors and editors.

Also, simply because coding is succinct, it resists change. The average Hebrew verse can house about a half-dozen coded spellings of the same name. Adding letters to one or more of the verse's words would not alter a previous encoding; subtracting letters would if one of the letters taken had been used to build the encoding (a one-in-four chance). Adding or dropping just one text word would disrupt some but not all of the spellings, while adding words at either end of the verse would have no effect.

Webster's defines truth as the "actual state of a matter," and "conformity with fact." The operative words are actual and fact. Actual facts are unassailable and indisputable.[15] The anagrams and coded spellings reported in this book are actual facts. Those facts may be misinterpreted in whole or in part but actual facts they remain. We hope that others will quickly move to join in interpreting the facts pouring from this newly opened cornucopia.

14. Despite this .001 limit, final outcomes total one-half percent of findings (.005), a difference due to the high number of coded spellings at the far-right tail of the distribution. Stated another way, to secure outcomes averaging .005, we had to set individual cutoffs at .001.

15. The thought comes from Golletz, *Consensus*, 84.

LOW STATUS OF WOMEN

Most leading authorities would agree with the statement, "The Bible was written and compiled by males who had no special interest in women's roles."[16] Others go further: "Few could dispute the overwhelming orientation of the Hebrew Bible to the male world"; "The Bible is written in androcentric language, [and] has its origin in the patriarchal culture of antiquity"; and "The Old Testament is man's 'book,' where women appear . . . simply as adjuncts of men . . . [It is] a collection of writings by males from a society dominated by males."[17] Virtually all Hebrew Scripture was written after kings were enthroned and temples established in Israel and Judah. Prior to this time (say until 950 BCE), the foci of activities were the family household, the clan, and the tribe. Scripture speaks of it as the period of the judges, and a pro-monarchy editor of the book of Judges has inserted the refrain, "In those days there was no king in Israel." That same person closes the book by adding, "All the people did what was right in their own eyes" (Judg 21:25).

In the uplands of Israel, the work contributed by women as mothers and wives was vital. Women birthed and nurtured children, processed food, cooked meals, and made and repaired clothing. As mid-wives, women were important health-care providers.[18] Women also furnished field labor to help their family wring a living from rocky soil, though the most important crop they produced were children, an essential contribution in an agricultural, hand-labor economy. Yet this came at a cost, for the risks of childbirth were considerable. Remember God's sentence upon Eve: "I will greatly increase your pangs in childbearing; in pain you shall bring forth children" (Gen 3:16).[19] Mortality rates uphold this truth. A scientific study shows that the average life span of women in the eastern Mediterranean during biblical times was twenty percent shorter than that of men.[20]

The authority of women in *pre*-monarchy Israel was extensive and included religious leadership within the household. Lack of separate

16. King and Stager, *Life in Biblical Israel*, 49. By count, men's names mentioned in HS outnumber those of women by an astounding nine to one.

17. Meyers, *Discovering Eve*, 4; Bird, *Missing Persons*, 13; and Fiorenza, *But She Said*, 21.

18. King and Stager, *Life in Biblical Israel*, 52.

19. Those words may have been written by Huldah. Her name is significantly coded beneath this and Gen 3:17, the following verse.

20. Nicholson, "Longevity." See chart: http://www.beyondveg.com/nicholson-w/angel-1984/angel.

buildings for worship at the earliest sites indicates that worship was fami-ly-centered, and probably led by women.[21] Archaeologists have unearthed thousands of female cult figurines at numerous sites in Israel dating be-tween the tenth and sixth centuries BCE, which is the period of the mon-archy. No male figurines have been reported. These small female figures were common in Judah, and they came from the debris of homes, not of sanctuaries. Devotions within households were prevalent and, judging by the sex of the figurines, represented women seeking "to secure fertility, safe childbirth, and/or adequate lactation."[22] The figurines may have been associated with the Canaanite goddess Asherah, the goddess of fertility who was the consort of the storm-god Baal.

When kings displaced judges as sources of law and protection, fe-male authority was diminished. During nearly four centuries of rule, the monarchs established centralized palace and military bureaucracies, both of which were male. Also, the northern and southern kingdoms vied for the allegiance of their subjects by offering sites of worship manned (liter-ally) with male priesthoods. Also, law supported religion. Much of the Pentateuch was written by members of a priesthood that was all-male and hereditary, and those first five books catalogue Israelite law.[23] The old-est adult male inherited, although a widow with an underage son could also inherit. If there were no male descendants, daughters could inherit property and marry men of their choice—if they selected within the tribe. Marriages were arranged. After a woman married, she joined the house-hold of her husband, a practice that offered continuity of land tenure. The bride then fell under the supervision of her new mother-in-law. At the death of her husband, the newly widowed woman could marry her hus-band's brother to perpetuate the deceased's name and ensure that property remained within the clan. A man could take several wives, though mo-nogamy remained the ideal. Also, a man could father children with any female slave owned within the household. Only a husband might initiate divorce proceedings, and after divorce he had no responsibility to support his ex-wife.

Phyllis Bird writes, "The picture of woman obtained from the Old Testament laws can be summarized . . . as that of a legal nonperson; where she does become visible it is as a dependent, and usually an inferior, in a

21. Meyers, *Discovering Eve*, 159. Meyers points out that the Micah story in Judges tells us that households had their own shrines.

22. Meyers, *Households*, 31, 57.

23. Meyers, *Discovering Eve*, 11.

male-centered and male-dominated society. The laws, by and large, do not address her, most do not even acknowledge her existence . . . Where ranking occurs she is always inferior to the male. Only in her role as mother is she accorded status equivalent to a man's."[24]

Interestingly, when most Hebrew Scripture was written, Israelite women appear to have been no worse off, and in some ways better off, than women in surrounding cultures.[25] While this excuses much, it does not address the problem of how women of the twenty-first century should interpret Scripture that seems to bind rather than liberate. However, Elisabeth Schüssler Fiorenza argues that, correctly understood, the Bible fosters the liberation of women. One of her strategies for achieving this is to "recover works written by women in order to restore critical attention to female voices and intellectual traditions."[26]

This is exactly what this book seeks to achieve. It will use coded spellings and anagrams to pry from Scripture the role that Huldah played in creating the Bible.

During the last several decades, this writer has enjoyed a monopoly on applying anagrams, coded spellings, and Word Links to Hebrew Scripture. As a result, this present search for the historical Huldah often assumes as given events that are as yet unrecognized by others. Here, for example, is a startling finding that serves to show how Huldah used coded spellings. It is the familiar opening of the book of Jeremiah:

> The words of Jeremiah son of Hilkiah . . . to whom the word of the LORD came . . . in the days of King Jehoiakim son of Josiah of Judah, and until the end of the eleventh year of King Zedekiah son of Josiah of Judah, until the captivity of Jerusalem in the fifth month. Now the word of the LORD came to me saying, "Before I formed you in the womb I knew you, and before you were born I consecrated you; I appointed you a prophet to the nations." Then I said, "Ah, Lord GOD! Truly I do not know how to speak, for I am only a boy." (Jer 1:1–6)

Encoded within this text are sixteen spellings of two athbash versions of Huldah-the-prophetess and one version of Huldah-the-queen-mother. One of the Huldah-the-prophetess renderings has three spellings and the

24. Bird, *Missing Persons*, 30.

25. Wegner, "Leviticus," 48. Wegner cites the research of Sarah B. Pomeroy in *Chattel or Person? The Status of Women in the Mishnah*.

26. Fiorenza, *But She Said*, 23, 28.

other has five.[27] Also stitched into the Jeremiah opening are no fewer than eight encoded Huldah-the-queen-mother spellings.[28] Each of these three different groupings stands as statistically significant—defined as having less than one chance in a thousand of being coincidental.[29] These Huldah encodings lie within vv. 3–6, with all three crossing v. 5, which carries the memorable words, "Before I formed you in the womb I knew you, and before you were born I consecrated you; I appointed you a prophet to the nations." The footnotes allow anyone who wishes to verify these coded spellings to do so.

How does one account for Huldah's coded presence in Jeremiah's call? Was Jeremiah in some way honoring the prophetess? That is unlikely. Readers will soon learn that Jeremiah repeatedly used anagrams to criticize Huldah—and he also employed coded spellings in the same way. Proof is close at hand. While three spellings of Huldah-the-prophetess are concealed within the verses quoted above, another seven underlie verses 16–17 in this same opening chapter.[30] There God says, "I will utter my judgments against them, for all their wickedness in forsaking me; they have made offerings to other gods, and worshiped the works of their own hands." The Huldah coding within the call verses (Jer 1:1–6) praise and probably describe the female prophet; the spellings that underlie verses 16–17 bristle with hostility toward her. Given Jeremiah's fulminations against Huldah (which this book will document), the best way to account for the coding beneath the prophetic call passage is that Huldah or someone very close to her wrote it, attributing it to Jeremiah. Those words of God very likely applied to Huldah herself. Huldah was the one whom God formed and knew in the womb, consecrated even before birth, and appointed a prophet to the nations. Perhaps Jeremiah had told Huldah about his call, and Huldah then expressed it in words of her own. But the fact must be that they were her own words, words spoken from her

27. דחתאאיירוקא, which is an athbash variation of חלדההנביאה, Huldah-the-prophetess, has three spellings using ten consecutive text words starting with word 4 in v. 5; ערלממתיצטם has five spellings starting at word 3 in v. 4.

28. Huldah-the-queen-mother, חלדההגבירה, is encoded eight consecutive times, from 3–12 to 3–21 for the first to 5–1 for the last. To illustrate, the sequence of letters (one per text word) for the 3–12 spelling is חרגדיל הבדהה.

29. The coding with three spellings in the Jeremiah preface has seven more in verses 16–17. The two batches together make the chapter's coding statistically significant.

30. Spellings of דחתאאיירוקא (one letter per text word) begin at words 16–6 through 16–12 and end at words 17–1 through 17–7, making seven coded spellings of Huldah-the-prophetess. This, of course, is an athbash variation.

own prophetic experience. Both Huldah and Jeremiah were familiar with Judah's court circles, and both were of an age.[31] Indeed, tradition says that they were related.[32] Possibly they learned their craft from the same master, for each was to become a consummate writer who could readily apply anagrams and coding to Scripture. In the small world of seventh-century Judah, the two prophets would have been well acquainted, though probably not as friends. Judging by Jeremiah's fierce criticisms, he and Huldah were anything but friends during the Exile.

In view of all this, it is most likely that the prophetic call that until now has been associated with Jeremiah in reality is Huldah's own call. Literally, Jeremiah would only have allowed the Huldah coding over his own dead body. The best scenario, then, appears to be that Huldah outlived Jeremiah and in her final years edited some portion of that great prophet's work.[33] While doing so, she inserted the marvelous, touching—and encoded—words that described her own call. Was it spite that led her to do so? Could it have been compassion? One could argue either or even both, though we choose compassion. She selflessly offered her own most personal experience to memorialize her fellow prophet. Vats of ink have been consumed in commenting on this passage, but until now not one drop has ever been used to write the name Huldah. The stunning discovery that Jeremiah's famous call really belonged to Huldah corrects that omission.

ANAGRAM BREAKTHROUGHS

One of the great events of the Exile was the Cyrus-led revolt of the 570s—an event that has so far escaped the notice of scholars. The uprising, with its disastrous aftermath, gave rise to much Scripture, some of which contained Cyrus anagrams. These anagrams offer a handy way to date passages. If they include a Cyrus anagram, they must have been created later than 575. Biblical writers used anagrams much as modern authors use italics—to make a point, to insult, or to associate a person with a trait, an event, or a condition. When Ezekiel accused, "You *played the whore* [Huldah anagram] with the Egyptians" (Ezek 16:26), he employed "played the

31. One expert estimates Jeremiah's year of birth as c 640 BCE (Lundbom, "Jeremiah," 686), and we calculate that Huldah was also born about 640.

32. Rothkoff, "Huldah," 1063.

33. Tertullian and Jerome say that Jeremiah died in Egypt, stoned to death by his exiled fellow countrymen (Lipinski, "Jeremiah," 1351). The reason for the execution is not known. Huldah would have outlived Jeremiah by some fifteen years.

whore" to conceal the Huldah anagram.[34] It was a direct attack upon her and her presumed dealings with Egyptian authorities. In his prophecies, Ezekiel seldom shied from repetition, and in chapter 16 he used that same root containing Huldah ten other times. Today's scholars should assume that virtually every literate sixth-century-BCE Jew knew exactly whom Ezekiel was addressing. Chapter 16 also contains four Cyrus anagrams.[35] These assure that the prophet wrote after the plot to take Jerusalem was already well advanced. Since Ezekiel prophesied so as to "make known to Jerusalem her abominations" (Ezek 16:2), Cyrus and his Israelite forces may already have taken that city, an event that probably occurred in 573 BCE.

This next illustration of anagrams comes from a text marking the middle of the exilic campaign. The Israelite army, camped before the city of Jericho, apparently needed a new commander.

> . . . when *Joshua* [Asaiah] was by Jericho, he looked up and saw a man standing before him with a drawn sword in his hand. *Joshua* [Asaiah] went to him and said to him, "Are you one of us, or one of our adversaries?" He replied, "Neither; but as com-mander of the army of the LORD I have now come." And *Joshua* [Asaiah] fell on his face to the earth and worshiped, and he said to him, "What do you command your servant, my lord?" The commander of the army of the LORD said to *Joshua* [Asaiah], "Remove the sandals from your feet, for the place where you stand is holy." And *Joshua* [Asaiah] did so. (Josh 5:13–15)

The name Joshua contains the anagram Asaiah. That person had been a minor official under King Josiah forty years earlier. Asaiah also had been in the delegation that called upon Huldah (2 Kgs 22:12), and he later was an active member of the Shaphan group.[36] By contrast, the fictional Joshua character could have been a creation of Dtr in this same monarchy-Exile period.[37] The verses above use Asaiah anagrams five times within a short span. The probability is miniscule that so many Asaiah anagrams could

---

34. The text word וּתֵזְנִי contained the letters for זונה, which is an athbash anagram of Huldah. Henceforth, [H] will stand for [Huldah anagram]. Other anagrammed names will be spelled out—for instance [Cyrus]. Where a single text word contains two different anagrams, the reading will be [H, Cyrus], [Cyrus, Ezra], or [Cyrus, Cyrus].

35. Using a verse-word format, 4–14 and 27–12 conceal the Cyrus anagram תהמל, 25–12 has רגב׳, and 52–12 contains נקקך.

36. Kavanagh, *The Shaphan Group*, 74.

37. Ramsey, "Joshua," 999.

occur coincidentally within a text of so few words.[38] The conclusion is that Joshua is probably Asaiah. Quite possibly he led Israelite forces during the Cyrus revolt. The venture ended very badly—previous work indicates that Asaiah may have been captured and that he later perished as a Babylonian substitute king. Psalm 23 might be an account of Asaiah's end.[39]

For the first time ever, we know about the campaign to capture Jerusalem and the way that it ended. Knowing this, what can one surmise about the odd story of the man with the sword who approached Joshua-Asaiah? The stranger announces that he comes as commander of the army of the Lord. Had the ultimate outcome been good, the chapter would have ended as it was first written—probably with the promise to the kneeling Joshua-Asaiah that God's army would deliver a triumph. But when the opposite proved true, the Dtr editor hastily had to cut the ending.[40] After all, how could the army of the Lord be allowed to lose? Something else supports this theory about the story's finish. The words "Remove the sandals from your feet, for the place where you stand is holy" are identical to those that God spoke to Moses out of the burning bush (Exod 3:5). The Dtr writer had constructed a parallel between Moses and Asaiah, a parallel that the author had to retract after the Babylonians crushed the uprising.

Here is another example of what anagrams have to teach. In Ezek 34:17–19, the prophet himself renders his opinion of the harm that the revolt caused. "I shall judge between sheep and sheep, between rams and goats: Is it not enough for you to feed on the good pasture, but you must tread down with *your feet* [Cyrus, Cyrus] the rest of your pasture? When you drink of clear water, must you foul the rest with *your feet* [Cyrus, Cyrus]? And must my sheep eat what you have trodden with *your feet* [Cyrus, Cyrus] and drink what you have fouled with *your feet* [Cyrus, Cyrus]?"[41] What seems at first reading to be pedestrian writing is really a revelation. The prophet cleverly arranged his vocabulary so that one text word had within its letters the characters of two athbash variations of Cyrus. Then he used that text word four times, fashioning eight anagrams. After Hebrew Scripture has surrendered all possible anagrams for all

38. The probability that five Asaiah anagrams would appear coincidentally within sixty-six text words is 3.12×10^{-17}.

39. Kavanagh, *The Shaphan Group*, 109.

40. The RSV and the NRSV translators also think that the story has been truncated.

41. In each of four cases, Ezekiel fashions two Cyrus anagrams—גרלם and רגבי—from רגליכם, "your feet." See Kavanagh, *The Shaphan Group*, 36–37, and *The Exilic Code*, 36, for further comments on the Cyrus revolt.

possible names, something may emerge to match these eight Cyrus anagrams. But until then, these Ezekiel verses hold the record for repetition.
Other Judahites also drew Ezekiel's ire, starting with Huldah. The
quotation above puts a Huldah anagram within "fouled" and the entire
passage conceals other anagrams: four for Baruch, two for Asaiah and
Ezra, and one each for Jehoiachin and Jacob. Huldah had good company
in that risky venture to retake Jerusalem. They included Jeremiah's amanu-
ensis, an ex-official of Josiah, the author of the P Source, Judah's exiled
king, and a principle of the Second Isaiah group.

Though Cyrus profited, for others there was hell to pay. One of those
presented the bill was Ezekiel himself. He was rounded up with numerous
other exiles, imprisoned, and subsequently executed as a substitute for Nebuchadnezzar. Isaiah 52:13—53:12 is an account of his final days.[42] Some
twenty years after the revolt failed, Cyrus first surfaced in Near Eastern
history and began to acquire nations, starting with the Medes.[43] The revolt
in Palestine began in 575 BCE, plus or minus a year or two. Cyrus was
not to conquer Babylon until 539, "freeing" the Jews when he did so. As
of today, no other student of Scripture has noticed this uprising. This is
too bad, because the revolt is the fulcrum that tipped the Exile downward
towards disaster. Also, a large amount of scripture addresses the tragic
aftermath of this event. Until scholars begin to understand the context of
such Scripture, cogent analysis of those texts will continue to be limited.

42. Kavanagh, *The Exilic Code*, 110–15.

43. In 553 Nabu-naid, the new king of Babylon, allied himself with Cyrus the
Persian. Olmstead, *Persian Empire*, 36. This was the first mention of Cyrus of which
historians are aware. Thus, biblical anagrams help to sight Cyrus two decades earlier
than those working in the related field of Persian history.

2

Huldah's Character

WHAT WAS HULDAH REALLY like? How did her contemporaries feel about her and how did they express those feelings? Anagrams can tell us. An anagram has the letters of one word among the letters of a text word that is of equal or greater length. There are close to eighteen hundred Huldah anagrams in Scripture, some negative but many of them positive. Saving most of the negative ones for a later chapter, the following will fit anagrams like pieces in a mosaic, seeking to reconstruct a picture of this extraordinary person. The starting point will be the martial anagrams—Huldah spellings crafted within the text words "mighty," "warriors," "horsemen," "shields," and their variations. Scripture contains about ninety of these martial anagrams, many of them within texts that were from Huldah's hand. Foremost is 2 Samuel 1, her moving eulogy to Saul. She placed that account in the mouth of David ("How *the mighty* [H] have fallen!").[1] David's tribute to Saul contains six Huldah anagrams, four of which are from the word stem for "mighty."

MARTIAL ANAGRAMS

Huldah uses the same signing technique in the Song of Deborah, a lyrical poem set in the period of the judges. It is about a commander of Israel's army who delivered her people from their Canaanite oppressors. Deborah was a military leader, a prophet, and a judge—the only female to whom

1. [H] will stand for a Huldah anagram. Other names within brackets will be spelled out. For example, [H, Cyrus] indicates both a Huldah and a Cyrus anagram within the italicized text word.

Scripture openly attributes those three positions. The Song of Deborah was Huldah's creation, or, at a minimum, her retelling of an older story. The subject of most of Judges 5 is Deborah's victory over the Canaanites, with the remainder of the chapter given to a poetic account of Sisera's death. Sisera, who commanded the Canaanite army, fled after Deborah defeated him and sought refuge with the woman Jael. She fed the exhausted Sisera, perhaps made love with him, and, after he had fallen asleep, drove a tent peg through his temple. Commentators classify this as ancient material—one says the Song of Deborah "is one of the oldest examples of Hebrew literature still in existence."[2] However, eight Huldah anagrams and 108 coded spellings reveal that Huldah's sure hand shaped (or reshaped) the whole chapter.[3] Its date would be in the period immediately before a Huldah-led expedition took Jerusalem in the late 570s. Perhaps Huldah added a veneer of antiquity to disguise her authorship or—less likely—she revised older material. One of her anagrams says, "Then down marched the remnant of the noble; the people of the LORD marched down for him *against the mighty* [H, Jehoiachin]" (Judg 5:13). The same Hebrew text word also accommodates a Jehoiachin anagram.

Another martial word that often concealed a Huldah anagram was "trumpet." Authors like Huldah completed the anagram by prefixing the letter *bet* to convert it to "with the trumpet."[4] Judges 7:18–20 describes a night attack by Gideon's forces upon the army of Midian. The three verses contain five Huldah anagrams, four of which are derived from "trumpet." Very likely this passage also came from Huldah's hand: "'When I *blow the trumpet* [H], I and all who are with me, then you also *blow the trumpets* [H] around the whole camp, and shout, "For the LORD and for Gideon!"' So . . . they *blew the trumpets* [H] and smashed the jars that were in their hands. So the three companies *blew the trumpets* [H] and broke [H] the jars . . . and they cried, 'A sword for the LORD and for Gideon!'"

Frank Cross writes of "a wedding of kingship and Conquest" in the Jerusalem cult.[5] He combines them under the rubric of Yahweh as the

2. Harvey, "Deborah," 809.

3. For the coded Huldah spellings, the probability of a text the size of Judg 5 containing 108 spellings is 6.7×10^{-7}. Readers should understand that at least fourteen others helped with the chapter. For brevity, call them the Shaphan group. See Kavanagh, *The Shaphan Group*, 87–110, 113. Separately, the probability of coincidence for the eight Huldah anagrams in the chapter is 6.1×10^{-5}.

4. The word בַּשּׁוֹפָר, "with the trumpet," yields the Huldah anagram בּוֹרֵשׁ.

5. Cross, *Canaanite Myth and Hebrew Epic*, 111.

Divine Warrior.[6] Much of the image of the Divine Warrior was formed by the mind of Huldah, the warrior-like queen mother. One can almost hear the martial beat of drums in these quotes from the Song of Deborah: "'LORD, when you went out from Seir, when you marched from the region of Edom, the earth trembled, and the heavens poured . . . water. The mountains quaked before the LORD, the One of Sinai, before the LORD, the God of Israel.'" And, "'the people of the LORD marched down for him against the *mighty* [H, Jehoiachin].'" Of course include: "'The stars fought from heaven, from their courses they fought against Sisera.'" And finally, "'So perish all your enemies, O LORD! But may your friends be like the sun as it rises in *its might* [Jehoiachin].'"[7] Huldah has also provided in the Song of Deborah a generous share of anagrams for her son Jehoiachin, probably so that readers may think of the exiled king of Judah as the Divine Warrior's agent. The chapter that follows will have more to say about this warrior theme.

It appears that Huldah was of non-Israelite extraction—that she probably was a Moabite. The book of Ruth was written during the period of Ezra-Nehemiah, a time of ethnic purges.[8] Ruth, a Moabite, married an Israelite and King David was a descendant of the union (recall that Huldah is the mother of King Jehoiachin in the Davidic line). The book contains only two Huldah anagrams, but one of them comes at the start of this passage: ". . . *the elders* [H], said, 'We are witnesses. May the LORD make the woman who is coming into your house like Rachel and Leah, who together built up the house of Israel'" (Ruth 4:11).[9] Rachel and Leah were Jacob's wives; they gave birth to those who founded the tribes of Israel. The second Huldah anagram in the book of Ruth appears in what the Moabite Ruth says to Naomi, her beloved Israelite mother-in-law: "'*Where* [H] you go, I will go; where you lodge, I will lodge; your people shall be my people, and your God my God'" (Ruth 1:16). These words of Ruth are among the most cherished in Scripture. Though the book probably was written a century after Huldah lived, a sympathetic author used an anagram to state Huldah's fidelity to Israel and to its God.

Interestingly, Huldah herself used "uncircumcised" to sign David's dirge over Saul (2 Sam 1:17–27). Here is that "uncircumcised" anagram set

6. Ibid., 91–111.

7. Judg 5:4–5, 13, 20, 31.

8. LaCocque, *Ruth*, 2.

9. The word "elders" in Ruth 4:11 also contains anagrams for Jacob, Ezra, Baruch, and Cyrus.

in the midst of a passage thick with martial Huldah encodings: "How *the mighty* [H, Jehoiachin] have fallen! Tell it not in Gath, *proclaim it* [H] not in the streets of Ashkelon; or . . . the daughters *of the uncircumcised* [H] will exult . . . For there the shield *of the mighty* [H, Jehoiachin] was defiled, the shield of Saul . . . From the blood of the slain, from the fat *of the mighty* [H, Jehoiachin] . . ." (2 Sam 1:19–22).

The problem of unions between foreign women and Judean men continued to vex the Israelites well beyond the Exile. And those who wrote Scripture later reached back to draw Huldah into their discussions, using her as a straw woman in their arguments. Nehemiah wrote, "Did not King Solomon of Israel sin on account of such women? *Among the many nations* [H] there was no king like him . . . nevertheless, foreign women made even him *to sin* [H]" (Neh 13:26). And it is no coincidence that two Ezra chapters with harsh solutions to the foreign wives problem are filled with concealed Huldah spellings.[10] Bear in mind that these were written a full century after Huldah's death. Nehemiah was on the mark about Huldah when he wrote, "You performed signs and wonders *against Pharaoh* [H] . . . You made a name for yourself, which remains to this day" (Neh 9:10).

SURPASSING BEAUTY

Huldah and Ezekiel met face to face when she and her son Jehoiachin were exiled to Babylon in 597. Huldah was then in her early forties. A dozen years later, in a chapter that bears a 585 date, Ezekiel rhetorically wrote, "'Whom do you surpass in beauty? Go down! Be laid to rest *with the uncircumcised* [H]!'" (Ezek 32:19). When he penned those words, Huldah was fifty-three. She must have been someone to behold! She was beautiful in her early twenties when a Davidic prince chose her as his wife and took her from her first husband; she was beautiful in her forties when Ezekiel saw her in Babylon; and she remained enduringly beautiful in her fifties when that same prophet marveled, "Whom do you surpass in beauty?" There are such women. However, Huldah was singular—given her spiritual, governing, literary, military, financial, and prophetic accomplishments. Here are some of the things that Huldah's lover says of her in Song of Songs: "O my dove, *in the clefts* [H] of the rock, in the covert of the cliff, let me see your face, let me hear your voice; for your voice is sweet, and your face is lovely"; "My heart, my sister, my bride, you have ravished my heart with a

---

10. Ezra 9 and 10 between them contain 345 coded Huldah spellings. Separately, the chapters each have zero probability that their spellings occur coincidentally.

Huldah

glance of your eyes, with one jewel *of your necklace* [H]"; and also "How fair and pleasant you are, O loved one, *delectable maiden* [H]!" (Song 2:14, 4:9, 7:6).[11] Quoting Ezekiel again, "Your fame spread *among the nations* [H] on account of your beauty, for it was perfect because of my splendor that I had bestowed on you, says the Lord GOD" (Ezek 16:14). Huldah's beauty, then, was legendary and God given.

Beauty aside, it was as a prophet that Huldah first shone. She was consulted in 622 BCE by Josiah's officials about the newly discovered temple scroll. Despite that start, Huldah had to struggle until the end to maintain her prophetic credentials, as this next verse shows (we know that its date is after 573 because it contains a Cyrus anagram). When Elisha heard that a king of Israel "had torn *his clothes* [H]" about curing a leper, he told the king, "Why have you torn your clothes? Let him come to me, that he may learn that there is a prophet in Israel" (2 Kgs 5:8). The sub-rosa message was that Huldah continued to retain her status as a prophet.[12]

Prophets had visions and so also did Huldah. Not all were pleasant. Three passages from Job are likely to have come toward the end of her life: Evil men "will be chased away like *a vision* [H] of the night"; "You scare me with dreams and terrify me with *visions* [H]"; and "Amid thoughts from *visions* [H] of the night" (Job 20:8, 7:14, 4:13). Next, Huldah herself probably composed God's memorable but discouraging charge to the prophet Isaiah: "Make the mind of this people dull, and stop their *ears* [H], and shut their eyes, so that they may not look with their eyes, and listen with their *ears* [H], and comprehend with their minds, and turn and be healed" (Isa 6:10). And there is this classic quotation from Joel: "I will pour out my spirit on all flesh; your sons and your daughters shall prophesy, your old men shall dream dreams, and your young men shall see *visions* [H]" (Joel 2:28 H3:1). Joel 2:28 also contains anagrams for Daniel, Jehoiachin, and Baruch, as well as the one for Huldah.

Huldah was a prominent Israelite woman—a rare thing—and thus especially susceptible to attack. "Their only plan is to *bring down* [H] a person of prominence," says a psalm (Ps 62:4 H5). Two Jeremiah anagrams confirm that the prophetess rose to queen mother, the highest position to

11. Neither coded spellings nor anagrams indicate that Song of Songs is solely about Huldah. However, she did play a role in composing parts of that book. See Kavanagh, *The Shaphan Group*, 106, 122.

12. The word "clothes" contains a Huldah anagram. Biblical authors used the term fifty-one times to convey to readers that Huldah was a subject or author of the particular passage. For example, in 2 Kgs 22:11, "When the king heard the words of the book of the law, he tore *his clothes* [H]."

which a Judean female could aspire. "Say to the king and *the queen mother* [H, Jehoiachin]: 'Take a lowly seat, for your beautiful crown has come down from your head'"; as well as "This was after King Jeconiah, *and the queen mother* [H, Jehoiachin] . . . had departed from Jerusalem" (Jer 13:18, 29:2). Psalm 2 and Prov 8 base their Huldah anagrams on the word for "rulers." The first is hostile to Huldah and the second is friendly. "The *rulers* [H] take counsel together, against the LORD and his anointed"; and "By me kings reign, *and rulers* [H] decree what is just" (Ps 2:2, Prov 8:15). A Job excerpt uses both "exalted" and "arrogantly" to describe Huldah: "with kings on the throne he sets them forever, *and they are exalted* [H]. And if they are bound in fetters and *caught* [Jehoiachin] . . . then he declares to them their work *and their transgressions* [Jehoiachin], that they are *behaving arrogantly* [H, Jehoiachin]" (Job 36:7–9). Plainly, the Job author has paired Huldah and Jehoiachin, treating them both as royalty. Date the Job passage after the 573 uprising, since King Jehoiachin is imprisoned.

A favorite for Huldah anagrams was "elders"—often with anagrams for other notables grounded within this same text word. For example, "The governor of the city, along with *the elders* [H, Jacob, Baruch, Cyrus, Ezra] and the guardians, sent word to Jehu: . . . 'We will not make anyone king; do whatever you think right'" (2 Kgs 10:5). The italicized text word conceals anagrams for Huldah, Jacob, Baruch, Cyrus, and Ezra.[13] These anagrams may even announce a decision of the leaders of the 573 revolt not to enthrone Jehoiachin until after Jerusalem was secure. Whether Jehoiachin should continue as king would have been a hot issue. This passage is especially rich because it (a) includes a Cyrus anagram that dates it within a year of 573; (b) shows that Huldah in her sixties is a recognized leader of the exiles in Egypt or Palestine; (c) places Jacob, Baruch, and Ezra (the author of the P Source) alongside her; and (d) puts Cyrus, who was then in his twenties, on that governing council of elders. A woman and a young foreign mercenary sitting on the Judean council of elders! It shows the strains that exile must have put on Judean custom and tradition. On the other hand, people of the stature of Huldah and Cyrus (and Second Isaiah, too) do not appear often in human history.

Another "elders" example with the same five embedded names shows the power that this council exercised: "If any did not come within three days, by order of the officials *and the elders* [H, Jacob, Baruch, Cyrus, Ezra] all their property should be forfeited, and they themselves banned from

13. "The elders" is וְהַזְּקֵנִים. An athbash anagram for Huldah is יָנֹו, for Jacob קְמָיה, for Baruch יֹוּנק, for Cyrus קָנֹוּן, and for Ezra זְקֹוּם.

the congregation of the exiles" (Ezra 10:8). Strangely, the verse lies in the book of Ezra. Perhaps the Restoration-era elders were citing the exilic precedent for such a coercive ruling.

Huldah anagrams appear in "elders" text words over twenty times, which is another example of her prominence during the Exile. Some of these will show that not every anagram supported her—that Huldah's opponents skillfully used the "elders" anagram against the prophet. Here they cram two Huldah and Baruch anagrams plus one each for Cyrus and Ezra into six text words. These convert Israelite elders into elders from the traditional enemies Moab and Midian: "So the *elders* [H, Cyrus, Baruch] of Moab and the *elders* [H] of Midian departed *with the fees* [Baruch, Ezra] for divination in their hand . . ." (Num 22:7). Notice that Huldah's prophecy becomes mere divination. One has to admire the craftsmanship.

Huldah lived into her mid-seventies and retained her extraordinary powers well into old age. The word translated as "old" not surprisingly is from the same Hebrew root as "elders." Here Jeremiah uses both shadings of the root: "Take with you some of *the elders* [H, Cyrus, Ezra] of the people and some of the *senior* [H, Cyrus] priests" (Jer 19:1). Cyrus anagrams accompany those for Huldah in both words, while Huldah herself is said to be among "the senior priests"—presumably referring to her Asherah role. The next text is similar. Earlier in Scripture, when answering Pharaoh's question about who would leave Egypt to worship the Lord, Moses said, "We will go with our young *and our old* [H, Jehoiachin, Baruch, Cyrus]; we will go . . . with our flocks and herds, because we have the LORD's festival to celebrate" (Exod 10:9). At this point, when the leaders in Egypt had launched their quest to retake Jerusalem, Huldah would have been sixty-five.

Separately, Jer 31:13 speaks of gathering scattered Israel, presumably after the Jerusalem defeat: "Then shall the young women rejoice in the dance, and the young men *and the old* [H, Baruch, Ezra, Cyrus] shall be merry. I will turn their mourning into joy." As one would expect, those who opposed the Jerusalem expedition used Huldah's age against her. In its pithy manner, the book of Job said, "It is not the old that are wise, *nor the aged* [H, Baruch, Ezra, Cyrus] that understand what is right" (Job 32:9). Isaiah 20:4 uses the identical word (with an identical foursome of anagrams) to paint a verbal picture of captives "both the young *and the old* [H, Baruch, Ezra, Cyrus], naked and barefoot" being led into exile.

WEALTHY HULDAH

During part of her life, Huldah enjoyed great wealth. Huldah anagrams often appeared in the Hebrew words translated as "treasuries," "purchase," "wealth," and "goods." For example, "You shall *purchase* [H] food from them for money"; "By your wisdom and your understanding you have amassed wealth for yourself, and have gathered gold and silver into your *treasuries* [H]"; "He shall return to his land with great *wealth* [H, Baruch, Cyrus]"; "Your wealth and your treasures I will give as plunder . . . throughout all *your territory* [H]"; "Do not let the wealthy boast *in their wealth* [H, Jehoiachin]"; "With silver and gold, with *goods* [H, Baruch, Cyrus] and with animals"; and "Menahem exacted the money from Israel, that is, from all the *wealthy* [H, Jehoiachin]."[14] Anagrams tell us that Huldah also was generous with her money. For example, Ps 146:7 says, ". . . who gives food to the *hungry* [H]." She also gave without stint to equip the rebel army for its campaign against Jerusalem: "a great army and *abundant supplies* [H, Baruch, Cyrus]" (Dan 11:13).

Ezekiel 27 is ostensibly about Tyre—the wealth the port had amassed by trading and the doom that overcame it. But the chapter is also about the trading acumen of Huldah and her son Jehoiachin. Ezekiel 27 is flecked with Huldah anagrams, nearly half of which come from a word that is unique to this text, a word that the NRSV translates as "wares." A sample reads, "When your *wares* [H, Jehoiachin, Jehoiachin] came from the seas, you satisfied many peoples; with your abundant wealth and merchandise you enriched the kings of the earth" (Ezek 27:33). The single italicized word houses one Huldah anagram and *two* Jehoiachin anagrams—and the chapter contains seven "wares" text words.[15] Here is just one of them: "Tarshish did business with you out of the abundance of your great wealth; silver, iron, tin, and lead they exchanged for your *wares* [H, Jehoiachin, Jehoiachin]" (Ezek 27:12). Obviously, Ezekiel knew his anagrams, painstakingly crafted the special word, and then used it often. Add "merchant" to the list of Huldah's accomplishments.

The Ezekiel chapter about Tyre raises the question of where Huldah and Jehoiachin did their trading. It might have been in Babylon, but Egypt makes more sense. Egypt's northern ports would have been closely tied in trade to Tyre and by the mid-580s, when she came to Egypt, Huldah

---

14. Deut 2:6; Ezek 28:4; Dan 11:28; Jer 15:13, 9:23; Ezra 1:4; 2 Kgs 15:20.

15. The text word is עִזְבוֹנַיִךְ. It contains the Huldah anagram יוֹנַ and the Jehoiachin anagrams יוֹכִנ and וֹבַזִי. Ezekiel 27 has 16 Huldah anagrams, which are far too many to be coincidental. The probability of coincidence is a miniscule 3.12 × 10⁻⁸.

would have been more mature. As the next chapter will show, the queen mother and her son spent about a decade in both Babylon and Egypt.[16] When in Egypt, profits must have flowed to Huldah from trade conducted with Tyre-based ships. Another quote from one of Ezekiel's chapters about Tyre supports this surmise: "By your great wisdom in trade you have increased your wealth, and your heart has become *proud* [H] in your wealth" (Ezek 28:5).

At forty-three, when Huldah was exiled to Babylon, she would have forfeited the wealth that she had accumulated as a member of Judah's royal family. Jeremiah put it this way: "Like the partridge hatching what it did not lay, so are all who amass wealth unjustly; in mid-life *it will leave them* [H, Jehoiachin], and at their end they will prove to be fools" (Jer 17:11). The words that follow speak of a glorious high throne in Judah, which tends to confirm the 597 dating. Using trade, the queen mother and her son restored their fortunes a dozen years later—after they joined other refugees in Egypt.

Clothes can be associated with wealth, and wealth with "clothes"— one of the words that formed Huldah anagrams.[17] Leviticus and Numbers have over forty of these, and they almost always involve uncleanness—a studied insult. Leviticus 15 uses variations of "wash his clothes" coupled with "be unclean until evening" nine times, each with a specific act leading to contamination and each pointing directly at Huldah.[18] For example, "Whoever touches her bed shall wash *his clothes* [H], and bathe in water, and be unclean until the evening" (Lev 15:21). "Until the evening" may be a stock reference to the end of the Exile. Understanding this negative aspect helps to clarify several puzzling texts. The first is, "He too stripped off *his clothes* [H], and he too fell into a frenzy before Samuel. He lay naked all that day and all that night. Therefore it is said, 'Is Saul also among the prophets?'" (1 Sam 19:24). This detractor implies that Huldah was the frenzied prophet who had spent a day and a night lying naked before an unknown someone represented by Samuel. The other passage involving a "clothing" anagram (Judg 11:35) is in the story of Jephthah's daughter. It is perhaps the most outrageous slur against Huldah in all of Scripture, and we shall treat it in a future chapter.

---

16. During the very period Huldah was in Egypt, from 585 to 574 BCE, Nebuchadnezzar was besieging Tyre. Katzenstein, "Tyre," 690.

17. After "clothes" is changed to "his clothes" (בגד to בגדיו), it forms the Huldah anagram וידב.

18. Lev 15:5–8, 10, 11, 13, 21, and 22 each contain Huldah "clothes" anagrams.

Depending on context, the word "clothes" can also be translated as "vestments," and someone close to Huldah used those anagrams in a positive fashion. Exodus 29:21 illustrates: "Then you shall take some of the blood that is on the altar . . . and sprinkle it *on Aaron* [Ezra anagram] and *his vestments* [H] and on . . . his sons' vestments with him; then he *and his vestments* [H] shall be holy, as well as his sons and his sons' *vestments* [H]." Three Huldah anagrams dot this verse and tie Huldah to Ezra ("Aaron" is an Ezra anagram), who held the title of high priest during much of the Exile.[19] Notice what pains the author takes to separate the vestments from those who wore them. Huldah would most probably have worn vestments when officiating in any Asherah worship. This author of Exod 29:21—probably Huldah herself—is stating that she had the exiled high priest's approval in conducting Asherah services. If so, this passage becomes one of the most important in Scripture in proving that Huldah's support of the Asherah did not diminish her support of Yahweh worship. As background, "the asherah seems to have played a role in the cult of Yahweh, in the Jerusalem temple and at various other sanctuaries . . . The asherah was a standard and legitimate part of the cult of Yahweh in non-deuteronomistic circles."[20]

Then—as now—royalty was closely watched. Using anagrams, First Isaiah says that Huldah drank more than she should: "Ah, you who are *heroes* [H, Jehoiachin] in drinking wine and valiant at mixing drink . . ." as well as "These also reel with wine and stagger with *strong drink* [H, Ezra]; the priest and the prophet reel with strong drink" (Isa 5:22; 28:7). Jeremiah added, "I will make her officials and her sages *drunk* [Cyrus], also her . . . *warriors* [H]" (Jer 51:57). Huldah's supporters countered with: "Spend the money for whatever you wish—oxen, sheep, wine, *strong drink* [H, Cyrus, Baruch], or whatever you desire" (Deut 14:26).[21]

The word "righteousness" with a *taw* added forms a Huldah anagram, a fact that both pro- and anti-Huldah writers in Scripture well

19. Kavanagh, *The Shaphan Group*, 45–66.

20. Olyan, *Asherah and Yahweh*, 9.

21. Second Samuel 1 relates how Hannah, while praying, was accused by Eli the priest of being drunk—a charge that she strongly rejected. This has the look of a denial by Huldah against false charges of drunkenness, though there are not sufficient anagrams or coded spellings to support that conclusion. Still, a single Huldah-Jehoiachin anagram appears at the start of the story and a word with a Cyrus anagram occurs towards its end. At best, we have an unconfirmed suspicion that Hannah's denial of drunkenness is really Huldah's.

understood.[22] The book of Psalms was particularly friendly to Huldah—so much so that a later chapter will identify which psalms she herself wrote. Huldah or one of her partisans inserted twenty-eight anagram-forming variations of "righteousness" into Psalms, and these were unfailingly supportive. Consider this trio of examples: "Give the king your justice, O God, and *your righteousness* [H, Cyrus] to a king's son"; "They have distributed freely, they have given to the poor; *their righteousness* [H] endures forever"; and "They shall celebrate the fame of your abundant goodness, and shall sing aloud of *your righteousness* [H, Cyrus]" (Pss 72:1; 112:9; 145:7). The first example ties Huldah to a king and a king's son, the second underlines her wealth and charity, and the third defends her reputation. According to the book of Psalms, righteousness was certainly among Huldah's attributes (for those who seek a fuller understanding of her character, the footnote enumerates the righteousness anagrams found in Psalms.[23] Glancing over these would be a quick way to get to know Huldah. More serious students can choose to study the verses that hold all 1,773 of Scripture's Huldah anagrams. (Appendix 1 shows their locations.)

That two of the quoted examples include Cyrus anagrams is especially informative. It means that Pss 72 and 145 were composed about 573 BCE, while both Huldah and Cyrus were on the scene. In several thousand years no one has succeeded in dating even a single psalm—yet the preceding sentence dates two of them. This is a fine example of the power of anagrams.

A single, little-noticed verse puts Huldah's literary mastery on display. In a short two lines within the book of Jeremiah, Huldah discloses that Sheshach and Babylon are equivalents—that the two sets of letters are interchangeable—and then with an anagram she signs her name to that disclosure: "How Sheshach [ששך] is taken, the pride of the whole earth seized! How Babylon [בבל] has become an object of horror *among the nations* [H]!" (Jer 51:41). Biblical authors used further rotations of the Sheshach-Babylon alignment of opposing letters to derive twenty-two ways to spell any Hebrew word—a technique that modern scholars have yet to perceive. Huldah not only achieved mastery of that craft but in Jer

---

22. The most usual form of "righteousness" yielding a Huldah anagram was צדקך. The Huldah athbash anagram was תדצק.

23. The Huldah anagrams formed in Psalms from "righteousness" are in 5:8 H9; 11:7; 22:31 H32; 31:1 H2; 36:6 H7, 10 H11; 40:10 H11; 51:14 H16; 69:27 H28; 71:2, 15, 16, 19, 24; 72:1; 88:12 H13; 89:16 H17; 98:2; 103:6, 17; 111:3; 112:3, 9; 119:40, 142; 143:1, 11; 145:7.

51:41 she also showed all who in the future would read her words how to take the first athbash step.

In summary, this chapter reviews what anagrams reveal about Huldah's character. They show that, like Deborah, she was a military leader, a prophet, and a judge. Huldah appears to have been a Moabite and of surpassing beauty, a beauty she retained into old age. Early in her life she rose to prominence, marrying a prince of Judah and later attaining the exalted status of queen mother. In Judah and also in Egypt, she served as a priestess in Asherah worship. In exile, Huldah gained great wealth through trading—wealth that she generously devoted to the poor and to financing the recapture of Jerusalem. Numerous psalms describe Huldah's righteousness. When she was in her fifties and sixties, she helped to govern the Egyptian exiles as an elder, and she led her people in revolt against Babylon. Anagrams also hint at Huldah's great literary breadth— something this book will catalogue in chapters to come. All in all, this brief anagram biography reveals an extraordinary person serving God in exceptional ways during dreadful times. The next several chapters will expand our knowledge of Huldah by assigning specific dates to events within her remarkable life.

3

Huldah's Biography, Part 1

THE TIMES IN WHICH Huldah lived were crucial to the formation of the Hebrew Bible. They also were tumultuous. In her lifetime she saw mono-theistic reform and backsliding; kings summoned to and then forcibly deposed from the throne; sieges, surrenders, executions, and deporta-tions; Jerusalem and the temple destroyed; and the initial triumph and climactic disaster of the Cyrus-led revolt. Working amidst this turbulence were the prophets, priests, and scribes who wrote and edited Scripture. Huldah herself participated, as did Jeremiah, Ezekiel, Second Isaiah, the author of the P Source, the Dtr team, the Shaphan group, and unknown others. Huldah's lifetime extended from about 640 to 564 BCE, a span of seventy-six years. For Hebrew Scripture, this was a period richer than any other—and Huldah helped to make it so.

The next two chapters will rely upon anagrams and coded writing to sketch a biography of Huldah the prophet. Once the outlines of her biography are clear, this book can fit issues and events to the Scripture she wrote and that others wrote about her. On its face, the Bible provides little information about Huldah. It mentions her name in only two places—in accounts about the scroll discovered during temple repairs in the reign of King Josiah. However, anagrams greatly expand scholarly access to the prophet. Scripture contains 1,773 Huldah anagrams, each inserted into an individual text word. As the opening chapter of this book says, "Biblical writers used anagrams much as modern authors use italics—to make a point, to insult, or to associate a person with an event, a trait, or a condi-tion." Sometimes the true context of an anagram is unclear. Most often, however, the answer is plain to see. Readers, of course, must finally decide such distinctions for themselves.

Table 3.1: Huldah's Life, 640–564 BCE

Year	Age	Event
640		Birth
622	18	Consults on temple scroll
615	25	Marries Jehoiakim, bears Jehoiachin
605	36	Sees King Jehoiakim burn prophecy
597	43	Becomes queen mother
597	43	Exiled to Babylonia with Jehoiachin
592	48	As elder in Babylonia visits Ezekiel
586	54	In Jerusalem during siege
586	54	To Mizpah after Jerusalem's fall
585	55	Gedaliah murdered, Huldah to Egypt
575	65	Cyrus revolt begins
574	66	Israelites take Jerusalem
573	67	Enemies retake Jerusalem, Huldah flees
572	68	Makes way to Bethel
564	76	Death

An overview of Huldah's life follows the dates in table 3.1. The prophetess was born around 640 BCE, about the same year as Jeremiah. According to Scripture, in 622 a committee from King Josiah consulted her about a scroll discovered during temple repairs. At the time, she was perhaps eighteen and married to the king's wardrobe keeper. Some seven years later, Huldah presumably was married to Jehoiakim when she bore him a son. Anagrams show that in 605 she witnessed her husband, who was now Judah's king, defiantly burn Jeremiah's prophecy. In 597, Huldah's husband Jehoiakim was removed from the throne, to be replaced by her son, Jehoiachin. This made Huldah Judah's queen mother. A scant three months later, however, Nebuchadnezzar deposed Jehoiachin and sent him and his newly minted queen mother to exile in Babylon. Anagrams indicate that in 593 she held the title of elder and attended a meeting at Ezekiel's home in Babylonia. In 586, eleven years after her exile, Huldah reappeared in Jerusalem—anagrams relate that she witnessed Nebuchadnezzar's capture of the city. However, Huldah escaped deportation when the victors permitted her to remain in Israel. About 585, following the assassination of Babylon's governor of Judah, the prophetess joined others seeking refuge in Egypt.

Around 575, after a decade in Egypt, Huldah helped to launch an invasion of Palestine. The foray enjoyed initial success but the Babylonians subsequently crushed it. Huldah escaped, and by 572 had settled near Bethel. There, after several years of illness, she died and was buried in 564. Table 3.1 shows these events and correlates Huldah's age with calendar dates and events.

In examining these events, one cannot always follow strict chronological sequence. The reason is that sometimes a sure subsequent event (B) necessitates a probable prior happening (A). For example, if it is easy to prove that Huldah was Jehoiachin's mother (B), then it follows that earlier she most likely married his father Jehoiakim (A). Also, 2,700 years have passed since Huldah lived, and Scripture—the primary source about her—openly mentions her only twice. Clearly one must add the arts of deduction and inference to hard coding data when constructing a biography of this great woman.

564: AT SEVENTY-SIX, HULDAH DIES AT BETHEL

The chronology of Huldah's life begins with her death. Second Chronicles 16:12–13 says that in the thirty-ninth year of his reign, King Asa contracted a disease "in his feet" that led to his death two years later. "In his feet" has within it a Huldah anagram.[1] The anagram and the lengthy reign lead one to suspect that Asa's thirty-nine years had something to do with Huldah. As it happens, King Nebuchadnezzar ruled Babylon for most of Huldah's adult life. His reign lasted forty-three years, extending through the late 560s. Examination showed that there were two consecutive coded spellings of a rare athbash of "Nebuchadnezzar" running from the third through the twelfth words of v. 12.[2] The thirty-ninth year of Asa's reign actually applied to Nebuchadnezzar! This confirms that the prophetess was stricken in Nebuchadnezzar's thirty-ninth year, which was early 566 to early 565. Second Chronicles 16:13 says that Asa (Nebuchadnezzar-Huldah) died in the forty-first year of his reign. That is, Huldah died between March of 564 and February of 563.

1. בְרגליו yields the Huldah athbash anagram ויבג. The same text word also contains ברגו, an anagram for Jehoiachin.

2. The two coded spellings of Nebuchadnezzar within 2 Chr 16:12 use התגרת עדדחמו, which is an athbash of נבוכדראצר.

By employing Asa and "feet," the Second Chronicles author added two twists to his reference. First, King Asa had removed his own queen mother because she had made an Asherah pole (2 Chr 15:16). Huldah herself held the same queen-mother office and, by all indications, had led in the worship of Asherah. Second, scholars say that the word "feet" is used elsewhere in Scripture as a euphemism for genitals, implying that Huldah died as a result of loose living.[3] The Chronicles writer takes a final swing at Huldah by saying about Asa, "Yet even in his disease he did not seek the LORD, but sought help from physicians."

Other passages also bear upon Huldah's death. Genesis 35:7–8 says that after Jacob the patriarch had completed an altar at Bethel, Rebekah's nurse Deborah died and was buried beneath a tree named the oak of weeping. Later chapters of this book will reveal that Huldah wrote the stories of both Rebekah and Deborah. The Genesis verse could be a fabrication because it is the only mention of a second person called Deborah. Besides, Huldah-the-prophetess is strongly encoded beneath Gen 35:7–8, the passage that mentions the nurse named Deborah.[4]

The Bethel site was located in the kingdom of Samaria. Not coincidentally, half a dozen verses within the books of Kings couple the terms "burial" and "in-Samaria."[5] Since the Hebrew word for "in-Samaria" contains an anagram for Huldah, it seems likely that the authors intentionally associated Huldah's burial site with what they considered the sinful northern kingdom. Possibly another brief obituary appears in 2 Chr 24:15. "Jehoiada *grew old* [H, Baruch, Cyrus] and full of days, and died."

What may be Huldah's own—and final—words are those that close Ps 39. She implores God, "Do not hold your peace at my tears, for I am your passing guest, an alien, like all my forebears. Turn your gaze away from me, that I may *smile* [H] again, before I depart and am no more" (Ps 39:12–13). In addition to the anagram, the closing words contain a Huldah coded spelling.[6]

3. Evans, "Asa," 470. Evans cites Williamson, *Chronicles*, 276–77.

4. The athbash version of Huldah-the-prophetess is הדחאאריורקא. Its three spellings in Genesis 35 use letters from consecutive text words starting at verse 7, words 11 and 12, and verse 8, word 2.

5. Pairing "burial" and "in-Samaria" are 1 Kgs 16:28; 22:37; 2 Kgs 10:35, 13:9, 13; 14:16. Second Chronicles 22:9 also has this combination.

6. טהמל, a Huldah athbash, runs from word 2 through word 6 in the final verse of Psalm 39.

This book began Huldah's biography with her year of death, 564 BCE. Now that biography turns to the first of two dates that Scripture openly certifies—the year 622 BCE.

622: AT EIGHTEEN, HULDAH CONSULTED ON SCROLL

In 622 BCE, during repairs to the Jerusalem temple, workmen discovered what they thought to be an ancient scroll[7] (experts think that this "book of the law" included what is now part of Deuteronomy. Further, the opinion of some is that reformers planted the scroll for discovery because they wanted to centralize worship at a cleansed Jerusalem temple). Officials carried the scroll to King Josiah who, upon hearing its contents, ordered further inquiry "of the LORD" (2 Kgs 22:8–13). A delegation "went to the prophetess Huldah the wife of Shallum son of Tikvah, son of Harhas, keeper of the wardrobe; she resided in Jerusalem in the Second Quarter, where they consulted her" (2 Kgs 22:14). Scripture tells us then that Huldah was a prophetess—one of the OT's seven female prophets—and of sufficient renown to be consulted on the important matter of the scroll. At that time, Huldah lived in the Second Quarter with her husband Shallum, a court functionary.

The Second Quarter was a residential district within Jerusalem. The single Hebrew word for it means "second," but can also mean "double" or "copy."[8] According to Wilda Gafney, the term is associated with repetitive teaching. Gafney notes that the Targums say Huldah "lives 'in the House of Instruction.'"[9] This is not only plausible but also likely, given what we now know about Huldah's writing accomplishments. Also, the text seems to go out of its way to mention something not germane to the story. The word appears in Scripture as a Jerusalem location three times.[10] Since the adjacent text word holds a Huldah anagram, the term "Second Quarter" appears to be associated only with the prophetess.

7. Scripture says that this happened during King Josiah's eighteenth year, which includes most of 622 and a short period in 621 BCE. For ease of notation, this book uses 622.

8. BDB 1041; Herion, "Second Quarter," 1065.

9. Gafney, *Daughters of Miriam*, 192 n. 106.

10. 2 Kgs 22:14; 2 Chr 34:22; Zeph 1:10.

640: HULDAH'S BIRTH YEAR

How old would Huldah have been when the group consulted her in 622? The year of her death is established at 564, fifty-eight years later. That year of death seems as solid as such things can be. Suppose that Huldah was eighteen when she first prophesied. Adding eighteen to those fifty-eight years would bring her age at death to seventy-six and set her birth year at 640. The year of birth, 640, can vary but, for the sake of this biography, a year or two either way makes little difference. If Huldah had been born in 642 and died in 564, she would then have been seventy-eight at death and twenty when she prophesied about the scroll. If instead Huldah came into the world four years later, then she would have prophesied at age sixteen and died at seventy-four. According to Scripture, Huldah was married when Josiah's committee asked her to consult on the temple scroll. There is no firm data on women's ages at marriage, but experts suggest that they married while still in their teens and sometimes in their early teens.[11] All in all, it is reasonable to assume that Huldah was born in 640 BCE, was eighteen years of age when she saw the scroll in 622, and was seventy-six in 564 when she died.

605: HULDAH, THIRTY-SIX, WATCHES HER HUSBAND BURN JEREMIAH'S PROPHECY

Anagrams offer another firm date in Huldah's life. Early in King Jehoiakim's reign, Jeremiah's disciple Baruch read an entire scroll of his master to a gathering of notables. The prophecy was about the disasters that Babylon would bring upon Judah. The occasion was a fast called for "all the people *in Jerusalem* [H] and all the people who came from the towns of Judah *to Jerusalem* [H]." Continuing, "Baruch read . . . from the scroll, in the house of the LORD, in the chamber of Gemariah son of Shaphan the secretary, which was in the upper court, at the entry of the New Gate of the LORD's house" (Jer 36:9–10). The year was 604, eighteen years after Huldah had given her judgment about the rediscovered temple scroll. Note that this first reading was in the scribes' room of the temple and that two anagrams tell us that Huldah was present. Huldah, even while married to Judah's king, may have been a practicing scribe.

The second reading took place immediately afterward in a different scribes' room—that of the palace. "Micaiah son of Gemariah son of

11. King and Stager, *Life in Biblical Israel*, 37.

Shaphan . . . went down to the king's house, into the secretary's chamber; and all the officials were sitting there . . . And Micaiah told them all the words that he had heard, when Baruch read the scroll in the hearing of the people" (Jer 36:11, 13). Then the officials sent for Baruch and instructed him, "'Bring the scroll that you read in the hearing of the people, and . . . sit down and read it *to us* [H].' So Baruch read it to them" (Jer 36:14–15). Again, the anagram announced Huldah's presence.[12]

The officials in the scribes' room recognized that King Jehoiakim himself had to hear Jeremiah's message, damning though it must have been. Those officials also understood that Baruch and Jeremiah might not survive such a hearing. First they told Baruch that he and Jeremiah must hide. Then they brought the scroll to the king. Jehudi, a royal official, "read it to the king and *all* [H] the officials who stood beside the king" (Jer 36:21). The italicized word "all" contains yet another Huldah anagram (the literal Hebrew of "all" is "in the ears of"). What comes next is one of the most chilling eyewitness accounts in Scripture: "Now the king was sitting in his winter apartment . . . and there was a fire burning in the brazier before him. As Jehudi read three or four columns, the king would cut them off with a penknife and throw them into the fire in the brazier, until the entire scroll was consumed in the fire that was in the brazier. Yet neither the king, nor any of his servants who heard all these words, was alarmed" (Jer 36:22–24).

The scroll was read in three places: in the scribes' room of the temple, in the scribes' room of palace, and in the king's apartment. Huldah's anagrams mark all three, implying that she was present in each location. If any specific places can ever lay claim to being a birthplace of Hebrew Scripture, it is those two scribal rooms. Perhaps Huldah composed some of hers within the temple or the king's palace. Indeed, there is an excellent chance that Huldah herself helped to write this very account in Jer 36. Consider the Huldah anagrams and the author's eyewitness command of the story. And besides, we know already that she probably composed at least part of the introduction to Jeremiah's book. Moreover—and at least as important as the anagrams—there is zero probability that the Huldah coding in Jer 36 can be coincidental.[13]

12. A Huldah anagram shows that she was also present when another prophet, Uriah son of Shemaiah, denounced Jerusalem and Judah "in words exactly like those of Jeremiah" (Jer 26:20). King Jehoiakim sent agents to seek him out in Egypt. They then brought him to Jerusalem, where the king had him killed.

13. Jeremiah 36 contains 201 coded Huldah spellings in the chapter's 618 text words. Scripture's other 304,878 text words have 46,894 spellings. A chi-square test

The chapter teems with the names of notables of Jehoiakim's time. Among them are six members of the Shaphan group—a term that identifies those who collectively produced several hundred chapters of Scripture.[14] Group members whose names appear in Jer 36 include Gemariah, Achbor, Micaiah, Baruch, Jeremiah, and Shaphan himself, who once had served as King Josiah's secretary (Huldah was also a member, though the Jeremiah chapter does not mention her). The named presence of this many group members suggests that they were collectively responsible for writing Jer 36. However, there is no coded evidence that they had any hand in it. Indirectly, this points to Huldah as one of the authors. This writer's current research strongly indicates that most writings in Scripture had more than a single author. Perhaps unknown others collaborated on composing that Jeremiah chapter. But for now, Huldah should head any list of suspects.

597: AT FORTY-THREE, QUEEN MOTHER HULDAH EXILED TO BABYLON

Biblical authors seemed to enjoy playing with anagrams. Sometimes they shamelessly altered text words so as to supply the lacking final letter needed to complete a desired anagram. Take, for example, the name Abigail. It appears sixteen times in Scripture, four of which include the prefix *waw* signifying "and." This added letter completes a Huldah anagram formed from "Abigail," who was one of Scripture's heroines. In a fifth case (2 Sam 25:18), however, the author simply inserts a *waw* into the midst of the name's other letters, to the confusion of future scholars.[15] The result achieved is that five of Abigail's sixteen appearances conceal Huldah anagrams—a balance that has zero probability of coincidence.

Here is another example of anagram whimsy. Whoever wrote the book of Esther liked to crowd multiple anagrams into single text words. In Esth 9:2, the word "and-the-satraps" contains at least a dozen different anagrams, five of which are variations of Ezra. Other text words in Esth 8 conceal six and nine anagrams, respectively.[16]

Another favorite practice was pairing anagrams within single text words. This provides the modern analyst with an extraordinary

---

shows that the Jer 36 spellings have zero probability of coincidental occurrence.

14. Appendix 1 of Kavanagh, *The Shaphan Group*, lists the chapters of Scripture written by the Shaphan group.

15. The Huldah anagram is וייבג and the altered Abigail word is אבוגיל.

16. The text words in Esth 8 are word 22 in verse 9 and word 15 in verse 10.

opportunity—to track such pairings across the breadth of Scripture and then to draw conclusions about relationships from those pairings. The initial question, of course, is whether the pairing is statistically exceptional. If so, the next question is why the author(s) intentionally made the pairing. Here is an important example. Within Scripture, anagrams for "Huldah" appear 1,773 times, while those for Jehoiachin occur in an even 1,800 places. Well and good, but strangely, within the ocean of Scripture's text words, Jehoiachin and Huldah anagrams find 246 text words in common. The odds are long against having even one of Scripture's three hundred thousand-plus words house both a Huldah and a Jehoiachin anagram. Having them coincidentally share 246 text words has no measurable probability.[17] Those who wrote those 246 text words purposefully fashioned those Huldah-Jehoiachin connections. Why did they do so?

Only two possible relationships come to mind: wife-husband and mother-son. Considering the first, a good estimate of Huldah's birth year is 640. Second Kings 24:8 says Jehoiachin was eighteen in 587 when he assumed the crown. Simple arithmetic puts their age difference at thirty-five years, which almost eliminates a relationship between husband and wife.[18]

That leaves the mother-son possibility, though this has a major difficulty. Second Kings 24:8 reads, "Jehoiachin was eighteen years old when he began to reign; he reigned three months *in Jerusalem* [H]. His mother's name was Nehushta daughter of Elnathan of Jerusalem." Scripture claims that the name of Jehoiachin's mother was Nehushta, not Huldah. A number of things belie that. First, the word translated as "in Jerusalem" contains a Huldah anagram. It comes just three text words before Nehushta. Next, Nehushta's father is said to be Elnathan of Jerusalem and his father, in turn, probably was Achbor, a member of the delegation that visited Huldah.[19] It could be said that Nehushta's family line leads straight to Huldah. The chain is Nehushta–Elnathan–Achbor, and Achbor called upon Huldah. If Nehushta was really Huldah, it seems that her own grandfather was one of those appointed by King Josiah to seek her advice, which accords with the pious-fraud theory of the temple scroll. That is, in 522 BCE, reformers—including Achbor—planted the scroll in the temple, confident that word of its discovery would reach the king.

17. A Venn diagram produces these chi-square proportions: 246 / 1,527 and 1,554 / 302,169. The P value = 0.

18. Second Chronicles 36:9 says that Jehoiachin was only eight when he began to reign. This would make the wife-husband disparity forty-three years rather than thirty-five.

19. Ward, "Elnathan," 94.

Nehushta means "snake," one of the symbols of Ashtoreth—a cult associated with Judah's queen mothers. The name is also rooted in the word for bronze. The reformer king Hezekiah "*broke in pieces*" (a Huldah anagram) the bronze serpent named Nehushtan that Moses had fashioned (2 Kgs 18:4).[20] It appears that naming Jehoiachin's queen mother Nehushta was a scriptural insult aimed at Huldah. Though interesting, these things are not decisive. What *is* decisive follows—two Jeremiah anagrams decide the question of the proper name of King Jehoiachin's mother. The word *gebira* is the formal title for queen mother. The term appears twice in the book of Jeremiah and another four times elsewhere. Only the Jeremiah occurrences prefix the letter *waw* to *gebira* so as to allow formation of a Huldah anagram (Jer 13:18, 29:2).[21] Here is one of those verses: "This was after King Jeconiah, and *the queen mother* [H], the court officials, the leaders of Judah and Jerusalem, the artisans, and the smiths had departed from Jerusalem" (Jer 29:2). The italicized words carry the Huldah anagram. Jeremiah uses the same anagram-bearing text word in 13:18, which predicts the doom of the king and his queen mother. The two Jeremiah anagrams determine the proper name of King Jehoiachin's mother. The queen mother's name was Huldah—not Nehushta. The term implying "snake woman" could have been invented to insult, but it also could have been the cultic name that Huldah used when she conducted worship before the Asherah goddess.

It is time to see where we have come and where we have still to go. Table 3.1a shows us. The shaded lines on the table are those already discussed. The parameters of Huldah's life were 640 and 564—her estimated years of birth and of death. In 622, the committee of court officials sought her advice as a prophetess on the recently discovered temple scroll. In 604, eighteen years later, Huldah witnessed King Jehoiakim burn Jeremiah's prophetic book one page at a time. Most of these events are documented by anagrams. The year 597 saw Huldah take the title of queen mother as her son Jehoiachin ascended the throne of Judah. Within a few months, however, both were forced into exile in Babylon. Referring again to the table, it is time to reach back to 615, the approximate year in which Huldah married Jehoiakim—a prince at the time—and bore him a son. The remainder of the chapter will cover this marriage and birth.

---

20. See Num 21:4–9 for the Moses account.

21. The word וּלְגְבִירָה in Jer 13:18 houses the Huldah anagram וּיָבּ. Jeremiah 29:2 is similar.

Huldah

Table 3.1a: Huldah's Life, 640–564 BCE

Year	Age	Event
640		Birth
622	18	Consults on temple scroll
615	25	Marries Jehoiakim, bears Jehoiachin
605	36	Sees King Jehoiakim burn prophecy
597	43	Becomes queen mother
597	43	Exiled to Babylonia with Jehoiachin
592	48	As elder in Babylonia visits Ezekiel
586	54	In Jerusalem during siege
586	54	To Mizpah after Jerusalem's fall
585	55	Gedaliah murdered, Huldah to Egypt
575	65	Cyrus revolt begins
574	66	Israelites take Jerusalem
573	67	Enemies retake Jerusalem, Huldah flees
572	68	Makes way to Bethel
564	76	Death

615: AT TWENTY-FIVE, HULDAH MARRIES JEHOIAKIM, DELIVERS SON JEHOIACHIN

Given that Jehoiachin was eighteen when Nebuchadnezzar took the young king and his mother to Babylonia in 597 (2 Kgs 24:8), Huldah bore her son in 615 (597 + 18 = 615). Because she became queen mother when Jehoiachin ascended the throne, Huldah would then have been the wife of his father, King Jehoiakim. Since their son Jehoiachin was eighteen in 597, she would have married the father in, say, 616 while King Josiah still reigned. Keep in mind that when the delegation first called upon Huldah six years earlier, she was the wife of one Shallum, "son of Tikvah, son of Harhas, keeper of the wardrobe" (2 Kgs 22:14). The Kings author enumerates two generations for Shallum, presumably to highlight Huldah's non-royal marriage. How does Huldah move from marriage with a commoner to marriage with a king-to-be? Because Scripture does not directly address this question, here is a scenario that can fit the historical situation.

Huldah was surpassingly attractive—beautiful, skilled, accomplished, and a magnet to men. She was a woman in a thousand, perhaps in a million—a woman fit for a king. But what happened to Shallum the wardrobe keeper, Huldah's first husband? While this is as yet unknown, there could be a real-life parallel between Shallum and Uriah the Hittite of David's time. King David arranged to have Uriah killed in battle after impregnating Uriah's wife Bathsheba.[22] Shallum may have perished in a similar way.

However, the love between Huldah and Shallum seems to have been imperishable, for there is evidence that Shallum survived his former wife's marriage to royalty. Chapter 7 of the Song of Solomon supports coded spellings well beyond coincidence for both Shallum and Huldah. In addition, Song 7:6 addresses the woman as "O loved one, *delectable* [H] maiden!" The opening verse exclaims, "O queenly maiden!" Elsewhere, the woman's lover says, "A king is held captive in the tresses" of her hair (Song 7:5). These verses imply that the lovers continued to be intimate after Huldah remarried a prince or king. Future work—perhaps done years from now and certainly by others—might address such questions.

Moving to chapter 4 of Song of Songs, except for its final verse, the chapter's words are spoken entirely by the man. That man probably is Shallum, because chapter 4 has a disproportionate number of coded Shallum spellings—plus three Huldah anagrams. Here are the closing words: ". . . *flowing streams* [H] from Lebanon. Awake, O north wind . . . Blow upon my garden . . . that its fragrance may be wafted abroad. Let my beloved come to his garden, and eat its choicest fruits" (Song 4:15–16).

But it seems that Huldah attracted others besides Shallum. When one of King Josiah's sons saw her, his conversation with his parents might have gone like this: Samson's "father and mother said to him, 'Is there not a woman among your kin, or among all our people, that you must go to take a wife from the *uncircumcised* [H] Philistines?' But Samson said to his father, 'Get her for me, because she pleases me'" (Judg 14:3). The passage contains a Huldah anagram derived from "uncircumcised" that probably refers to her Moabite blood. Samson's father could have represented King Josiah, but which of Josiah's four sons was Samson? The obvious choice is Jehoiakim, who subsequently became king and fathered Jehoiachin with Huldah. The marriage followed by the birth would have taken place around 615 BCE, while Josiah was still on the throne.[23] Hopes would have

---

22. Huldah coded spellings throughout the David-Bathsheba tale in 2 Samuel 11 are respectable, but not statistically significant.

23. Possibly levirate marriage was involved. If so, then Huldah married one of Josiah's other sons before wedding Jehoiakim. Johanan, who did not reign (and probably died when a youth), is one candidate. Shallum, the youngest son, is another. Separately, Huldah in 622 seems to be angry at Josiah, for she says in 2 Kgs 22:14, "Tell the

Huldah

been high, the Josiah reforms well advanced, and Judah still independent—though precariously so.

Several passages tell what Huldah thought about the birth of a royal son. The first is Hannah's vow to God about a male son: "If only you will . . . *remember me* [H, Jehoiachin], and . . . give to your servant a male child, then I will set him before you as a nazirite until the day of his death. He shall drink neither wine nor intoxicants, and no razor shall touch his head" (1 Sam 1:11). Further along, the text contains a Cyrus anagram, so the passage's composition date probably was long after Jehoiachin's birth. Whatever that date, Jehoiachin did not become a nazirite, nor did he live like one.

The next birth passage is a classic. The words are among the most celebrated in Scripture, in part because George Frederic Handel used them in *The Messiah.* The biblical source is Isaiah 9.

> [2]The people who walked in darkness have seen a great light; those who lived in a land of deep darkness—on them light has shined. [3]You have multiplied the nation, you have increased its joy; they rejoice before you as with joy at the harvest, as people exult when dividing plunder. [4]For the yoke of their burden, and the bar across their shoulders, the rod of their oppressor, you have broken as on the day of Midian. [5]For all the boots of the *tramping* [Jehoiachin] warriors and all the garments rolled in blood shall be burned as fuel for the fire. [6]For a child has been born for us, a son given to us; authority rests upon his shoulders; and he is named Wonderful Counselor, *Mighty* [Jehoiachin] God, Everlasting Father, Prince of Peace. [7]His authority shall grow continually, and there shall be endless peace for the throne of David and his kingdom. He will establish and uphold it with justice and with righteousness from this time onward and forevermore. The zeal of the LORD of hosts will do this. (Isa 9:2–7 H1–6)

Shown above are some of the verses that hold twenty-six coded spellings of Huldah variations. Almost 90 percent of the text words conceal Huldah encodings. However, there is a strange absence of coding in vv. 4–5. That section includes a Jehoiachin anagram ("tramping"), and another ("mighty") appears in v. 6. Not quoted above are vv. 8–11. These are also densely encoded, but within text that is hostile to Huldah. Altogether, vv. 2–11 are statistically significant in their Huldah encodings. There is

man" instead of the more courteous "Tell the king." The Talmud calls her haughty for doing so (*Meg* 2.6 in Neusner, *Talmud,* 7:72).

40

zero probability that they occurred coincidentally.[24] Aside from a small clump in vv. 14–15, the second half of Isaiah 9 is bare of coded Huldah spellings. Enemies seem to have appended to Huldah's original paean of thankfulness a verbal attack on her, Jacob, and perhaps others.[25] In summary, because of coding and anagrams, Huldah certainly composed vv. 2–7. The text after v. 7 originated with Huldah's enemies.

Contemporary scholars differ widely on the context appropriate for Isa 9:2–7. Is the child pre-exilic, post-exilic, or even simply above history?[26] What person could have been described as "Wonderful Counselor, Mighty God, Everlasting Father, Prince of Peace"? Coding and anagrams allow us to conclude several things. First, Huldah composed this passage and the child announced in verse 6 was of royal blood. Also, the Jehoiachin anagrams strongly suggest that he himself was either the child or the child's father. In addition, Jehoiachin coding is strong throughout the passage.[27] If Jehoiachin was the *child*, then Huldah was the mother and the date of composition was 615.

But if Jehoiachin was the *father*, the Isaiah 9 passage's date should be advanced to mid-Exile, and Huldah herself was not the child's mother. At least one passage with a Huldah anagram supports this possibility. Solomon says in prayer that his father David walked before the Lord "'*in uprightness* [H] of heart toward you; and you . . . have given him a son to sit on his throne today'" (1 Kgs 3:6). Cyrus and Jehoiachin anagrams stand in the following verse, which dates the passage to the later 570s. As discussed elsewhere, Huldah equated Jehoiachin with King Solomon. This suggests that when Solomon spoke of receiving a son to sit upon David's throne, the thought was really Jehoiachin's. Perhaps the heir apparent was born in Egypt or en route to the recapture of Jerusalem.

In about 574 BCE the Cyrus-led forces took Jerusalem and began to reestablish the nation of Judah. During the short time that they held the city, the Jews probably installed Jehoiachin as king. If so, the newborn could have been his son. Isaiah 9, then, would have been written to paint his future. Something along these lines makes sense for two reasons. First, verses 3 through 5 are militant. Examples are "dividing plunder," "on the

---

24. Isaiah 9:2–11 (H1–10) contains 26 Huldah coded spellings in 125 text words, while the remainder of HS has 2,657 such spellings in 305,371 text words. The chi-squared probability of coincidence equals zero.

25. A Jacob-Israel parallel in v. 8 refers to the prophet named Jacob.

26. Seitz, "First Isaiah," 481.

27. Fifty Jehoiachin coded spellings within 125 text words yield a chi-square probability of 8.23×10^{-10}.

day of Midian," "trampling warriors," and "garments rolled in blood." The other reason Isa 9:2–7 might be dated after the rebels took Jerusalem is that the second part of Isaiah 9 sounds much like a description of Judah after neighboring fighters had slaughtered its defenders. That would account for the verbal attack on the prophet Jacob and the scorn heaped on the elders, dignitaries, and prophets who had led their people to ruin.

Here is an explanation that could fit the entire chapter. Huldah wrote some part of Isa 9:1–7 to celebrate Jehoiachin's birth in 615. In about 574, she revised it to cover a different birth immediately after the Judahites had freed Jerusalem. But when the revolt failed, critics added vv. 8–21 to Huldah's revised preface, mocking her vision of a new age under David in which "he will establish and uphold . . . with justice and with righteousness from this time onward and forevermore" (Isa 9:7). This sounds complex, but the compositional history of Isa 9 probably *is* complex. To complicate it further, 1 Chr 3:17–18 lists seven sons of Jehoiachin, and ration tablets excavated in Babylon name five Jehoiachin sons.[28] The year 592 is a sure date for one of the ration tablets. With so many princes on the scene, the weight of evidence could shift back toward a birth date of 615, with Jehoiachin himself as the "Wonderful Counselor, Mighty God, Everlasting Father, Prince of Peace." The mother of this extraordinary child would be the woman who composed the birth announcement—Huldah herself. However, the identity of the child in Isa 9 for now must remain unsettled.

A notable line from the book of Joel probably reflects upon Huldah's Isaiah 9 vision. "Then afterward I will pour out my spirit on all flesh; your sons *and your daughters* [Jehoiachin] shall prophesy, your old men shall dream dreams, and your young men shall see *visions* [H]" (Joel 2:28 H3:1). In the Hebrew, Joel 3 is a short insert between chapters 2 and 4. The insert's three Huldah anagrams make it nearly certain that the Huldah connection is not coincidental.[29] The dreams-visions passage in Joel is by, or at the least about, Huldah the prophetess.

For some eighteen years, Huldah would have been a royal personage in Judah. By position, she was one of King Jehoiakim's wives and, with the birth of Jehoiachin, she became a contender for queen mother. It stands to reason that someone of Huldah's beauty and force of character would have become the first among equals. The Huldah anagram in this next verse about King David's son Absalom suggests that she led in the court:

28. Weidner, "Jojachin," 923–35; cited by Albright, "King Jehoiachin," 52.

29. The chi-square probability is 4.18 × 10⁻³ that the three Huldah anagrams are not coincidental.

"Thus Absalom did to every Israelite who came to the king for judgment; so Absalom *stole* [H] the hearts of the people of Israel" (2 Sam 15:6). Also, Jehoiachin—like King David's son Solomon—did not come to the throne as the eldest son. It appears that Huldah, like Solomon's mother Bathsheba, engineered her son's succession. This excerpt from First Kings gives that 597 drama a more ancient setting: "But the priest Zadok . . . and the prophet Nathan . . . and David's own *warriors* [H, Jehoiachin] did not side with Adonijah. Adonijah *sacrificed* [Jehoiachin] . . . fatted cattle . . . and he invited all his brothers, the king's sons, and all the royal officials of Judah, but he did not invite the prophet Nathan . . . or *the warriors* [H, Jehoiachin] or his brother Solomon" (1 Kgs 1:8–10). The rest of this lengthy chapter relates how Bathsheba, Nathan, and the king's warriors secured approval from the dying King David and stage-managed the anointing and crowning of Solomon—even as his brother Adonijah celebrated what he anticipated would be his own enthronement.

The anagrams cited above only hint at the truth behind this text. In addition, 1 Kings 1 conceals *over six hundred* coded Jehoiachin spellings. These are formed from natural or athbash spellings of all six versions of that person's Hebrew name. Probabilities for both the Huldah and the Jehoiachin encodings make it certain that these are no accident.[30] Behind the story of Solomon's investiture seems to be an eyewitness version of how Jehoiachin became king. Huldah and her group ignored primogeniture and contrived to crown her son Jehoiachin (he was to reign for only three months before Nebuchadnezzar sent him and his mother into exile).

Another anagram in 1 Kings 1 indicates that Shaphan, King Josiah's ex-Secretary, assisted Huldah in the coup (Shaphan became a leader of the exiles in Egypt after about 586). The chapter also has a single Cyrus anagram that would date 1 Kings 1 to the decade following 575. These also support the theory that Huldah helped to write the chapter.

The next chapter will resume Huldah's biography, picking up its thread when she became queen mother and then soon after was exiled to Babylon with her son Jehoiachin. The date is 597 and Huldah is by now middle-aged.

---

30. Huldah coded spellings total 190 in 1 Kings 1, with 32,852 in the rest of Hebrew Scripture; Jehoiachin spellings are at 622, with 44,934 in Scripture's remainder. Chapter 1 contains 813 text words and the rest of Scripture has 304,683. Chi-square tests produce P values of 9.79×10^{-23} for Huldah occurrences and 0 for those of Jehoiachin. Coincidence for each name is out of the question. Spellings for each name cover forty-seven of the chapter's fifty-three verses, so it can be assumed that the same author(s) wrote the entire chapter.

4

Huldah's Biography, Part 2

THIS CHAPTER WILL COMPLETE the biography of Huldah the prophet, starting with her exile to Babylon in 597 BCE. For the reader's convenience, the previous chapter's table showing Huldah's life is included below. The last chapter covered the shaded events. This chapter will discuss things yet to come, which are shown without shading on this table.

Table 4.1: Huldah's Life, 640–564 BCE

Year	Age	Event
640		Birth
622	18	Consults on temple scroll
615	25	Marries Jehoiakim, bears Jehoiachin
605	36	Sees King Jehoiakim burn prophecy
597	43	Becomes queen mother
597	43	Exiled to Babylonia with Jehoiachin
592	48	As elder in Babylonia visits Ezekiel
586	54	In Jerusalem during siege
586	54	To Mizpah after Jerusalem's fall
585	55	Gedaliah murdered, Huldah to Egypt
575	65	Cyrus revolt begins
574	66	Israelites take Jerusalem
573	67	Enemies retake Jerusalem, Huldah flees
572	68	Makes way to Bethel
564	76	Death

597–585: MIDDLE-AGED HULDAH EXILED, NEXT IN
BESIEGED JERUSALEM, THEN TO MIZPAH

In 597, Huldah as queen mother accompanied her son Jehoiachin on his
journey into exile in Babylonia. A passage from Samuel may report this
event: "So the king left, followed by *all his* [H, Jehoiachin] household, except ten concubines whom *he left behind* [Jehoiachin] to look after the
house. The king left, *followed by all* [H, Jehoiachin] the people; and they
stopped at the last house" (2 Sam 15:16–17). Ostensibly, this text is about
King David; for knowing readers, however, the cluster of anagrams steers
it to the 597 departure of Huldah and Jehoiachin for Babylon. Another
text names Jehoiachin and identifies Huldah through anagrams and with
the words "king's mother." Here is the passage: "He carried away all Jerusalem, all the officials, all *the warriors* [H, Jehoiachin], ten thousand captives
. . . He carried away Jehoiachin to Babylon; the king's mother, the king's
wives . . . The king of Babylon brought captive to Babylon all the *men of
valor* [H, Jehoiachin]" (2 Kgs 24:14–16).

During her stay in Babylon, Huldah must have attended Nebuchadnezzar's court and apparently was free to visit the Judeans' exilic settlements. Undoubtedly she composed Scripture, perhaps in collaboration
with Judean court officials exiled with the young king. Anagrams provide
a glimpse of her and other dignitaries visiting the prophet Ezekiel. His
chapter 8 bears the exact date of September 17, 592 BCE. The opening
line of that prophecy says, "As I sat in my house, *with the elders* [H, Cyrus,
Baruch] of Judah sitting before me, the hand of the Lord GOD fell upon
me there" (Ezek 8:1). A series of visions of idolatry in the Jerusalem temple
follows, and the first of them contains another Huldah anagram (Ezek 8:2).
The word "elders" in Ezek 8:1 contains anagrams not only for Huldah but
also for Cyrus and Baruch. Because 592 is far too early for Cyrus the Great
to have been attending meetings (he might have been six years of age),
the preface to Ezekiel 8 must have been inserted by an editor—probably
Huldah herself. The Cyrus question aside, what we have is her eyewitness
account of the meeting. Something else is of interest—Baruch also was
there. He was Jeremiah's able and trusted scribe. Scripture records that
Baruch accompanied that prophet to Egypt in about 585, yet seven years
earlier, in 592, he was in Babylonia.

Evidence testifies that Huldah edited the book of Ezekiel. It contains
fifteen specific dates, a feature that is unique to the prophet—and important for establishing the chronology of Huldah. Six of those fifteen dates
contain Huldah anagrams—for example: "In the seventh year, in the fifth

month, *on the tenth* [H, Jehoiachin] day of the month . . ." and "In the *twenty* [Jehoiachin]-seventh year, *in the first* [H] month . . ." (Ezek 20:1; 29:17).[1] Evidence discussed elsewhere indicates that Ezekiel died as a substitute king early in 569.[2] If Huldah edited the book of Ezekiel, she would have done so at Bethel prior to her death in 564. If she were the editor, she would have used her own knowledge or that of acquaintances to assign dates that included Huldah anagrams.

According to anagrams, Huldah as an elder met with Ezekiel in Babylonia in 592. Anagrams also show that six years later, in 586, Huldah was back in Jerusalem when Nebuchadnezzar laid siege to the city.[3] The Second Kings account reads, ". . . in the ninth year of his reign, in the *tenth month* [H, Jehoiachin] . . . Nebuchadnezzar king of Babylon came, he and all his army, against Jerusalem, and encamped against it" (2 Kgs 25:1). Thus, when the siege began, Huldah was in Jerusalem. It is not clear whether Jehoiachin accompanied her. Evidence establishes that the young king resided in Babylon in 592.[4] It is surprising to find Huldah back in Jerusalem, but would she have returned there without Jehoiachin? Upon reflection, Huldah as queen mother would never willingly have separated herself from her royal son. But evidence from this book's final chapter will indicate that Jehoiachin had been imprisoned for an unknown reason earlier than the 560s, when Scripture says he was freed from jail (2 Kgs 25:27). But why did the authorities allow Huldah—with or without her son—to leave? Almost certainly the Babylonians kept track of the families of their puppet kings, and probably they required them to be at court from time to time. But perhaps Huldah's masters sent her to Jerusalem because—with good reason—they distrusted their vassal, King Zedekiah. He, of course, was in the process of allying Judah with Egypt against Babylon.

This possibility moves toward likelihood because Jeremiah was in the same anti-Egypt pro-Babylon camp. After Jerusalem fell, Nebuchadnezzar's chief lieutenant Nebuzaradan went out of his way to spare the prophet, offering Jeremiah his choice of staying in Judah or going to

1. The six dating verses in Ezekiel that contain Huldah anagrams are Ezek 8:1; 20:1; 24:1; 29:17; 30:20; and 40:1. The probability that the six could be coincidental is about one in 19,000. The full list of twenty verses is available in Boadt, "Ezekiel," 713.

2. Ezekiel apparently was executed as a substitute king after the solar eclipse of January 5, 569, brought him to the Babylonian throne. See Kavanagh, *The Exilic Code*, 111.

3. The year in which the siege began is in question. It seems to have been either 588 or 586 BCE. Althann, "Zedekiah," 1070.

4. Weidner, "Jojachin," 923–35; cited by Albright, "King Jehoiachin," 51–52.

Babylon as a free person (Jer 39:11–14). Huldah coded spellings indicate that Nebuzaradan gave Huldah a similar choice.

Although the author of 2 Kings 25 was parsimonious in using Huldah coded spellings, he or she did it to good effect. The italicized portion shows the ten text words that carry a single coded spelling of Huldah-the-queen-mother.[5] Separately, the italics highlight yet another Huldah anagram. Both techniques confidentially announce that Huldah escaped deportation. "Nebuzaradan the captain of the guard carried into exile *. . . all the rest of the population. But the captain of the guard left some of the poorest people of the land* [Huldah-the-queen-mother coding] to be vinedressers and *tillers of the soil* [H]" (2 Kgs 25:11–12).[6]

Where did Huldah go after Nebuzaradan released her? Again, coded Huldah-the-queen-mother spellings provide the answer. The text hiding three consecutive encodings of that compound is italicized: "*. . . at Riblah in the land of Hamath. So Judah went into exile out of its land. He appointed Gedaliah son of Ahikam son of Shaphan as governor over the people who remained in the land of Judah,*" whom King Nebuchadnezzar of Babylon had left" (2 Kgs 25:21–22). As the new governor, Gedaliah certainly was sympathetic to his own grandfather Shaphan and to what remained of the circle of Josiah-era reformers. Anagrams show that Nebuzaradan also reprieved Baruch, Ezra (the author of the P Source), and Jacob.

585: AT FIFTY-FIVE, HULDAH FLEES TO EGYPT

Unfortunately for Huldah and the others, Governor Gedaliah did not govern for long. Within a year or so of his appointment, an agent of neighboring Ammon assassinated him. To avoid Babylonian reprisal, Huldah and others at Mizpah fled to Egypt. The time was early in 585, and Huldah would have been fifty-five. It is certain that she was on her way to Egypt by March 3 of 585. On that date, Ezekiel prophesied the doom of Pharaoh at the presumed hand of Babylon. But the prophecy (Ezekiel 32) is at least as much an attack on Huldah as it is on Pharaoh. The prophet, writing

5. One of the five coded spellings in 2 Kings 25 is under v. 27, which deals with Jehoiachin's execution as a substitute king twenty-five years after Jerusalem's fall. This could imply that Huldah died with her son in Babylon in 561, instead of her more probable death near Bethel in 564. The parallel description of Jehoiachin's death in Jer 52:31–34 lacks such coding.

6. The encoded word is חלדההגבירה. The encoding begins at v. 11, word 15, and ends at 12–5. Using one letter per text word, the sequence is חבההלל ירדגה. The Huldah anagram in word 12–7 is ו.בב.

from Babylon, marshaled sixteen anagrams against Judah's queen mother. Sixteen is a lot—no chapter in Scripture has more.[7] This example contains five of those Huldah anagrams: "all of them *uncircumcised* [H], killed by the sword . . . for they spread terror in the land of the living. And *they* [H] do not lie with the fallen *warriors* [H, Jehoiachin] of long ago who went down to Sheol . . . for the terror *of the warriors* [H, Jehoiachin] was in the land of the living. So you shall . . . lie among *the uncircumcised* [H] . . ." (Ezek 32:26–28). The Jehoiachin anagrams imply that Jehoiachin left his Babylonian prison and made his way to Egypt to join other exiles there.

Ezekiel 32 is rich in information. First, Huldah is looking toward a Babylonian invasion of Egypt and pictures Jehoiachin as a warrior ("the mighty"). Also, she draws Ezekiel's anger because she sides with Egypt rather than Babylon. Furthermore, based on this chapter's new coding information, scholars can now firm up the year of Gedaliah's murder. Scripture says that he was assassinated "in the seventh month" (Jer 41:1), which by our calendar was October. We know that Huldah and others were in Judah in October of an unstated year and in Egypt by March 3, 585—five months later—when Ezekiel dated his own chapter that condemned both Pharaoh and Huldah. In conclusion, readers can safely assume that 586 was the year of Gedaliah's assassination.[8]

585–575: FROM FIFTY-FIVE TO SIXTY-FIVE, HULDAH IN EGYPT

Huldah remained in Egypt for almost a dozen years. A single chapter from the book of Jeremiah proves her presence. Jeremiah 44 is twice as long as most OT chapters and is awash in Huldah coded spellings. The carefully wrought text contains 171 of them—variations of Huldah, Huldah-the-prophetess, Huldah-the-queen-mother, and Huldah-the-wife-of-Shallum. The author has concealed at least one encoding under twenty-eight of the chapter's thirty verses, and the total of Huldah encodings eliminates coincidence.[9] Without doubt, Huldah is the focus of Jeremiah's baleful forecast.

7. The probability that the concentration of Huldah anagrams occurred coincidentally is tiny—7.9×10^{-15}.

8. Althann, "Gedaliah," 924 says that 586 BCE is most logical, given the context.

9. The two chi-square proportions are 171 / 46,924 and 623 / 304,873. The first proportion is Huldah spellings in the chapter over spellings in the rest of Scripture. The second is text words in the chapter over text words in the rest of Scripture. The probability of coincidence is 1.2×10^{-11}.

Jeremiah addressed his words to exiles living in locations at the eastern edge of the Nile's delta and in Upper (southern) Egypt. The prophecy declares that God had desolated Judah because its people had made offerings to other gods. And despite this lesson, those who had escaped to Egypt had resumed their detestable practices. Jeremiah spoke heatedly of worship of the queen of heaven—worship that apparently had a large female following. As a result of this worship, those who had fled to Egypt would never be able to return to Judah. Instead, they would perish in Egypt by famine, pestilence, or the sword.

Jeremiah 44 records an actual debate between the prophet and Huldah's followers—perhaps even Huldah herself. It took place in Pathros, which was the area of Upper Egypt between modern Cairo and Aswan. Jeremiah's own words show that both husbands and wives vehemently rejected Jeremiah's arguments. They said, "We will . . . make offerings to the queen of heaven and pour out libations to her, just as we and our ancestors, our kings and our officials, used to do in the towns of Judah . . . We used to have plenty of food, and prospered, and saw no misfortune. But from the time we stopped making offerings to the queen of heaven and pouring out libations to her, we have lacked everything . . ." (Jer 44:17–18). Huldah probably led the debate against Jeremiah, because the chapter's heaviest Huldah coding lies beneath the words quoted above. Both sides argued their own interpretation of recent Judean history. King Manasseh had established worship of female deities, Josiah had excised them, and Jehoiakim and Zedekiah had reinstituted them. After the Babylonians destroyed Jerusalem, those who fled south reestablished the cult.

Worship of the queen of heaven in Egypt apparently was transplanted from Jerusalem (see Jer 7:17–18), though it has not been identified elsewhere in the ANE. It probably combined features of several fertility goddesses—including the Asherah—and could even have included a female companion for Yahweh. There is evidence that "before the reforming kings in Judah, the Asherah seems to have been entirely legitimate."[10] Jeremiah said that exiles—especially wives—who had resumed their impure worship in Egypt would perish. Those in Egypt countered that when they stopped such practices, bad things commenced to happen, but that since they had resumed that worship, things were going well. Jeremiah's final word was that God was going to watch over the exiles for bad and not for good. They would indeed die. Kathleen O'Connor notes that Jeremiah

---

10. Olyan, *Asherah and the Cult of Yahweh*, 72.

Huldah

accused wives alone of false worship while the offense of their husbands was reduced to failing to control their wives.[11]

And where was Huldah in this? Given Jeremiah's heavy encoding of Huldah in Jeremiah 44, she probably was at the center of the dispute. When Huldah presided in Jerusalem as Jehoiachin's queen mother, we know from Jeremiah himself that she had a throne and wore a diadem. The Lord told Jeremiah to declare, "Say to the king *and the queen mother* [H, Jehoiachin]: 'Take a lowly seat, for your beautiful crown has come down from your head'" (Jer 13:18). Huldah certainly had the authority to be chief patron of the Asherah worship in Jerusalem before her exile. Further, the heavy Huldah coding in Jeremiah 44 indicates that she was deeply involved in the queen of heaven cult a few years later in Egypt.

Huldah and Jeremiah were the same age and both grew up in or near Jerusalem. Tradition holds that they were kinsmen, which is certainly possible given the small circle of Judah's elite.[12] When Josiah's ministers consulted Huldah in 622 about the newly discovered scroll, she gave a reply that was wholly deuteronomistic—that is, the Lord would bring disaster upon Israel because its people had followed other gods (2 Kgs 22:16–20). Jeremiah, of course, followed the same line and vigorously pushed the Josiah reforms. But a quarter century later, while still in Judah, the two held divergent views. Huldah wore the crown of queen mother and probably led in worshiping the queen of heaven. For his part, Jeremiah was prophesying against her and her practices. Later still, when Huldah and Jeremiah were in their fifties, the two old acquaintances were debating in Upper Egypt whether a woman could continue to honor the queen of heaven while remaining an adherent of Yahweh.

In his chapter 44, Jeremiah speaks to "all the Judeans living in the land of Egypt, at Migdol, *at Tahpanhes* [Jacob, Jozadak], at Memphis, and in the land of Pathros" (Jer 44:1). The exiles were scattered, and possibly their leadership was also. "Tahpanhes" has Jacob and Jozadak anagrams, and the account of the debate (Jer 44:15–30) at Pathros contains anagrams for Daniel, Asaiah, Ezra, and Jacob (again). The governing structure that the Judean exiles in Egypt used appears to be that of elders. Across Scripture as a whole, Huldah anagrams occur repeatedly in the word "elders"— twenty-two times, a frequency that cannot be coincidental.[13] Flatly stated,

11. O'Connor, "Jeremiah," 181.

12. Ginzberg, *Legends* 4: 282.

13. In a chi-square test, the probability that 22 of Huldah's 1,773 anagrams would fall upon 22 of the 123 "elders" occurrences by coincidence is zero. The "elders-Huldah"

50

this proves that Huldah served as one of the elders of the exilic community in Egypt (consider, too, that she had held the title of elder in Babylon fifteen years before when she visited Ezekiel). The position of elders had a long tradition in the ANE and in Israel, too. "Elders are . . . grown-up men, powerful in themselves, by reason of personality, prowess, or stature, or influential as members of powerful families."[14] The expert sees elders as a constant in Israel's life, "as prominent under the monarchy as they were before it."[15] One would expect the exiles in Egypt to continue their long-established practice of rule by elders. However, one would not expect that Huldah, a woman, would have become one of them. Of course, over twenty years earlier, she had briefly held the prestigious position of queen mother, and among exiles this must have carried weight. Nevertheless, it still would have required great force of personality to join that select circle of leaders.

When she arrived in Egypt, the prophetess would have been in her mid-fifties, and she probably remained in Egypt for about eleven years. It seems that Jehoiachin was with her, but we find no indication that he acted as a king-in-exile. Let his status remain unresolved.

Josephus writes that a Babylonian invasion of Egypt started five years after the final fall of Jerusalem, or about 581.[16] Judean refugees in Egypt would certainly have fought against Nebuchadnezzar. The campaign must have concluded in a year or so, leaving the Judean settlements in Egypt with a cadre of experienced fighters. Using their Egyptian sanctuary, in the early 570s Baruch, Jacob, Ezra, Jozadak, Shaphan, Huldah, and others assembled funds and soldiers to retake Jerusalem. This writer has shown elsewhere how anagrams help to outline the extensive preparations made by the leaders of the Egyptian exiles.[17]

It is time to update the table showing Huldah's biography. So far, this chapter has discussed her exile to Babylon in 597, her return to Jerusalem in time for the 586 siege, and her subsequent flight to Egypt where, as an elder, she debated Jeremiah and made preparations to retake Jerusalem. By then, Huldah was in her sixties. Still to come was one of the Exile's most important events—the Cyrus revolt, which will be discussed next. Table 4.1a shades the events in Huldah's life already covered.

---

combination occurs in a variety of books. Only Joshua has more than two of them.

14. Hinton, "Elder," 72.

15. Ibid., 73.

16. *Ant* 9:7.

17. Kavanagh, *The Shaphan Group*, 49–59.

Huldah

Table 4.1a: Huldah's Life, 640–564 BCE

Year	Age	Event
640		Birth
622	18	Consults on temple scroll
615	25	Marries Jehoiakim, bears Jehoiachin
605	36	Sees King Jehoiakim burn prophecy
597	43	Becomes queen mother
597	43	Exiled to Babylonia with Jehoiachin
592	48	As elder in Babylonia visits Ezekiel
586	54	In Jerusalem during siege
586	54	To Mizpah after Jerusalem's fall
585	55	Gedaliah murdered, Huldah to Egypt
575	65	Cyrus revolt begins
574	66	Israelites take Jerusalem
573	67	Enemies retake Jerusalem, Huldah flees
572	68	Makes way to Bethel
564	76	Death

In 577 or 576, the elders in Egypt reached out to Cyrus, then in his early twenties.[18] The senior leadership must have come to agreement with him, for there is strong evidence that he met repeatedly with Huldah and Baruch and probably with other elders as well. Each of the twenty-two "elders" text words proving that Huldah held that office also contains anagrams for Baruch and Cyrus.[19] Again, this cannot have been coincidental. Here is an example. The Lord tells Moses, "They will listen to your voice; and you *and the elders* [H, Baruch, Cyrus] of Israel shall go to the king of Egypt and say to him . . ." (Exod 3:18). While the elders—Huldah and Baruch among them—had authority, apparently they answered to Moses

18. Mallowan in "Cyrus," 9, picks 598 as the Persian's birth year. Though young, Cyrus probably was experienced in war. For comparison, at eighteen, Alexander commanded a wing of his father's army. Isaiah 22 describes the final battle at Jerusalem and mentions chariots and horsemen from Elam, an area on the Iranian plateau. This indicates that Cyrus brought with him a contingent of Persian mercenaries.

19. The "elders" text words that contain Huldah, Baruch, and Cyrus anagrams are found in these verses: Exod 3:18; Lev 9:1; Num 11:30, 22:7; Deut 5:23, 27:1; Josh 7:6, 8:10, 23, 9:11, 23:2; Ruth 4:11; 2 Kgs 6:32, 10:5; 1 Chr 15:25, 21:16; Ezra 10:8; Ps 105:22; Isa 24:23; Jer 19:1; Lam 1:19; and Ezek 8:1. The Huldah anagram is יזרח, the Baruch anagram ייזקן, and the Cyrus anagram קזונז.

52

(who might have been Shaphan, King Josiah's ex-Secretary).[20] This Exodus example suggests that Cyrus was in Egypt during the organizational phase of the revolt. To assemble an army near Egypt would have necessitated negotiations with Pharaoh, and may also have meant battling the Egyptians to gain release.

The Israelite leaders could have made no better choice than Cyrus. Though young in the mid-570s, he was to become a great statesman and military commander. Thirty-five years after joining the Israelites in Egypt, Cyrus, at the head of his Persians, marched into Nebuchadnezzar's fabled capital and took down the Babylonian Empire. Cyrus the Great ranks with Alexander, Genghis Kahn, Tamerlane, and Napoleon as history's foremost conquerors.

575–572: IN LATER SIXTIES, HULDAH IN CYRUS REVOLT

Huldah accompanied Israel's army north as it fought and defeated Judah's former neighbors, who had seized the Exile to expand into Israel's territory. Though the prophetess was in her later sixties, coded spelling shows that she played an active part in the campaign. The book of Joshua described the battles, and major sections of it were from her hand.[21] By way of illustration, Huldah's whimsical pen describes the battle of Jericho. The word for "trumpet" forms a Huldah anagram, and the account of Jericho's fall has seven of them. For example, the Lord instructs Joshua, "On the seventh day you shall march around the city seven times, the priests blowing the *trumpets* [H]" (Josh 6:4). And what exile would fail to understand that Jericho's mighty battlements also represented the massive double walls that Nebuchadnezzar had built to protect his Babylon?

In that same chapter, "The LORD said to Joshua, 'See, I have handed Jericho over to you, along with its king and *soldiers* [H, Jehoiachin]'" (Josh 6:2). "Soldiers" shields anagrams for Huldah and for Jehoiachin, which means that her exiled son apparently was among the commanders of the liberating army. Joshua 6 also completes the tale of Rahab, the prostitute with whom Israel's spies had earlier taken shelter when reconnoitering

---

20. Kavanagh, *The Shaphan Group*, 80–82.

21. Seven chapters in Joshua—9; 10; 12; 13; 15; 19; and 20—have sufficient Huldah coded spellings to achieve zero probability of being coincidental. Of those, chapters 12, 13, and 15 also had active cooperation from members of the Shaphan group. Separately, Huldah played a somewhat less dominant (though statistically discernable) role in composing chapters 16–18. See Kavanagh, *The Shaphan Group*, 113.

Jericho. The Rahab story, in both chapters 2 and 6 of Joshua, used the text word "spy," which fittingly houses a Cyrus anagram[22] (Cyrus later became famous for his use of subversion and espionage to further his military aims. He was to capture the capitals of both Lydia and Babylon without resorting to arms).

Joshua 10 is another chapter with numerous Huldah encodings. Two verses of poetry are especially noteworthy. The Lord "said in the sight of Israel, 'Sun, stand still at Gibeon, and Moon, in the valley of Aijalon.' And the sun stood still, and the moon stopped, until the nation took vengeance on their enemies" (Josh 10:12–13).[23] This is a favorite theme of Huldah's—the Lord's use of heavenly bodies to intervene militantly on the side of Israel. Elsewhere, the Song of Deborah runs, "The stars fought from heaven, from their courses they fought against Sisera" (Judg 5:20), while Habakkuk has, "The moon stood still in its exalted place, at the light of your arrows speeding by, at the gleam of your flashing spear" (Hab 3:11). Huldah wrote each of these, enlisting the Lord on the side of his people. Perhaps she had in mind that the Babylonians sought to terrorize their captive subjects with the natural movements of the sun, moon, and planets. During the Exile of the Jews, there were eighty-one solar and lunar eclipses over Babylon.[24] By calculation, about half of these resulted in the execution of a substitute king. Most victims, of course, were not Jews, but Ezekiel, Jehoiachin, Jehoiakim, and Zedekiah died in this fashion, and possibly Asaiah and other leaders did as well.[25] Huldah would have known each one of these leaders personally. Also, both her own husband and her son died as substitute kings.

Was Huldah active as a warrior? In her long life she certainly had opportunity. She survived two Jerusalem sieges, one of them of several years' duration. In the first she was in her forties, in the second in her fifties. During Nebuchadnezzar's lengthy siege that ended in 586, women probably helped to "man" the city's battlements—and if they did, Huldah would have led. When she was in her sixties, she accompanied the Israelite

22. Huldah coding encompasses the Rahab-related portion of Josh 6, but only covers one-third of the twenty-four verses of Joshua 2. Perhaps Huldah finished the Josh 6 part of the Rahab story that someone else began in Joshua 2.

23. Beginning at word 12 in v. 12, Huldah spells ערל□, an athbash of Huldah, four times. Word 12–1 starts another spelling.

24. Kudlek and Mickler, *Eclipses of the Ancient Near East.*

25. Kavanagh *The Exilic Code*, *Secrets*, and *The Shaphan Group* each have a discussion of substitute kingship. With the exception of Walton, "Substitute King Ritual," no other scholar has taken note of this important practice.

army as it fought its way northward toward Jerusalem in the course of the Cyrus-led revolt. During that time, Huldah undoubtedly witnessed—and perhaps directed— plenty of fighting.

The traces she has left in Scripture are fascinating. She invented (or revivified) the character of Deborah, the warlike heroine of the book of Judges. And even more importantly, numerous applications of the Hebrew words "warriors" and "mighty" form Huldah anagrams. For example, in the Song of Deborah, anagrams within "against the mighty" in Judg 5:13 and 23 alerted contemporary readers about both Huldah and her son King Jehoiachin.[26] (It also alerts us that Huldah wrote the Deborah poetry in the 570s, during or immediately before the Cyrus revolt. This would have been the only time that Jehoiachin was available to lead in open fighting, as opposed to siege warfare.)

In some sixty passages, Scripture's authors used the root for "warrior" to form a Huldah anagram. Close to half of these appear in Chronicles, and they are invariably favorable. For example, "They helped David against the band of raiders, for they were all *warriors* [H, Jehoiachin anagrams] and commanders in the army" (1 Chr 12:21). First Chronicles 7, 11, and 12 contain the bulk of these friendly anagrams, most of which are about David's soldiers.[27] One can conclude both that those chapters are about the revolt and that a portion of Chronicles was either by Huldah or one of her supporters.

A single passage in 1 Chronicles 5 illuminates the opposition that targeted Huldah and the mid-Exile revolt that she led: "These were the heads of their clans . . . *mighty* [H, Jehoiachin] warriors, famous men . . . But they transgressed against the God of their ancestors, and prostituted themselves to the gods of the peoples of the land . . ." (1 Chr 5:24–25). Very likely, a later hand penned the insult that begins with "But they transgressed . . ." This is the only instance within Chronicles of a "warrior" anagram negative to Huldah—though it probably is a positive anagram that opponents converted to an insult.

The "warrior" anagram was used frequently in describing the conquest of the Promised Land during the Cyrus revolt. Here are several: "All *the warriors* [H, Jehoiachin] among you shall cross over armed before your kindred and shall help them"; "Joshua chose thirty thousand *warriors* [H,

---

26. The text word בגבורים yields ריב, which is an athbash for Huldah.

27. The Huldah-warrior anagrams in Chronicles are 1 Chr 5:24; 7:2, 5, 7, 9, 11, 40; 11:10, 19, 26; 12:1, 4, 21, 25, 30; 19:8; 28:1; 29:24; 2 Chr 13:3; 14:8; 17:13, 14; 23:9; and 32:3.

Jehoiachin] and sent them out by night"; and "The LORD said to Joshua, 'See, I have handed Jericho over to you, along with its king and *soldiers* [H, Jehoiachin]'" (Josh 1:14, 8:3, 6:2).

Virtually every prophetic book used the "warrior" anagram against Huldah. Generally, the prophets did this by painting mighty men as Israel's enemies. For example, "The heart of the *warriors* [H, Jehoiachin] of Edom in that day shall be like the heart of a woman in labor" (Jer 48:41). Note the added woman-in-labor touch. The Later Prophets contain close to twenty of these negative "warrior" anagrams.[28]

The very best of the Huldah-warrior anagram passages is this poignant poetry, which has been previously quoted. Ostensibly, it is David's death-dirge over Saul; instead, it might mourn the death of Huldah's husband Jehoiakim. Huldah uses no statistically significant encodings of her name to sign this scripture. Rather, she relies entirely upon anagrams.

> Your glory, O Israel, lies slain upon your high places! How the *mighty* [H, Jehoiachin] have fallen! Tell it not in Gath, *proclaim* [H] it not in the streets of Ashkelon; or the daughters of the Philistines will rejoice, the daughters of the *uncircumcised* [H] will exult. You mountains of Gilboa, let there be no dew or rain upon you, nor bounteous fields! For there the shield of the *mighty* [H, Jehoiachin] was defiled, the shield of Saul, anointed with oil no more. From the blood of the slain, from the fat of the *mighty* [H, Jehoiachin], the bow of Jonathan did not turn back, nor the sword of Saul return empty . . . How the *mighty* [H, Jehoiachin] have fallen, and the weapons of war perished! (2 Sam 1:19–22, 27)

572: AT SIXTY-EIGHT, HULDAH FLEES WHEN REVOLT CRUSHED

April 28, 573 BCE is the last exact date that the book of Ezekiel provides. The chapter so dated launches the prophet's blueprint for restoration of the temple, and it also opens with a Huldah anagram: "In the twenty-fifth year of our exile, at the beginning of the year, on the *tenth* [H] day of

---

28. The negative Huldah-warrior anagrams in the prophetic books are in Isa 13:3; 21:17; 31:1; Jer 5:16; 26:21; 48:14, 41; 49:22; 51:56, 57; Ezek 32:12, 27 (2); Hos 10:13; Amos 2:16; Obad 9. Positive Huldah-warrior anagrams in the prophets are found in Joel 2:7: 3:9, 11; Nah 2:3. Joshua, 2 Samuel, Kings, Nehemiah, Ecclesiastes, and Songs contribute a few more anagrams, most of which are positive.

the month . . ." (Ezek 40:1). We think that this dates the battle marking Jerusalem's recapture by enemies—either by Nebuchadnezzar or by an alliance of neighbors.[29] Appropriately, Ezekiel laid out the dimensions of the new city in a chapter dated on the day, month, and year of the city's most recent destruction. The anagrams are scarce, but the long (and not engaging) chapter is crammed with Jehoiachin coded spellings.[30] Given the context, the spellings indicate that King Jehoiachin was captured at the Jerusalem site.

This line from Joel has the ring of an appeal to others for help as hostile armies approach: "Come quickly, all you nations all around, gather yourselves there. Bring down your *warriors* [H], O LORD" (Joel 3:11). "Those who are swift *of foot* [H] shall not save themselves, nor shall those who ride horses save their lives," reads an unsympathetic Amos 2:15. "Their *warriors* [H] are beaten down . . . 'Terror is all around!'" adds Jeremiah (Jer 46:5). Several of the Lamentations chapters surely came from this time, if only because they contain Cyrus anagrams: "My priests *and elders* [H, Cyrus] perished in the city while seeking food to revive their strength" and "Lift your hands to him for the lives of your children, who *faint* [H] for hunger . . . The young and *the old* [Cyrus] are lying on the ground in the streets; my young women and my young men have fallen by the sword" (Lam 1:19; 2:19, 21).

Isaiah 22 has within it an account of the battle "in the valley of *vision* [H]" (Isa 22:1). Most likely this was the 573 battle of Jerusalem. Indeed, the chapter's first seven verses contain six Huldah anagrams. Like a newscaster, the author leads with this: "All *your rulers* [H] have fled together, without the bow they were captured. All of *you who were found* [H, Cyrus, Baruch] were captured, though they had fled far away" (Isa 22:3). Those "who were found" were captured, but we know that at least Huldah and Cyrus escaped. The reporter continued, "'Let me weep bitter tears; do not labor to comfort me for the destruction of the beloved [RSV reads "daughter"] of my people'" (Isa 22:4).[31] "The daughter of my people" might refer to Huldah herself. The next few lines contained yet three more Huldah anagrams. She may have written this herself: "For the Lord GOD of hosts

29. The 573 date might instead mark when Israel's armies liberated Jerusalem. If so, some of table 4.1's dates would require adjustment by a year or so.

30. Ezekiel 40 contains 256 coded spellings of Jehoiachin variations. There is zero probability that so many spellings could have been coincidental. Huldah coded spellings total 159, and their P value is .007, which is somewhat worse than our .001 standard.

31. The RSV properly uses "daughter," while the NRSV substitutes "beloved."

has a day of tumult and trampling and confusion in the valley *of vision* [H], a battering down of walls and a cry for help to the mountains. Elam bore the quiver with chariots *and cavalry* [H] . . . Your choicest valleys were full of chariots, *and the cavalry* [H] took their stand at the gates" (Isa 22:5–7). The chapter also contains the notable phrase "Let us eat and drink, for tomorrow we die" (Isa 22:13).

From Babylon, the prophet Ezekiel injected hope into the battle's dismal outcome. God commands his prophet, "'Breathe *upon these slain* [H, Jehoiachin], that they may live.' I prophesied as he commanded me, and the breath came into them, and they lived, and stood on *their feet* [Cyrus], a vast multitude" (Ezek 37:9–10). The aftermath of the Jerusalem battle is the proper context for this famous chapter about the valley of dry bones.

Slavery was the fate of those who escaped death: "I will send survivors to the nations, to the coastlands far away that have not heard of my fame or seen my glory; and they shall declare my glory *among the nations* [H]"; "Though I scattered them among the nations, yet in far countries they shall *remember* [H, Jehoiachin] me, and they shall rear their children and return"; and "As for the people, he *made slaves of them* [H] from one end of Egypt to the other" (Isa 66:19, Zech 10:9, Gen 47:21).

Huldah herself evaded her enemies, but by the narrowest of margins. "My bones cling to my skin and *to my flesh* [H], *and I have escaped* [H, Ezra, Baruch, Cyrus] by the skin of my teeth" (Job 19:20).[32] This reveals that Ezra (the author of the P Source) and Baruch accompanied Huldah and that Cyrus also escaped with her. Previously, we had thought that the Persian deserted the rebel army before the final battle at Jerusalem.

Seemingly, Gen 19 is about the rescue of Lot and his family from the destruction of Sodom and Gomorrah. In actuality, the chapter tells of the escape of Huldah, Cyrus, and others from doomed Jerusalem. Genesis 19:2 packs three Cyrus anagrams into three text words. The rest of the chapter (vv 17–22) contains five Huldah anagrams hidden within the text words translated as "flee" and "escape." The cover story for Huldah's escape was about Lot. His situation was immediate and dire. An angel urged Lot, "'*Flee* [H] for your life; do not look back or stop anywhere in the Plain; *flee* [H] to the hills, or else you will be consumed.' And Lot said . . . 'I cannot *flee* [H] to the hills, for fear the disaster will overtake me and I die. Look,

---

32. "And I have escaped" is וָאֶתְמַלְּטָה. It contains anagrams for Huldah (חלדה), Baruch (חמדה), Cyrus (חדמל), and Ezra (מטמו). It is an amazing and graceful construction that, in view of the side-by-side Huldah anagrams, probably was composed by the prophetess herself. Job 19:22 contains yet a third Huldah anagram and v. 26 still a fourth.

that city is near enough . . . Let me *escape* [H] there . . . and my life will be saved!'" The angel then agrees to delay destruction of the cities and tells Lot, "Hurry, *escape* [H] there, for I can do nothing until you arrive there" (Gen 19:17–22). Zoar was the immediate destination of the fugitives. It lay at the southeastern edge of the Dead Sea depression.[33] The Dead Sea is the lowest surface on earth, with severe heat in most seasons.[34] Huldah's flight to Zoar after the battle of Jerusalem probably took place early in May of 573. Interestingly, Scripture associates the settlement at the edge of the Dead Sea with Moab (Isa 15:5, Jer 48:4), and Huldah herself probably was of Moabite descent.[35] She would have been sixty-eight years of age when she sought refuge there.

After fleeing to Zoar in 573, Huldah made her way northward to the vicinity of Bethel, which is some fifteen miles beyond Jerusalem. At Bethel, she lived and wrote for nine years, until her death in 564. That brings Huldah's biography full circle, from 640 to 564.

Her son Jehoiachin probably was captured during the Jerusalem battle. It is likely that he spent the years from 573 to 561 imprisoned in Babylonia. In early April of 561, the authorities released him in order to crown him as a substitute king—which is contrary to the misleading account that ends the book of Second Kings. Jehoiachin died heroically after an extended hunger strike.[36] As for Cyrus, he would have made his way north and east until he reached either the Medes (to whom he was royally connected) or his native Persia. Perhaps a guard of soldiers accompanied him and Huldah to Zoar, perhaps not. Until this sighting, historians have had no glimpse of Cyrus before 553 BCE, the date when the Persian allied himself with Babylon.[37]

The last words of this biographical sketch belong to Huldah herself. Though Ps 31 is short, it has 102 Huldah-related spellings. (The probability of coincidence is 4.1×10^{-22}.) Several Cyrus anagrams testify that she composed the psalm in her final years.

---

33. Astour, "Zoar," 1107; Harland, "Sodom," 395.

34. The Dead Sea is thirteen hundred feet below sea level.

35. For more on the Zoar-Moab connection, see Astour, "Zoar," 1107.

36. Jehoiachin's substitute kingship is explained in Kavanagh, *The Exilic Code*, 42–61.

37. In 553, Nabu-naid, king of Babylon, allied himself with Cyrus the Persian. Olmstead, *Persian History*, 36.

Huldah

> Into your hand I commit my spirit; you have redeemed me,
> O LORD, faithful God. You hate those who pay regard to worth-
> less idols . . . Be gracious to me, O LORD, for I am in distress;
> my eye wastes away from grief, my soul and body also. For my
> life is spent *with sorrow* [H], and my years with sighing; my
> strength fails because of my misery, and my bones waste away.
> I am the scorn of all my adversaries, a horror *to my neighbors*
> [Jehoiachin], an object of dread to my acquaintances; those who
> see me in the street flee from me. I have passed out of mind like
> one who is dead . . . For I hear the whispering of many . . . as they
> plot to take my life. (Ps 31:5, 6, 9–13 H6, 7, 10–14)

Huldah's final years were not pleasant—she was sorrowful, shunned, and ill. The prophet had no conception that the words she contributed to Scripture would be scanned by a billion believers. One of those was Jesus of Nazareth. Upon the cross he chose Huldah's final words as his own, which implies that he knew Huldah's story. "Then Jesus, crying with a loud voice, said, 'Father, into your hands I commend my spirit.' Having said this, he breathed his last" (Luke 23:46, see Ps 31:5 H6).

5

Huldah's Critics

HULDAH RANKS WITH ELIJAH, Isaiah, and Jeremiah as one of the most controversial characters in Hebrew Scripture. The female prophet's major enemies were her fellow prophets Jeremiah and Ezekiel and, of the two, Ezekiel was far and away the most vociferous. To this short list must be added someone who drafted parts of the Minor Prophets as well as several members of the Dtr team that assembled the Deuteronomistic History. Measured by encodings, Micaiah authored more of the DH than anyone else, and he may have been a critic of the exiled queen mother. However, Huldah herself helped put that history together, and so did several of her allies, notably Daniel, Jacob, and Ezra (the author of the P Source). In the future, scholars using coding and anagram techniques will be able to specify authors who are critical of Huldah, and perhaps identify the academies that wrote anti-Huldah texts. The time period for such passages might run from 622 BCE, when Huldah rendered her opinion on the newly found temple scroll, to about 560, shortly after her death. Those academies are more likely to be in Babylonia and Egypt than in Israel.

A principal source of contention was whether or not to worship a female deity. This was true during the closing years of the monarchy and true also during the several stages of Judah's exile. Another question that covered the late monarchy and stretched far into the Exile was whether to side with Babylon or Egypt. For example, it must have shocked the Judean exiles in Egypt to read of Jeremiah's and Ezekiel's support for Nebuchadnezzar against Pharaoh at a time when Judean exiles were enlisting with Egypt. Of course, the greatest area of conflict would have been the expedition in the 570s to take back the Promised Land. Those in Babylonia would have feared a pogrom against them brought about by rebellion of their countrymen—and this repression very likely killed Ezekiel himself (he died as a substitute king about 569).[1] As this book testifies, the 570s revolt and its dismal outcome inspired a great deal of Scripture. Scholars have not been successful in analyzing that Scripture because they do not yet understand what lies behind it. A final zone of dispute was the power and character of one woman, first in Judah during the late-monarchy period and then in the Exile's Diaspora. Huldah was a female of extraordinary abilities, and she challenged and sometimes changed vital matters of law, rule, worship, property, priesthood, and prophecy.

HULDAH'S VOCIFEROUS CRITICS

Specific criticisms of Huldah fall within a range of Scripture but especially in the book of Ezekiel. Virtually all the passages employ Huldah anagrams. To begin, an unknown writer in Kings used anagrams to depict Huldah as Jezebel. King Ahab took the foreigner Jezebel to wife and "erected an altar for Baal . . . which he built *in Samaria* [H]." Another example is "*the harlotries* [H] and the sorceries of your mother Jezebel" (1 Kgs 16:32; 2 Kgs 9:22). Anagrams make clear that when "Jezebel" was written, "Huldah" was meant. Huldah was the harlot and the sorceress.

In the story of Jephthah's daughter, the father shifts the blame for the impending death of his own daughter to that daughter, and the unknown author of this Judges account, in turn, passes the guilt to Huldah: "He tore *his clothes* [H], and said, 'Alas, my daughter! You have brought me very low; you have become the cause of great trouble to me'" (Judg 11:35). That message was, of course, intended for Huldah herself. Of all the anti-Huldah passages that Scripture contains, the story of Jephthah's daughter may be the most stone-hearted. The daughter's life is to be sacrificed so that the father may keep the thoughtless oath pledged to God in exchange for a military victory. And the daughter—read Huldah—is blamed for the tragic result. Presumably, the author expected that, in a culture of misogyny, faulting the daughter for Jephthah's own rigidity would be sympathetically received by his male readers.

Perhaps this was the same Judges author who wrote about the Levite's concubine.[2] The word "concubine" contains one or more athbash anagrams

1. For a discussion of Ezekiel's death as the Suffering Servant, see Kavanagh, *The Exilic Code*, 107–33.

2. For further reading, see Trible, *Texts of Terror*, 65–87; Ackerman, *Warrior, Dancer*, 235–9.

for Huldah. Here are three brief excerpts from the story: "The man seized *his concubine* [H, H, Cyrus, Daniel, Baruch], and put her out to them. They wantonly raped her . . ."; "grasping *his concubine* [H, H, Cyrus, Daniel, Baruch] he cut her into twelve pieces"; and "Then I took *my concubine* [H, Cyrus, Daniel, Baruch] and cut her into pieces" (Judg 19:25, 29; 20:6).[3] The author of this revolting story has crammed five Huldah anagrams and three anagrams each of Cyrus, Daniel, and Baruch into the bloody account of the Levite's concubine. Huldah, Daniel, Baruch, and Cyrus led the catastrophic expedition against the Promised Land during the 570s. The author singled out Huldah for special mention by fashioning a pair of her anagrams in two of the concubine uses, and also by portraying her as a concubine. Probably she played the leading role in organizing the foray. Once again, the Cyrus encoding marks the Judges passage as written after 575—the likely date that the Persian took command of the Israelite forces. And given the bloodiness of the concubine's dismemberment, the Judges story must have appeared after the 573 slaughter at Jerusalem.

The minor prophet Nahum joined in the assault upon the queen mother with three derogatory anagrams within thirteen Hebrew text words: "Horsemen charging, flashing sword and glittering spear, piles of dead, heaps of corpses, dead bodies without end—they stumble *over the bodies* [H]! Because of the countless *debaucheries* [H] of the prostitute, gracefully alluring, mistress of sorcery, who enslaves nations through her *debaucheries* [H, Jehoiachin]" (Nah 3:3–4). Again, a hostile author used anagrams to picture Huldah as a debauching prostitute and a "mistress of sorcery."[4]

JEREMIAH SPEAKS OUT

The prophets Huldah and Jeremiah were of the same age and as youths lived, wrote, and taught within a few miles of each other. Like the author of Nahum, Jeremiah used anagrams to defame Huldah. Here are some of the four dozen anagrams that Scripture preserves: "You have polluted the land *with your whoring* [H, Jehoiachin, Jehoiachin] and wickedness," "Israel

---

3. "His concubine," בפילגשו, contains two Huldah athbash anagrams, ריבג and שפגב, as well as anagrams for Cyrus, Daniel, and Baruch. "My concubine" holds only one Huldah anagram plus those for Cyrus, Daniel, and Baruch.

4. As a matter of interest, the book of Nahum leads every other book in Hebrew Scripture in coding groups per text word. This proves that, by mid-Exile, encoding was highly advanced and that at least one of Huldah's critics was as skilled in it as she was.

. . . went up on every high hill and . . . *played the whore* [H]," and "All your lovers are *crushed* [H]" (Jer 3:2, 6; 22:20). Accusations about worshiping foreign gods were common: "*Offerings* [H, Jehoiachin] to other gods"; "*Stubbornly* [H] follow their own will and have gone after other gods"; "Kindle a fire in the temples of the gods of Egypt; and he shall *burn* [H] them and . . . *break* [H] the obelisks of Heliopolis"; and "Your children *have forsaken me* [H, Jehoiachin], and have sworn by those who are no gods" (Jer 1:16; 13:10; 43:12, 13; 5:7).

Jeremiah also used Huldah's wealth against her: "'Let me go to the rich and speak to them . . .' But they all alike *had broken* [H] the yoke"; "Do not let the wealthy boast *in their wealth* [H, Jehoiachin]"; "Your wealth and your treasures I will give as plunder . . . throughout *all your territory* [H]" (twice); and "So are all who amass wealth unjustly; in midlife it *will leave them* [H, Jehoiachin]" (Jer 5:5; 9:23; 15:13; and 17:3, 11).

The word translated as "mighty" or "warriors" contained a Huldah anagram, and Jeremiah employed it freely: "Their quiver is like an open tomb; all of them are *mighty warriors* [H]"; "Teach them my power *and my might* [H, Jehoiachin]"; "King Jehoiakim, *with all his warriors* [H, Jehoiachin] and all the officials"; "*Their warriors* [H, Jehoiachin] are beaten down"; "How can you say, 'We are heroes *and mighty warriors* [H]?'"; "A sword *against her warriors* [H]"; and "The hearts *of the warriors* [H, Jehoiachin] of Moab . . . shall be like the heart of a woman in labor" (Jer 5:16; 16:21; 26:21; 46:5; 48:14; 50:36, 48:41). In the last example, Jeremiah uses both Huldah's Moabite origin and her womanhood against her. In Jer 48:22, he repeated the simile but substituted Edom for Moab. In 6:24, Jeremiah dropped the foreign reference and used only "anguish has *taken hold of us* [H, Baruch, Cyrus, Daniel], pain as of a woman in labor."

Three times (in Jer 5:9, 29; and 9:9) Jeremiah played upon Huldah's official position as queen mother: "Shall I not bring retribution *on a nation* [H] such as this?" Separately, another seven anagrams said, "I will scatter them *among nations* [H]"; "Say to the king and *the queen mother* [H, Jehoiachin]; 'Take a lowly seat, for your beautiful crown has come down from your head'"; "Ask *among the nations* [H]: Who has heard the like of this?"; "I am going to bring such disaster upon this place that *the ears* [H] of everyone who hears of it will tingle"; "the LORD has an indictment *against the nations* [H]"; "I will make you least *among the nations* [H, Jehoiachin], despised by humankind"; and "How Babylon has become a horror *among the nations* [H]!" (Jer 9:16; 13:18; 18:13; 19:3; 25:31; 49:15; 50:23).

Jeremiah also took words like "stubborn" or "destruction" and consistently used them to criticize his fellow prophet Huldah: "For evil looms out of the north, and great *destruction* [H]"; "In the *stubbornness* [H] of their evil will"; "Everyone walked in the *stubbornness* [H] of an evil will"; "Destroy them with double *destruction* [H]!"; "Follow their own *stubborn* [H] hearts"; "Desolation and great *destruction* [H]!"; and "Battle is in the land, and great *destruction* [H]!" (Jer 6:1; 7:24; 11:8; 17:18; 23:17; 48:3; 50:22).

Jeremiah worked over many years, and the wide distribution of these anagrams shows that he kept at his attacks. Imagine the cumulative effect upon Huldah of this constant rain of destructive word plays. She must have dreaded the sight of her childhood friend's latest writing. To add to Huldah's anxiety, Jeremiah was relentlessly critical of her son Jehoiachin, though perhaps with better reason. The male prophet frequently fashioned his language to form Huldah-Jehoiachin anagrams within the same text word. And the book of Jeremiah contains scores of Jehoiachin encodings in addition to the ones printed above. The bitterness of modern political campaigns is mild by comparison.

EZEKIEL ATTACKS HULDAH

Jeremiah's Huldah anagrams were but a prolonged summer shower compared to the deluge of criticism that poured from the pen of Ezekiel. Measured against Jeremiah's text, the book of Ezekiel contains twice the number of anagrams targeting Huldah and, if anything, they are even more venomous. In selected chapters, the prophet concentrated his anagrams. Chapters 16, 23, 27, and 32 have more than a dozen each, while the rest of his chapters still average three apiece. In fact, Ezekiel seldom wrote without directing insults at Huldah. To date, no other scholar has discovered that biblical writers used anagrams. This is too bad because anagrams clarify hundreds of Scripture's passages. To show what anagrams can do, this chapter offers multiple specific examples of how Ezekiel used them against Huldah.

A major theme of Ezekiel's writings was Huldah's leadership of Asherah worship. The prophet devotes at least sixteen anagrams to it: "Your altars shall become desolate, and your incense stands *shall be broken* [H]"; "Your idols *broken* [H] and destroyed"; "Their abominations *among the nations* [H]"; "Estranged from me *through their idols* [H]"; "Who *separate* [H] themselves from me, taking their idols into their hearts"; "Made for yourself male images, and with them played the *whore* [H]"; "Your *whoring* [H, Jehoiachin, Jehoiachin, Daniel] with your lovers, and because of all your abominable idols"; "Samaria . . . you have committed more *abominations* [H, Jozadak] than they, and have made your sisters appear *righteous* [H]"; "They are more *in the right* [H, Jehoiachin, Cyrus, Baruch] than you"; "Do not defile yourselves with the *idols* [H] of Egypt"; "Nor defile yourselves with their *idols* [H]"; and "My holy name you shall no more profane with your gifts and your *idols* [H]" (Ezek 6:4, 6; 12:16; 14:5, 7; 16:17, 36, 51, 52; 20:7, 18, 39). And Ezekiel had still more to say about Huldah and her idols: "A city! . . . making its idols, *defiling* [H] itself"; "Defiled *by the idols* [H] that you have made"; "You played the whore with the nations, and polluted yourself with their *idols* [H]"; "'Because you have forgotten me . . . therefore bear the consequences of your lewdness and *whorings* [H, Jehoiachin]'"; "For the blood that they had shed upon the land, and *for the idols* [H] with which they had defiled it"; and "*Their idols* [H] and their detestable things" (Ezek 22:3, 4; 23:30, 35; 36:18; 37:23).

Ezekiel often used Huldah's attractiveness against her by using sexual word plays. Chapter 16 is crowded with them. On its surface, the chapter portrays Jerusalem as the Lord's adulterous wife, and probably Ezekiel intended it that way. However, knowing anagrams as we now do, it is a certainty that he also meant to level that charge at the prophet Huldah. Here are some of the lines: "You trusted in your beauty, and played the *whore* [H, Jehoiachin] because of your fame, and lavished your *whorings* [H] on any passer-by"; "Made for yourself colorful shrines, and on them played the *whore* [H]"; "You also took your beautiful jewels . . . and made for yourself male images, and with them played the *whore* [H]"; "In all your abominations and your *whorings* [H, Jehoiachin]"; "You played the *whore* [H] with the Egyptians"; "You played the *whore* [H] with the Assyrians, because you were insatiable; you played the *whore* [H] with them, and still you were not satisfied"; "You gave your gifts to all your lovers, bribing them to come to you . . . *for your whorings* [H, Jehoiachin, Jehoiachin, Daniel]. So you were different from other women *in your whorings* [H, Jehoiachin, Jehoiachin, Daniel]"; and "Your lust was poured out and your nakedness uncovered in your *whoring* [H, Jehoiachin, Jehoiachin, Daniel] with your lovers" (Ezek 16:15, 16, 17, 22, 26, 28, 33–34, 36).

The *Jewish Study Bible* notes that rabbinic interpreters have been uncomfortable with Ezekiel's lewd portrayal of Jerusalem. They might have felt even more strongly had they recognized the chapter as a personal attack upon Huldah.[5] Ezekiel 16 also contains anagrams for Huldah's allies Daniel, Jacob, Baruch, Cyrus, and for the priestly brothers Ezra and Jozadak, as well as for her son King Jehoiachin. That was distinguished company, though judged by weight of accusation, Huldah was Ezekiel's main target.

Ezekiel and Huldah knew each other personally, and a Huldah anagram announces to insiders that Huldah attended a meeting with Ezekiel at his house in Babylon in 592 (Ezek 8:1). But personal acquaintanceship did not assuage Ezekiel's fury. Ezekiel 23 uses the same sort of language and anagrams as Ezekiel 16. In Ezek 23, Jerusalem and Samaria are adulterous sisters, but Ezekiel concentrates his anger on Jerusalem and—through anagrams—on Huldah herself. Here are examples, all but two of which use the letters in "whoring" to form anagrams: "They played the *whore* [H] in Egypt"; "She bestowed her *favors* [H] upon them"; "She did not give up her *whorings* [H]"; "Her *whorings* [H], which were *worse* [H] than those of her sister"; "But she carried her *whorings* [H] further"; "Her *whorings* [H] so openly and flaunted her nakedness"; "Your *whorings* [H, Jehoiachin] shall be exposed. Your lewdness and your *whorings* [H, Jehoiachin] . . ." (Ezek 23:3, 7, 8, 11, 14, 18, 29; see also 23:19 and 35).

Like Huldah's other detractors, Ezekiel attacked her foreign origin. Ezekiel 28:10 pronounces, "You shall die the death of the *uncircumcised* [H] by the hand of foreigners; for I have spoken, says the Lord GOD." In chapter 32, the prophet repeatedly used uncircumcised to denounce Huldah for rallying the Jews to help Egypt against Nebuchadnezzar. This opening line addresses the famously beautiful Huldah: "'Whom do you surpass in beauty? Go down! Be laid to rest with the *uncircumcised* [H]!' They shall fall among those who are killed by the sword . . . The *mighty* [H, Jehoiachin] chiefs shall speak . . . out of the midst of Sheol: 'They have come down, they lie still, the *uncircumcised* [H] killed by the sword'"; "Who went down *uncircumcised* [H] into the world below"; "Their graves all around it, all of them *uncircumcised* [H]"; "You shall be broken and lie among the *uncircumcised* [H]"; "With the *uncircumcised*, with those who go down to the Pit"; "Laid to rest among the *uncircumcised* [H]" (Ezek 32:19–21, 24, 25, 28, 29, 32; see also 32:26, 30; and 31:18). Ezekiel aimed the surface words of these prophecies at the Egyptians, with anagrams, of course, directed at Huldah. This means that Ezekiel, writing from Babylonia, sided with Nebuchadnezzar rather than the Egyptians, with whom

---

Huldah had allied the exiled Jews. Ezekiel applied the "uncircumcised" anagram ten times in chapter 32, and then added another six anagrams from other text words (such a concentration of Huldah anagrams was not coincidental).[6]

No biblical writer was more fervently anti-Huldah than her fellow prophet Ezekiel. For example, note how he uses the word "righteousness" against her. "The righteousness *of the righteous* [H, Jozadak] shall not save them when they transgress . . . Though I say to the righteous that they shall surely live, yet if they trust in *their righteousness* [H] and commit iniquity, none of *their righteous deeds* [H] shall be remembered . . . yet if they turn *from their sin* [Cyrus, Ezra] and do what is lawful . . ." they shall live (Ezek 33:12–14). According to Ezekiel, because Huldah turned from righteousness to iniquity, she must perish. (Cyrus and Ezra, however, were offered olive branches.) The prophet repeats this thought a few lines later: "When the righteous turn from their *righteousness* [H], and commit iniquity, they shall die for it" (Ezek 33:18). In a previous prophecy, Ezekiel had covered the same ground: "When the righteous turn away from their *righteousness* [H] and commit iniquity . . . None of the *righteous* [H] deeds that they have done shall be remembered; for . . . sin they have committed, they shall die" (Ezek 18:24). Advocates for Huldah must have been pointing out her good works, but Ezekiel was having none of it. Again, the main object of his attack was Huldah, as other anagrams nearby attest. Ezekiel 18:20 says, "The person who *sins* [H] shall die . . . the righteousness of the *righteous* [H] shall be his own, and the wickedness of the wicked shall be his own." Elsewhere, Ezekiel or a disciple fashions an anagram hostile to Huldah from the Hebrew word for "sin offering": The prince "shall provide the *sin offerings* [H] . . . to make atonement for the house of Israel"; and "Blood of the *sin offering* [H]" (Ezek 45:17, 18; see also 40:39; 43:7, 21; 46:20).

An unnamed writer in Deuteronomy shared Ezekiel's opinion about Huldah's righteousness. Those Israelites who argued against attempting to retake Jerusalem in the 570s must have been dismayed when their fellow countrymen actually succeeded—however briefly. They use "righteousness" anagrams to shift credit for the conquest away from the rebels because of the wickedness of those they conquered. The Deuteronomy passage reads, "Do not say to yourself, 'It is because of *my righteousness* [H] that the LORD has brought me in to occupy this land'; it is rather

---

6. The probability that a chapter the size of Ezek 32 could contain 16 Huldah anagrams by coincidence is 7.9×10^{-15}.

because of the wickedness of these nations that the LORD is *dispossessing* [H] them before you. It is not because of *your righteousness* [H] or *the uprightness* [H] of your heart that you are going in to occupy their land . . ." (Deut 9:4–5). This quotation can easily be dated. It must have been composed in that brief window between Jerusalem's capture by the Israelites and the crushing defeat that followed. The prior chapter dated the final battle at April 28, 573 BCE. Assuming that the date is correct, Huldah's opponents would have composed Deut 31 in the winter of 574 or the spring of 573.

ANTI-HULDAH ANAGRAMS

Returning to Ezekiel, as expected, that prophet objected to the way Huldah exercised the prophetic office. He wrote, "If the sentinel sees the sword coming upon the land and blows the *trumpet* [H] and warns the people; then if any who hear the sound of the trumpet do not take warning . . . their blood shall be upon their own *heads* [H] . . . But if the sentinel sees the sword coming and does not blow the *trumpet* [H], so that the people are not warned . . . their blood I will require at the sentinel's hand" (Ezek 33:3–4, 6). Huldah was a prophet, but because she married Jehoiakim, who subsequently became king, Ezekiel might also have considered her a shepherd. At least he used that word to form a Huldah anagram: "Prophesy against the shepherds of Israel: prophesy, and say to them—to the *shepherds* [H] . . . Ah, you shepherds of Israel who have been feeding yourselves! Should not shepherds feed the sheep?" (Ezek 34:2). Shortly thereafter, the prophet accused, "You have not bound up the *injured* [H] . . . but with force and harshness you have ruled them" (Ezek 34:4).

Like Jeremiah, Ezekiel criticized Huldah for her prosperity. He said, "Violence has grown into a *rod* [H] of wickedness. None of them shall remain, not their abundance, not their wealth; no pre-eminence among them" (Ezek 7:11). However, in a chapter on Tyre, Ezekiel admiringly emphasizes Huldah's wealth from trading: "Your *borders* [H] are in the heart of the seas . . . Of fine embroidered linen from Egypt was your *sail* [H]" (Ezek 27:4, 7). Also, "In *clothes* [H] of blue and embroidered work, and in *carpets* [H, H, Jehoiachin] of colored material, bound with cords and made secure; in these they traded with you" (Ezek 27:24). Perhaps Ezekiel wrote those lines before the venture against the Promised Land, because he had much that was good to say about the exiled queen mother and her son (see also Ezek 27:5, 12, 14, 16, 19, 22, 33). However, toward the end of chapter 27 the prophet concluded, "Your riches, your *wares* [H, Jehoiachin, Jehoiachin], your merchandise, your mariners and your pilots, your caulkers, your dealers in merchandise, and all your warriors within you, with all the company that is with you, sink into the heart of the seas on the day of your ruin" (Ezek 27:33). This next verse houses an accusation within a compliment: "By your great wisdom in trade you have increased your wealth, and your heart has become *proud* [H] in your wealth" (Ezek 28:5).

During her long life, Huldah often experienced war. She survived two sieges at Jerusalem, resisted several Babylonian invasions of Egypt, may have fought against Pharaoh in order to leave Egypt, was with the Israelites as they battled to retake the Promised Land, and witnessed the final showdown against Nebuchadnezzar before Jerusalem. In such times, Ezekiel consistently threatened her with harm. Here are some of the numerous examples: "I am going to break the staff of bread *in Jerusalem* [H, Daniel]; they shall eat bread by weight and with fearfulness; and they shall drink water *by measure* [H] and in dismay"; "I bring more and more famine upon you, and *break* [H] your staff of bread"; "When a land sins against me . . . I stretch out my hand against it, and *break* [H] its staff of bread and send famine upon it"; "The sword is given to be *polished* [H]"; "King Nebuchadrezzar of Babylon, king of kings, together with horses, chariots, *cavalry*, [H, H] and a great and powerful army"; and "When I brandish my sword before them, they shall tremble every *moment* [H, Baruch] for their lives" (Ezek 4:16, 5:16, 14:13, 21:16, 26:7, 32:10).

Ezekiel prophesied that military disaster awaited his own nation's forces. This particular verse applied to the alliance with Egypt: "I will cause your hordes to fall by the swords of *mighty ones* [H, Jehoiachin], all of them most terrible among the nations. They shall bring to ruin the pride of Egypt" (Ezek 32:12). Ezekiel despised Egypt as he despised Huldah. Here is more Scripture that strikes at both: "I have set fire to Egypt, and all who help it are *broken* [H]"; "I am against Pharaoh king of Egypt, and will break his arms, both the strong arm and the one that was *broken* [H]"; "I will scatter the Egyptians *among the nations* [H]"; and "Scatter the Egyptians *among the nations* [H] and disperse them throughout the countries" (Ezek 30:8, 22, 23, 26). This next verse clearly shows on which side Ezekiel stood: "I will strengthen the arms of the king of Babylon, and put my sword in his hand; but I will *break* [H] the arms of Pharaoh" (Ezek 30:24).

The following verse has three Huldah anagrams with two more for her son: "They do not lie with the *fallen* [H] *warriors* [H, Jehoiachin] of long ago who went down to Sheol . . . for the terror of the *warriors* [H, Jehoiachin] was in the land of the living" (Ezek 32:27). The prophet stuck with his theme of slaughter: "'They shall cut off your nose *and your ears* [H], and your survivors shall fall by the sword"'; "I will fill its mountains with the slain; on *your hills* [H] . . . those killed with the sword shall fall"; and "They shall not *defile* [H] themselves by going near to a dead person" (Ezek 23:25; 35:8; 44:25). The sword would take some and exile would take the rest. Huldah was among the rest to be taken: "'Some of you shall escape the sword *among the nations* [H] and be scattered through the countries"'; Israel shall "'eat their bread, unclean, *among the nations* [H] to which I will drive them"'; The exiles "'shall remember me *among the nations* [H] where they are carried captive"'; "'I will scatter you *among the nations* [H] . . . and I will purge your filthiness out of you"'; and "'As I carry you captive *among the nations* [H], into countries you have not known"' (Ezek 6:8; 4:13; 6:9; 22:15; 32:9).[7]

Huldah received her share of rebuke from Ezekiel for organizing the failed campaign against Jerusalem. This anagram shows that others belonged in that same boat with Huldah: "I, the LORD, have heard all the *abusive* [H, Cyrus, Baruch, Jehoiachin] speech that you uttered against the mountains of Israel, saying, 'They are laid desolate, they are given us to devour'" (Ezek 35:12). "They are given us to devour" hints at the initial victories in the Cyrus-led venture. Ezekiel in Babylonia survived long enough to comment further. He also wrote, "O mountains of Israel . . . the desolate wastes and the deserted *towns* [H], which have become a source of plunder and an object of derision" (Ezek 36:4). The prophet seems to accuse the Cyrus-Huldah coalition of seeking alliances against Babylon and so profaning God: "I had concern for my holy name, which the house of Israel had profaned *among the nations* [H] to which they came"; and "For the sake of my holy name, which you have profaned *among the nations* [H] to which you came" (Ezek 36:21, 22; see also v. 23).

Ezekiel was obsessed with Huldah. At least a score of times he likened her to a whore, and he has left a woeful legacy within Holy Scripture that is beginning to be addressed. Other writers of the period—notably Jeremiah—shared or copied Ezekiel's misogynistic views, though champions like Jacob, Daniel, and Ezra rallied to Huldah's defense. This book

---

7. For other Huldah anagrams about exile in the book of Ezekiel, see Ezek 11:16; 12:15; 20:23; 29:12; 36:19; and 38:4.

about Huldah should advance the discussion by showing that Huldah herself was the object of many—perhaps most—of the attacks upon women within Hebrew Scripture. Ezekiel seems by nature to have been an angry man, but why single out Huldah as the principle object of his feelings? This writer leaves that to others to determine.

As for Ezekiel, let the last word be a good one. Chapter 37 is the memorable story of the valley of dried bones. The prophet said, "I looked, and there were sinews on them, and *flesh* [H] had come upon them, and skin *had covered them* [Ezra]; but there was no breath in them. Then he said to me, 'Prophesy to the breath, prophesy, mortal, and say to the breath: Thus says the Lord GOD: Come from the four winds, O breath, and breathe upon these *slain* [H, Jehoiachin], that they may live.' I prophesied as he commanded me, and the breath came into them, and they lived, and stood *on their feet* [Cyrus], a vast multitude" (Ezek 37:8–10). The prophet says that after the mortal defeat of Cyrus and the Israelites, the Lord would raise his nation again. And in that resurrected host would be Huldah herself, as well as Ezra, Jehoiachin, and Cyrus. It was a story of hope told against a backdrop of hopelessness.

The next chapter will discuss the portions of Scripture that Huldah helped to shape.

6

What Huldah Wrote

CODED SPELLING IS ONE of the two pioneering methods in biblical studies that this book presents—the other being anagrams. This volume's consistent aim is to identify portions of Hebrew Scripture that contain exceptional concentrations of Huldah coded spellings. Of course to find the exceptional, one must compare it against normal, a benchmark. For coded spellings, normal is always the entire text of Hebrew Scripture. Here is a specific example. The name Huldah in coded spellings occurs 4,233 times within Scripture's 305,496 text words. This 4,233 / 305,496 becomes the benchmark for all Huldah occurrences. Genesis 24, the story of Isaac's long-distance courtship of Rebekah, has thirty such spellings concealed under 918 text words. Are Genesis 24's thirty spellings exceptional? The chi-square test shows that they are indeed.[1] The probability of coincidence is about one in 550,000, and the lower the probability of coincidence, the higher the probability of purposeful coding.

A WIFE FOR MY SON

Computers enable one to skip any sampling and instead use the entire Hebrew Bible as the norm. Also, this approach requires only slightly more effort to measure Huldah frequency in all 929 chapters than to establish that frequency for just Genesis 24. It is common practice in biblical studies to concentrate upon a single book, period, or person, but this new

---

1. The chi-square proportions are 30 / 918 and 4,203 / 304,578. That is, 30 spellings in 918 text words compared to spellings and text words in the balance of Scripture. The probability of coincidence is 1.796×10^{-6}, or about 1 in 550,000.

approach outfits scholars with seven-league boots. In just weeks instead of years, it can provide them with a Bible-wide view of the subject they choose. Finally, athbash multiplication and name variations greatly increase the number of tests that any scholar can run at one time against any passage. For instance, variations such as Huldah-the-prophetess have allowed this writer to test Genesis 24 for 132 different coded spellings, and then to weigh results against their collective all-Bible norm. Genesis 24 houses statistically significant spellings of over one dozen of those Huldah variations. This is more than enough to promote the chapter to statistically significant status. It follows that Genesis 24 is by or about Huldah.

Is this judgment premature? In a way, it is. More than one thousand other Hebrew names await the same sort of testing that Huldah has received. Presumably a few of them will also show results similar to those of Huldah. When that time comes—and may it be soon—scholars should modify the words that "Genesis 24 is by or about Huldah" to "Genesis 24 is *also* by or about Huldah." That is, the statistically based conclusions in this book will stand, though others may take their places alongside them. And imagine what scholars may come to understand about the whole Hebrew Bible when all name variations have been tested against all Scripture. Instead of a dearth of information, there will be a plentitude.

Here is a firsthand example of what we can expect. Genesis 24 tells of an unnamed servant who was sent to Mesopotamia by his aged master Abraham to "'go to my country and to my kindred and get a wife for my son Isaac'" (Gen 24:4). This was to avoid having to select "'a wife for my son from the daughters of the Canaanites, among whom I live'" (Gen 24:3). The long chapter relates how the servant encounters the comely Rebekah and convinces her and her father that she should become Isaac's bride.[2] After the journey home, the conclusion is a happy one: Isaac "took Rebekah, and she became his wife; and he loved her" (Gen 24:67). The coding of Huldah and of her son Jehoiachin in Genesis 24 is heavy. With this coding in mind, one would surmise that the exiled queen mother arranged a marriage for her then-unmarried son Jehoiachin by sending back to Israel for a bride, and so avoided having to choose a Canaanite—presumably Babylonian—wife for him. We now know that Huldah and Jehoiachin were in Babylonia during the decade following 597, and that the young king was eighteen when he began his exile.

---

2. Huldah did not shy from lengthy chapters. Significant coded spellings indicate that she wrote or helped to write four out of six of Scripture's longest chapters—Genesis 24; Numbers 7; Psalm 119; and 1 Samuel 17.

The exiles would have been highly interested in a marriage that could carry on the Davidic line, and Genesis 24 could well be a romanticized account of what actually happened. Presumably, the bride's actual name is encoded under the text. It could have been Rebekah, or perhaps Jecoliah, who probably was Jehoiachin's wife when the Babylonians executed him in 562.[3] Either way, Genesis 24 has a sixth-century date. Baruch is a candidate for the role of Abraham's resourceful servant who made the journey, completed difficult arrangements, and brought Rebekah to Jehoiachin. The chapter has ten Baruch anagrams, but this is still five short of statistical significance for the chapter. Baruch should remain a person of interest, but let the question remain open pending further coding work.

As to date, Huldah probably composed Genesis 24 during her Babylonian sojourn (597–586). A complication is that the text contains two Cyrus anagrams. If Huldah wrote this when Cyrus was present, a better guess about composition date would be during her final years (572–564). Still, two Cyrus anagrams are exactly the number that a chapter this large should randomly produce. Given that, students of Scripture can reasonably assign a 597–586 date to chapter 24's composition. More important than the composition date, however, is the time when the quest for a bride took place. Plausibly, the queen mother would have been seeking a suitable wife for the youthful king not long after 597, when Huldah and Jehoiachin arrived in Babylonia.

SCOPE OF HULDAH'S WORK

The lesson from Genesis 24 is that with reasoned imagination and coding techniques one can relate the Exile's events to specific passages, chapters, and sometimes even to whole books of Scripture. However, most of that lies in the future. For the present, here is an overall view of the chapters and books of the Hebrew Bible that were written by or about Huldah. Scripture has 929 chapters. One hundred forty-four of those have Huldah coded spelling totals that are exceptionally high. Add to this number thirty-one more chapters with statistically significant numbers of Huldah anagrams. There is some overlap between chapters with numerous anagrams and those with high coded-spelling totals. Taking this into account,

3. Kavanagh, *The Exilic Code*, 10, shows that Jecoliah was a female name that the Priestly Benediction concealed. The Babylonians probably killed her along with Jehoiachin, who may have been her husband. The benediction at the end of Numbers 6 is a farewell to Jehoiachin after his execution in 562 BCE.

168 of Scripture's 929 chapters have significant Huldah markings. This is an amazing number considering that Huldah has never previously been thought of as an author of Hebrew Scripture. Still, exceptional coded results do not automatically confer authorship. In a number of those chapters, Huldah's opponents encoded her name to criticize her. Also, many portions of Scripture were produced by groups of experts acting together, so caution is in order when using the terms "author" and "wrote."

Huldah frequently worked with others in producing Scripture. An earlier book documented this association with the other fourteen prophets, scribes, and officials called the Shaphan group.[4] Huldah's name is significantly coded in two-thirds of the group's work. Judged by coding in the Shaphan-group chapters, others contributed at least as much—often more—than she did. After eliminating duplicates, the chapters add 118 to Huldah's count. Taken together, 168 plus 118 makes 286 chapters that Huldah to one degree or another wrote, assisted in, or provoked.[5]

Hebrew Scripture has thirty-nine books, starting with Genesis and ending with Second Chronicles. Dealing with books instead of just chapters offers another measure of Huldah's impact upon Scripture. A dozen books contain statistically significant totals of Huldah spellings, with representation from all four branches of the Bible—the Pentateuch, the historical books, the prophets, and the writings. The Pentateuch and history books yield but one Huldah concentration each—Numbers and Joshua. The prophets, with Ezekiel and Isaiah, have two. And last, but far from least, the writings with Ezra, Nehemiah, Esther, Daniel, Psalms, Proverbs, and First and Second Chronicles round out the dozen.[6] Surprisingly, Ezra, Nehemiah, and Esther made the list, though they came into being well after Huldah's lifetime. Ezra in particular seems to look back with sympathy upon Huldah's efforts to rebuild Jerusalem. The heaviest coding concentrations are in Daniel and Proverbs—facts that should help establish the provenance of both books. Ten of Daniel's twelve chapters are

4. For a discussion of the Shaphan group, see Kavanagh, *The Shaphan Group*, 67–85.

5. Huldah wrote or influenced 31 percent of Scripture's chapters. Knowing Huldah's penchant for longer chapters, her share of Scripture's total text words will probably be at least one-third.

6. Some chapters of Ezra and Daniel are in Aramaic rather than Hebrew. The key thing in coding is number of letters per text word—the more letters per word, the better a text can support coding. However, the number of letters per word in the books of Ezra and Daniel is virtually the same as for Scripture as a whole. It appears that the coded-spelling technique was applied as smoothly to Aramaic texts as it was to those written solely in Hebrew.

heavily coded with Huldah spellings; Proverbs has twenty-three of thirty-one such chapters.

A focus of future scholarly work is certain to be the book of Psalms. No fewer than eighteen psalms bear significantly coded Huldah signatures, including important ones like Pss 51, 89, and the massive 119. Psalm 31 contains Huldah's final words—and those of Jesus, too. The significant encoding in Ezekiel underlines the prophet's animus against Huldah. And unlike the authors of Psalms, Ezekiel used anagrams rather than coded spellings to emphasize his feelings about Huldah.

Table 6.1 presents an overview of Huldah's influence on the Bible. This table ranks the leading books in Scripture by percentage of chapters that contain significant Huldah coding, anagrams included. Except for Numbers, Joshua, Ezekiel, and Isaiah, the leading concentrations of Huldah coded spellings and anagrams come from the so-called writings, which are thought to be among the Bible's more recently written books. Daniel, Ezra-Nehemiah, Chronicles, Proverbs, and Psalms lead in percentage of significant chapters. Note that Huldah—this singular individual—was significantly involved with 16 percent of Hebrew Scripture. While books with heavier coding are high points of Huldah's influence, they in no way set its limits. She wrote and we enjoy Scripture far beyond these boundaries.

Table 6.1: Books with High Percentages of Significant Huldah Coding

Books	Significant Chapters	% Significant Chapters
Daniel	10	83%
Ezra-Nehemiah	15	74
Joshua	8	33
Chronicles	19	29
Numbers	10	28
Proverbs	7	23
Ezekiel	8	17
Isaiah	9	14
Psalms	18	11
All Huldah	104	11%
Rest of OT	46	5%
All	150	16%

The book of Daniel exceeds all others in percentage of significant chapters with Huldah coding. Daniel is a difficult challenge for those seeking to classify it. The book is written in both Aramaic and Hebrew, is filled with historical inaccuracies, and is thought by some to have originated as late as the second century BCE. Moreover, its hero is a legendary character named Daniel, who supposedly lived successively under Nebuchadnezzar, Darius the Mede, and Belshazzar (son of the final Babylonian king). A leading expert writes, "All but the most conservative scholars now accept the conclusion that the book of Daniel is not a product of the Babylonian era but reached its present form in the 2d century B.C.E. Daniel is not a historical person but a figure of legend."[7] It is possible to reconcile this conclusion with most Huldah-related findings, though even these cannot straighten out the book's tortuous authorship history. The Huldah findings, however, should help others who address that task.

Daniel 2–11 contains heavy Huldah encoding—over 4,000 Huldah-related spellings. Each of these ten chapters has, effectively, a zero percent chance that its encodings are coincidental. Therefore, those who wrote, edited, or reedited the chapters honored original Huldah spellings and added new encodings as they composed fresh text. Huldah died in 564, two years before Nebuchadnezzar's demise. This may limit any of the Daniel material that Huldah wrote in Dan 2–4, since the remaining chapters speak of other rulers. Also, Daniel 1 and 12, the first and last chapters, lack Huldah coding. This suggests that they were added after the rest of the book was complete.

Contrary to what "all but the most conservative scholars" may think, Daniel himself was a historical person, not a figure of legend. A study of overlapping Huldah and Daniel anagrams in Scripture links the two closely together, showing that their anagrams were intentionally formed within the same scriptural verse with improbable frequency.[8] Unquestionably, Huldah was a historical person and unquestionably—pending repeal of the laws of probability—anagrams of Huldah and Daniel share an extraordinary proportion of verses. It follows that Daniel himself was an actual person who lived during the same period as Huldah. Many of those overlapping anagrams come from the word formed by "in Jerusalem," which was used repeatedly in Kings and Chronicles. In 597, Huldah was

7. Collins, "Book of Daniel," 30.

8. Daniel anagrams occur in 1,573 verses and Huldah anagrams in 1,674 verses. Huldah and Daniel anagrams share 348 verses, while Scripture contains 23,191 verses. Drawing upon a Venn diagram, the chi-square proportions are 348 / 1,326 and 1,225 / 20,292. The probability that such overlapping would occur by coincidence is zero.

exiled to Babylon, where she undoubtedly came to know Daniel. Recently defeated Judah needed heroes badly, and Huldah had the skill to portray the exilic prodigy. She had ample opportunity to write part of the book of Daniel, and probably she did so—in company with virtually all of the other Shaphan Group members.[9] As a hypothesis, the material they wrote during the first decade of the Exile forms the core of today's much-altered book of Daniel. Later in the Exile, anagrams and coded Daniel spellings indicate that he was with the Israelite army as it fought its way north during the Cyrus revolt. If Daniel escaped capture at the battle of Jerusalem, he may also have helped Huldah to write Scripture at Bethel during the last years of her life.

The figure of Ezra is akin to that of Daniel. Coding shows that Ezra was indeed real, that he lived during the Exile, and that he was an ally of Huldah's during the struggle to win and hold Jerusalem. An entire chapter of another book traces Ezra's work as the author of the P Source as well as the rivalry with his brother Jozadak for the high priesthood.[10] However, those who hold that Ezra was an imaginary character in the books of Ezra-Nehemiah are also correct.[11] His proper era was the Exile, not the Restoration. The authors of Ezra-Nehemiah have memorialized Ezra's attempts to restore Jerusalem by moving him forward a full century in time and pairing him with Nehemiah, though their awkwardness has allowed many to detect the fiction.

Biblical writers did a similar thing with Huldah. Three-quarters of the Ezra-Nehemiah chapters have statistically significant Huldah encodings—*Huldah*, not Ezra encoding.[12] Three-quarters is more than four times Scripture's norm for significant Huldah coding. Though Ezra was a real person, Scripture intentionally misleads readers by placing him in the Restoration rather than in the Exile. As to Huldah, the text does not mention her at all, but her name is intensely encoded—even though she lived during the sixth-century Exile rather than during the fifth-century Restoration (experts place the composition date of Ezra-Nehemiah at around 400 BCE or a little later).[13]

9. Kavanagh, *The Shaphan Group*, 122, contains a list of Shaphan-group members whose names are significantly coded in Daniel 2–5, 8, and 11. Daniel and Huldah are included in that list.

10. Ibid., 45–66 ("Ezra and Jozadak BAs Sketch Exile's History").

11. For a discussion of this issue, see North, "Ezra," 726–28.

12. Ezra is encoded in four Ezra-Nehemiah chapters, compared with seventeen for Huldah.

13. Klein, "Ezra-Nehemiah," 732.

What caused the authors of Ezra-Nehemiah to conceal these matters? Here are some speculative answers. During the short period that rebel forces held Jerusalem, Huldah and Ezra led in rebuilding the city. The Huldah coding and the pseudo-Ezra character seem to refer to these previous activities. Next, Huldah and Ezra during their lifetimes were on opposite sides of the controversy about marriage to foreign women; and later, proponents on both sides used coding of pseudo-Ezra and Huldah to advance their arguments. Despite their prominence during the Exile, neither Huldah nor Ezra was openly mentioned in Scripture (with a few obliquely phrased exceptions). Subsequently, partisans of each must have agreed to continue that silence about their hero and heroine when they drafted the balance of Scripture. Most importantly, these things show the stature of both as well the pall that the abortive Cyrus revolt continued to cast over Judean life. More narrowly, the book of Ezra-Nehemiah illustrates the powerful influence that Huldah the prophet continued to exercise upon Scripture.

Like Ezra and Nehemiah, the two books of Chronicles have, in this analysis, been treated as a single book. Experts think that each was originally just one volume. Some scholars are of the opinion that the books of Chronicles share authorship with Ezra-Nehemiah.[14] True or not, the two collections do have at least one strong similarity, for both contain an exceptional number of coded Huldah spellings. This common trait strengthens the possibility that Chronicles-Ezra-Nehemiah was once a single work composed around the same time—c 400 BCE, a good century and one-half after Huldah's death. Again, this points to the enduring renown of the prophetess.

Seen together, the books of Numbers and Joshua go far toward covering the revolt of the 570s. That is, at least the eighteen chapters with significant Huldah spellings deal with that brief period. The Huldah chapters speak of preparations for the wilderness expedition, rebellions on the march, dealing with corpses, warfare in Canaan, offerings at feasts, setting boundaries, distributing land amongst the tribes, and even pasturing rights for the Levites. These are the very activities in which the revolt's leadership would have been involved—preparing for the campaign, fighting it, allocating land, re-establishing cult practices, and beginning to govern. Table 6.1 includes only significant Huldah chapters in Numbers and Joshua. However, an almost equal number of chapters can be credited to

14. Klein, "Chronicles," 993.

the Shaphan group, of which both she and Ezra were members.[15] Sanctions for directives in the book of Numbers came from the Lord via Moses; in the book of Joshua, the spokesperson was Joshua himself. Earlier work in another book posits that, at least in the exilic chapters, Moses and Joshua were actually Shaphan and Asaiah.[16] Both had served as officials in Josiah's court long before and, according to Scripture, both died before the rebels reached the Promised Land (Deut 34:5, Josh 24:29).

Scholars have identified both Deuteronomistic and Priestly Source shadings in Joshua and Numbers. The likely reason is that both views were represented within the Shaphan group. Although Huldah had plenty of writing help, coding and anagram results show that she had a strong hand in the actual drafting. A related conclusion is that those who analyze Scripture may soon be able to dispense with letter abbreviations like P and Dtr—at least for texts written from the Exile forward. Instead, scholars may choose to substitute the actual personal names encoded within Scripture.

HULDAH'S GREATEST ACHIEVEMENT

Perhaps Huldah's greatest gift to Scripture is her gift with words. Aside from Second Isaiah (with whom she worked), no other writer had her facility and depth. At the root of it was her ability to portray the feminine side of human nature. Passages that follow will illustrate this by exploring Huldah's connection with some of the women of Scripture. The examples will demonstrate Huldah's excellence in using the Hebrew language in the service of her God.

Her greatest achievement may be Judg 5, the Song of Deborah, which will be quoted at length to show its full narrative power. The chapter is a rarity in Scripture because both coded spellings (ninety-eight) and anagrams (eight) of Huldah are statistically significant. It reads in part:

LORD, when you went out from Seir, when you marched from the region of Edom, the earth trembled, and the heavens poured, the clouds indeed poured water. The mountains quaked before the LORD, the One of Sinai, before the LORD, the God of Israel
. . .

15. Shaphan-group chapters include Numbers 1–3; 19; 26; 28–29; 36; and Joshua 12–13; 15–19. See Kavanagh, *The Shaphan Group*, 112–13.

16. Ibid., 39 and 80.

> You arose, Deborah, arose as a mother in Israel . . . To the
> sound of musicians [Daniel] at the watering places, there they
> repeat *the triumphs* [H] of the LORD, *the triumphs* [H] of his
> peasantry in Israel.
> Then down *to the gates* [H] marched the people of the LORD.
> Awake, awake, Deborah! Awake, awake, utter a song! Arise,
> Barak, lead away your captives . . . the people of the LORD
> marched down for him against *the mighty* [H, Jehoiachin]
> . . . into the valley they rushed out *at his heels* [H, Jehoiachin].
> Among *the clans* [Cyrus] of Reuben [Jacob] there were great
> searchings of heart . . .
> The kings came, they fought; then fought the kings of Ca-
> naan, at Taanach [Daniel] . . . The stars fought from heaven,
> from their courses they fought against Sisera [Daniel]. The tor-
> rent Kishon [Baruch] swept them away, the onrushing [Ezra]
> torrent, the torrent Kishon [Baruch]. March on, my soul, with
> might! Then loud beat the horses' hoofs [Jacob] . . . They did
> not come to . . . the help of the LORD against *the mighty* [H,
> Jehoiachin]. (Judg 5:4–5, 7, 11–13, 15, 19–23)

Deborah may be the pre-eminent female character in Hebrew Scripture, and Huldah either created her or fashioned her from an earlier tradition.[17] Like Judges-era Deborah, Exile-period Huldah victoriously led her people in war—yet by association could still be called "a mother in Israel." Judged by Cyrus anagrams, the Song of Deborah could have originated in the early 570s when Huldah and other leaders in Egypt contacted Cyrus and sought to heat up the war fever around the Diaspora. Or more likely it came later during the campaign that led to Jerusalem's capture. "When you marched from the region of Edom" hints at this, and so does the descrip-tion of the battle against the Canaanite kings. In either case, the Song of Deborah was written in the 570s. Readers will notice how many anagrams crowd this battle scene. Hidden within the text are the names of Israel's ex-ilic leaders who were in Egypt at the campaign's start—Daniel, Ezra, Jacob, Baruch, Jehoiachin, and of course Cyrus the Persian and Huldah herself.

In the Song, Huldah profiles two other female characters. The first is Jael, who slew the Canaanite general Sisera, while the second is the un-named mother of that commander. Here is the later portion of Deborah's song that tells their stories. The fleeing Sisera takes refuge with Jael:

---

17. Huldah had a great deal of skilled help in composing Judges 5. Each of the other fourteen members of the Shaphan group also contributed significant coded writ-ing to the chapter. See Kavanagh, *The Shaphan Group*, 113.

Most blessed of women be Jael . . . He [Sisera] asked water and she gave him milk, she brought him curds in a lordly bowl. She put her hand to the tent peg and her right hand to the workmen's *mallet* [Cyrus]; she struck *Sisera* [Daniel] a blow, she crushed his head, she shattered and pierced his temple. He sank, he fell, he lay still at her feet; at her feet he sank, he fell; where he sank, there he fell dead.

Out of the window she peered, the mother of *Sisera* [Daniel] gazed through the lattice: "Why is *his chariot* [Baruch] so long in coming? Why tarry the hoofbeats of *his chariots* [Baruch]?" Her wisest ladies make answer, indeed, she answers the question herself: "Are they not finding and dividing the spoil?—A girl or two for every man; spoil of dyed stuffs *for Sisera* [Daniel], spoil of dyed stuffs embroidered, two pieces of dyed work embroidered for my neck as spoil?" (Judg 5:24–30)

Neither Jael nor Sisera's mother is squeamish about the ways of war. Huldah seems to go out of her literary way to make clear that women could be just as bloodthirsty as men. Also, observe how skillfully, in Judg 5:20, she takes her readers from the summit of God's cosmic battle for his people ("The stars fought from heaven, from their courses they fought against Sisera") to the intimacy of a self-deluding mother awaiting her son's overdue return from battle. The Song of Deborah might be Huldah's greatest work, but it was far from being the only engaging one. Here is another.

ABIGAIL, BATHSHEBA, AND HULDAH

Abigail, who became King David's second wife, was originally married to a surly man, Nabal by name, who refused aid to David when he was a fugitive. Abigail hurriedly interceded and secretly supplied David with food. Later, she made a lengthy speech that dissuaded David from taking her husband's life. David thanked her saying, "Blessed be your good sense, and blessed be you, who have kept me today from bloodguilt and from avenging myself by my own hand!" (1 Sam 25:33). Subsequently, David wooed Abigail and made her his wife. When a *waw* is added to the name "Abigail," the altered word supports a Huldah anagram. Seven of the name's sixteen occurrences in Scripture have such a *waw* addition. Six form "and Abigail," while the seventh solved the anagram problem by substituting—without apparent cause—a Hebrew *waw* for another letter in "Abigail." The result of all this is that the name "Abigail," in just sixteen appearances, supports seven Huldah anagrams. Can these seven Huldah anagrams be coincidental? The answer is no. The probability is zero that by coincidence seven of the sixteen "Abigail" occurrences could also be Huldah anagrams.[18] Imagine choosing while blindfolded seven red balls and nine black balls in sixteen draws from a vat containing 1,773 balls, seven of them red and the remaining 1,766 colored black. The odds against picking all seven red balls (the Huldah anagrams) in sixteen pulls are eighty-three billion to one.

Abigail is Huldah, and the Bible's story line might reflect an actual period in Huldah's life. Scripture says that Abigail "was clever and beautiful" (1 Sam 25:3), which certainly described Huldah. Also, Nabal and David might actually have been Shallum (Huldah's first husband) and Jehoiakim (her second). Further, as Abigail's pleading saved Nabal's life, Huldah's pleading might have saved Shallum's.[19] This is supposition, but what is not supposition are those Huldah anagrams lodged within "Abigail" text words. It appears that Huldah created Abigail, fashioning her in the prophet's own image.

Bathsheba is another strong woman in Scripture. After King David caught sight of her bathing on her rooftop, he sent for Bathsheba and lay with her, though she was another man's wife. When David learned that Bathsheba was pregnant, he arranged for the death of her husband, brought the woman to the palace, and married her. Second Samuel 11 narrates the famous romance, and this writer can find no indication that Huldah was the chapter's author, or that events such as these might have been biographical ones for Huldah herself. First Kings 1 is a different matter, however. It too is about Bathsheba but the events that it relates take place when David is on his deathbed. The chapter contains 190 coded spellings of Huldah, Huldah-mother-of-Jehoiachin, and Huldah-wife-of-Shallum. Although the chapter is a long one, 190 coded spellings make it a certainty that the text is by or about Huldah.[20] Moreover, the same chapter contains

18. "Abigail" has 16 occurrences, 7 of which also contain Huldah anagrams, while 9 Abigail and 1,766 Huldah anagrams have no overlap. The probability of coincidence = a combination of (16 choose 7) (1,766 choose 9) / 1,774 choose 16 = 1.21 × 10⁻¹¹. The seven text words with overlapping anagrams are in 1 Sam 25:14, 18; 27:3; 30:3; 2 Sam 2:2; and 1 Chr 2:16, 17. "Abigail" with the unusual spelling (אבוגיל) is in 1 Sam 25:18.

19. In passages that must have originated years after Huldah married Jehoiakim, the text continued to produce significant encodings of Huldah-wife-of-Shallum. It appears that Shallum the wardrobe keeper survived his wife's marriage to Jehoiakim. It is even possible that Shallum and Huldah resumed their relationship after King Jehoiakim's death.

20. The chi-square proportions are 190 / 26,020 and 813 / 304,683. The first

622—622!—coded spellings of Jehoiachin, Huldah's son. First Kings 1 is autobiographical. It is by the mother and about mother and son, Huldah and Jehoiachin.

The opening chapter of First Kings relates how Queen Bathsheba secured the kingship of Israel for her son Solomon from the rightful heir Adonijah, David's oldest son. With help from Nathan the prophet, Bathsheba convinced the dying David to reaffirm that Solomon was his successor. Acting under the old king's instructions, Solomon quickly assumed the throne. For a time, young Solomon spared his brother's life. However, in a subsequent chapter, Adonijah sought to marry one of King David's concubines. Bathsheba herself brought that request to Solomon, but the new king refused it and ordered Adonijah's execution.

All this intrigue from David's court is complex enough to be true. But one suspects it reports something close to what happened in the sixth century, not the tenth. More than three centuries later, Huldah as prospective queen mother saw to it that Jehoiachin succeeded her husband Jehoiakim as Judah's king. Succession accounts about Jehoiachin, however, are muddled. What *is* clear is that the queen mother Bathsheba of 1 Kings 1 is a mirror of the queen mother Huldah. First Kings 1 may tell us how young Jehoiachin actually came to the throne in 597 BCE (he was to reign for only three months before he, like his father, was sent into exile).

First Kings 2, the following chapter, bears no marks of Huldah's authorship. It does, however, contain a verse that shows the standing of a Huldah-era queen mother: "So Bathsheba went to King Solomon, to speak to him on behalf of Adonijah. The king rose to meet her, and bowed down to her; then he sat on his throne, and had a throne brought for the king's mother, and she sat on his right" (1 Kgs 2:19). If this was not written by Huldah, it was written with Huldah in mind. To conclude with Bathsheba, her name appears in three other verses that contain underlying Huldah coded spellings—2 Sam 11:3, 12:24, and 1 Chr 3:4. The Chronicles verse also contains a Huldah anagram.

---

proportion is Huldah spellings in 1 Kings 1 over spellings in the rest of Scripture, and the second is text words in the same categories. The probability that the Huldah spellings are coincidental is 1.54×10^{-38}. Coding about other members of the Shaphan group often accompanies such heavy Huldah coding. This is not the case in 1 Kings 1, however.

HULDAH AND THE FEMALE PROPHETS

In all of Hebrew Scripture, only four females are named as prophets—Moses' sister Miriam, Deborah, Huldah, and an individual named Noadiah. Deborah seems to be Huldah's creation, while Noadiah is an historical person. She opposed Nehemiah a century and one-half after Huldah's time, and rates but a single line in Scripture. Nehemiah prays, "Remember Tobiah and Sanballat, O my God, according to these things that they did, and also *the prophetess Noadiah* and the rest of the prophets who wanted to make me afraid" (Neh 6:14, italics added). Surprisingly, Huldah coding is heavy throughout that chapter, including beneath the Noadiah verse.[21] It is not clear what conclusion to draw from this, though one could venture that the author saw Noadiah in the line of female prophets that ran from Huldah.

As to Miriam the prophetess (Exod 15:20), there is only faint proof that Huldah created her or her title. The mention of "prophetess" comes at the conclusion of the Song of Miriam, which has but a single Huldah anagram and modest Huldah coding. These are concentrated in a passage ending at v. 15. It says, "The peoples heard, *they trembled* [Huldah]; pangs seized the inhabitants of Philistia. Then the chiefs of Edom were dismayed; trembling seized the leaders of Moab; all the inhabitants of Canaan melted away" (Exod 15:14–15).[22] This sounds as though it was written during the initial stages of Israel's invasion of Judah in the 570s. A few verses later—perhaps while Huldah was helping to draft the Song of Miriam—she added, "Then the prophet Miriam, Aaron's sister, took a tambourine in her hand; and all the women went out after her with tambourines and with dancing" (Exod 15:20).

As discussed, Miriam, Deborah, Huldah, and Noadiah were named as female prophets. In addition, Scripture has several other candidates, the daughters of Heman among them. The sons of Heman were members of a Levitical guild appointed to provide singing and prophecy in the Jerusalem temple. First Chronicles 25:5 says that God had given Heman three daughters along with his fourteen sons to play with cymbals, harps, and lyres. They worked at the direction of their father who was "under the orders of the king." It follows that Heman's daughters also prophesied—certainly in worship and perhaps even to the king. Are Heman's daughters connected with Huldah? They probably are. First Chronicles 25 contains

21. Taken as a whole, Nehemiah 6 is significantly encoded with Huldah spellings.

22. The text words in Exod 15:11–15 conceal significant Huldah encodings. The probability of coincidence is 6.9×10^{-5}.

138 Huldah coded spellings and falls just below the strict level of statistical significance.[23] Perhaps Huldah was reminding her readers of a tradition of female prophecy that stretched from early in the history of Israel's worship.

What were Huldah's ties with other female prophets? Isaiah chapter 8 identifies a female prophet and at the same time contains heavy Huldah coding.[24] The prophet Isaiah says, "I went to the prophetess, and she conceived and bore a son" (Isa 8:3). The weight and variety of the coding suggests that this is biographical. Huldah is the mother, but whom does the father represent? And what about the ill-fated child who bears a lengthy name that is roughly translated as "Hasten for spoil, hurry for plunder"? This could well be a passage that is hostile to sixth-century Huldah. Ezekiel attacked "the daughters of your people, who prophesy out of their own imagination" (Ezek 13:17), but they appear to have been practicing sorcery and casting spells.[25] Like the Isa 8 prophetess passage, this probably was an attack upon Huldah. In any event, a group of women during Huldah's time were prophesying in Judah, probably in Jerusalem.

In contrast is this famous passage from the book of Joel: "Then afterward I will pour out my spirit on all flesh; your sons and your daughters shall prophesy, your old men shall dream dreams, and your young men shall see *visions* [H]. Even on the male and female slaves, in those days, I will pour out my spirit" (Joel 2:28–29 H3:1–2). With help from some Shaphan-group members, Huldah wrote this and the verses that immediately follow.[26] Three Huldah anagrams within five verses plus mention of both slaves and survivors in Joel 2 establish Huldah's authorship and date the text after the Jerusalem catastrophe of 573.[27] When she wrote this, Huldah was in her early seventies. Joel 2:28–32 has a dreamlike quality. "Afterward" and "in those days" replace specific times and summon the reader to see beyond history. That time beyond time will include equal-

23. Kavanagh, *The Shaphan Group*, 123. The significance level of 1 Chronicles 25 is .002, slightly above the standard of .001. Daniel's coding is found alongside Huldah's within this chapter.

24. Forty-seven coded spellings of Huldah-wife-of-Jehoiakim, Huldah-wife-of-Shallum, Huldah-mother-of-Jehoiachin, Huldah-prophetess, and Huldah-queen-mother produce these chi-square proportions: 47 / 26,173 and 299 / 305,197. P = 8.85 × 10⁻⁵.

25. Zimmerli, *Ezekiel 1*, 296.

26. Kavanagh, *The Shaphan Group*, 116.

27. The Huldah anagrams yield a chi-square probability of coincidence of 4.18 × 10⁻⁵. On the other hand, Huldah coded spellings have a P value of .016, which misses this book's standard of .001.

ity between prophets of both sexes, since both sons and daughters will prophesy. Huldah carries the parallelism forward: old men and young men, dreams and visions, male and female. Had Shakespeare been a biblical scholar, he might have said of Huldah, "Age cannot wither her, nor custom stale her infinite poetic abilities."

The concluding verse in Joel 2 merits quotation: "Then everyone who calls on the name of the LORD shall be saved; for in Mount Zion and *in Jerusalem* [H] there shall be those who escape, as the LORD has said, *and among the survivors* [H] shall be those whom the LORD calls" (Joel 2:32 H3:5). Huldah herself was among those who survived the battle of Jerusalem. She was declaring in Scripture that this was the Lord's decision and not her own. She had not left her troops in the lurch but rather had been one of "those whom the LORD calls" to be a survivor—and she used two anagrams to support her claim. Date the Joel chapters in the early 560s.

Table 6.2 helps to summarize the nature of Huldah's authorial relationships with leading female characters and/or prophets in Scripture.

Table 6.2: Relationship of Huldah to Other Biblical Women

Women	Prophets	Coding Degree
Deborah	P	Heavy
Jael		Heavy
Sisera's Mother		Heavy
Abigail		Anagrams
Bathsheba		Heavy, Anagrams
Noadiah	P	Heavy, Hostile
Miriam	P	Faint
Heman's Daughters	P	Heavy
Isaiah's Prophetess	P	Heavy, Hostile
Ezekiel's Daughters	P	None, Hostile
Joel's Daughters	P	Heavy, Anagrams

Bathsheba is among the most memorable woman of the Hebrew Bible and at least half of her cameo appearances have close (and probably biographical) ties to Huldah. Anagrams bind the "clever and beautiful" (1 Sam 25:3) Abigail to Huldah. The resourcefulness of both Abigail and Bathsheba in dealing with their royal partner reflects well upon Huldah, who shaped the language of their stories. The connections of the war-leader Deborah and the ruthless Jael to Huldah their creator are wide and—once one understands about anagrams and coded spellings—plain to see. Both personify the warrior in Huldah. As to the passage about the prophetess who bears Isaiah's son, named "Hasten for spoil, hurry for plunder" (Isa 8:3), it must have been a slur on Huldah's military leadership, written either before or after the campaign against the Promised Land.

Next, textual evidence is strong that Huldah herself led in composing the lovely prophetic passage about how "your sons and your daughters shall prophesy" (Joel 2:28 H3:1). It may have been among her final writings. On the negative side, one detects only faint ties between Huldah and Miriam. Also, Huldah has no encoded connection to the group of female liturgical prophets denounced by Ezekiel, though they may have been her disciples.

Finally, there is Noadiah, the female prophet who opposed Nehemiah. It is notable that Nehemiah 6, the chapter in which Noadiah makes a brief appearance, is significantly encoded with Huldah spellings. The distance in time between the two women is some 150 years, yet Huldah is vividly remembered—to the extent that coded spellings measure such remembrance. Also, her influence reached far beyond female prophecy. Huldah knew Jeremiah, Ezekiel, and Second Isaiah well, and probably worked closely with at least Second Isaiah. Moreover, Huldah herself wrote Jeremiah's famous call—"Before I formed you in the womb I knew you, and before you were born I consecrated you; I appointed you a prophet to the nations" (Jer 1:5); probably the particulars of Jeremiah's call came out of Huldah's own experience. Whether or not that is true, the words were hers. In conclusion, Huldah stood in the mainstream of Hebrew prophecy—including males as well as females. It is far past time to honor her for that and for her substantial contribution to our Hebrew Bible.

Huldah did more than record the female prophets. She also implanted within Scripture the names of Judah's queen mothers. The Hebrew word translated as "in Jerusalem" contains an anagram for Huldah.[28] There are seventeen such anagrams in First and Second Kings, each associated with the mother's name of a reigning king in Jerusalem. Here is a typical entry: "Josiah was eight years old when he began to reign; he reigned thirty-one years *in Jerusalem* [H]. His mother's name was Jedidah daughter of Adaiah of Bozkath" (2 Kgs 22:1). These seventeen entries form a chain of queen mothers that stretches from the queen mother of King Solomon's son to the queen mother of the last king of Judah.[29] That extensive listing omit-

28. The Huldah athbash anagram is בורש. Its letters are contained within בירושלם.

29. The queen mothers are listed in 1 Kgs 14:21; 15:2, 10; 22:42; 2 Kgs 8:26; 12:2; 14:2; 15:2, 33; 18:2; 21:1, 19; 22:1; 23:31, 36; 24:8, 18. Chronicles has only nine such mentions and Jeremiah one.

ted the mothers of only two of Judah's kings—those of Joram, a king who "departed with no one's regret" (2 Chr 21:21), and of Ahaz, who installed a foreign altar in the Jerusalem temple. Clearly, this list of the mothers of the seventeen Judean kings is formulaic. Huldah, working with the deuteronomistic editors, composed it and then applied the formula again and again. However, Huldah's arrangement also included her signature so that every time her anagram appeared in the Kings text, Huldah announced her editorial presence. But, perhaps under the noses of her male counterparts, the prophetess was doing even more. She was inserting into the account of Judah's monarchs a history of its queen mothers. This work alone marks Huldah the prophetess as Scripture's foremost feminist.

And what does this indicate about the extent of her participation in the books of Kings? First, one would expect Huldah encodings to be denser in the dozen chapters that list Judah's queen mothers—but, if anything, coding is lighter. Only three of the chapters that identify queen mothers (1 Kings 15; and 2 Kings 12 and 15) contain statistically significant Huldah spellings or anagrams (this writer assumes that statistical significance is strong evidence of authorship). Huldah may well have taken a writing lead in those three queen-mother chapters, but what of the other chapters? On those she probably was editing older material, working with other authors who did more of the writing. Whatever occurred, with her record of Judah's queen mothers Huldah left a lasting feminist imprint on the books of Kings. And it was fitting that she memorialized those women. Huldah was, after all, the last of the line of Judah's queen mothers.[30]

Huldah's work in numerous chapters of Kings with her history of Judah's queen mothers evidences that she was a skillful editor. Her well-disguised writing of the call of Jeremiah in that book's very first chapter is another example of editorial excellence. Now add to that the Huldah anagrams in the Ezekiel chapter dates and the pattern they evince. And there is more proof ahead of her skill in shaping collections of writings into more comprehensive books. The next chapter will show that Huldah contributed at least one of the greatest texts in Scripture—Deuteronomy's Shema. Also still to come are her insertion of the promises to the patriarchs and her editing of the Genesis creation stories. In the future, others will be able to identify even more examples of her skillful touch, confirming yet again that Huldah had much to do with shaping our present version of the Hebrew Bible.

30. Zedekiah was the last king of Judah, but his mother was a generation older than Huldah. Zedekiah's mother probably was deceased when Huldah became queen mother in 597.

7

Huldah's Place in the Deuteronomistic History

THIS CHAPTER REVEALS—FOR THE first time ever—the identity of the Deuteronomist, the members—including Huldah—of that collective group, the decade during which most of Deuteronomy was written, and that book's context and primary purpose.

Almost seventy years ago, Martin Noth published his thesis that a single individual, whom he called Dtr, had written most of the book of Deuteronomy. The book itself was cast in the form of an almost continuous speech by Moses. Dtr had also reshaped the following six books of Scripture—Joshua, Judges, 1–2 Samuel, and 1–2 Kings. The aim of this founding biblical genius was to divide the history of Israel into four major periods: the time of Moses, the conquest of the Promised Land, the era of the judges, and the period of the monarchy. The seven books together carry the scholarly abbreviation of DH, for Deuteronomistic History. Other scholars have since modified Noth's theory, but only modestly. Summarizing this large body of work, Steven McKenzie has written that "the existence of the DH has achieved almost canonical status" within biblical studies.[1] The search for Dtr's identity has become the Holy Grail of biblical scholarship.

This book and this chapter bear Huldah's name—*Huldah: The Prophet Who Wrote Hebrew Scripture* and "Huldah's Place in the Deuteronomistic History." But what role in the DH did Huldah play? To properly answer that question, this writer had to address the seemingly eternal problem of Dtr's identity. However, this writer started that quest with an

1. McKenzie, "Deuteronomistic History," 161.

advantage—twenty-five years of full-time study has led to finding how biblical authors identified themselves. Knowing that, it was possible first to simplify the system and then computerize a method of extracting this information. The biblical author encoded a name, place, or thing (for example, "Jacob," "Bethel," or "siege") by taking a single letter from consecutive text words. Simultaneously one must apply a pre-coding technique to scramble the letters of any Hebrew word. Chapter 1 describes this Bible-based system termed "athbash." By rotating facing rows of letters, Hebrew authors generated twenty-two ways to spell any word.

But caution is in order. This "final" system comes with built-in limitations. First, the encoded name can be either the author or the subject of a biblical text. Determining whether the concealed name is author or subject is mostly a matter of judgment, though frequency studies can often clarify. Next, there is the matter of coincidence. Because coding often happens by chance, one must eliminate virtually every such coincidental occurrence. The social sciences commonly use a .05 probability breakpoint to determine whether or not something occurs by chance, which is 1 in 20. By contrast, this writer's computer search program uses .001, which is 1 in 1,000. This is fifty times more selective than the social-science standard.

But can the biblical text support such coding? The research discussed here relies upon the Leningrad Codex of the Masoretic Text, which has a better than 95 percent letter-for-letter congruence with the Qumran Isaiah scrolls.[2] That takes the MT back to about 150 BCE—not a bad starting time. Though there is little scholarly doubt that the MT is not the original text, it is the closest to one that we have. Moreover, the coding discussed here is succinct and thus change resistant. The average Hebrew verse can house eight or so coded spellings of the same name. While a break at verse end causes no damage to pre-existent coding, a fracture in the middle will simply wipe out coding in the "original" text and leave no record.

Inserting blocks of new material will import new encodings into original text. Those who edited earlier writings also knew coding and added their own encodings to whatever passages they amended. Thus, virtually all coded spellings that the computer identifies (a) are either original or added and (b) have passed rigorous probability tests. These additions are often easy to spot. This book's first chapter gives the example of the Wonderful Councilor / Prince of Peace passage in Isa 9. It mixes text that is both friendly and hostile to Huldah to produce an outcome that has zero chance of coincidental occurrence. While the MT is not the "original" text,

2. Burrows, *Dead Sea Scrolls*, 304.

it has within it many—perhaps most—of the words written by the Bible's original authors intermixed with coded passages added by editors. Sifting out the original (though diminished) coding placed by those who wrote the opening drafts of Scripture can be rewarding indeed.[3]

"The proof of the pudding is in the eating." The meaning of this old proverb is that "to fully test something you need to experience it yourself."[4] It is useless to argue that pudding set before us should be discarded because its baking pan has a dent. Why not taste the pudding, examine the coding? The payoff will prove to be handsome.

MASSIVE SEARCH FINDS DTR LEADERS

By applying encoded spellings with fast computers, in just four months this writer has identified the Dtr members and calibrated their chapter-by-chapter influence within the book of Deuteronomy. However, behind this four-month blitzkrieg lie years of data accumulation, costly programming outlays, and a quarter century of full-time labor.

Scripture itself contains the names of close to two thousand persons, but spelling differences, compound names (like X-son-of-Y), and especially athbash variations greatly expand this figure. In addition, archaeology has contributed several hundred other names from signature seals. In all, names to be tested totaled about twenty-five thousand. Programmer John Page used fast computers to run each and every name against the entire Hebrew text—from Gen 1:1 through 2 Chr 36:23. The task, which took months to accomplish, established frequencies and assigned chapter-by-chapter probabilities for every Hebrew word. The computer identified bunching of the same encoded word within any chapter. If that bunching passed the rigorous probability tests discussed earlier, it became a significant group (groups averaged about ten coded spellings apiece). A group is defined as a statistically significant concentration of the same coded spelling within a single chapter.

Counting groups is a handy way to compare the coding strength of different names within a single chapter—or within a batch of chapters such as the Dtr chapters in Deuteronomy. The completed calibration of Judean personal names against the entire OT text produced 1.7 million groups, and Deuteronomy 5–28's portion of that was just under twenty-five

---

3. The earliest layers of coding may even offer clues to the identities of the J and the E Sources, though this chapter about Huldah will not pursue these possibilities.

4. http://www.phrases.org.UK/meanings/proof-of-the-pudding.html.

thousand groups.[5] Even twenty-five thousand groups would be too much hay to harvest, except that a modern spreadsheet can be sorted to show which individuals recorded the highest number of coded groups. This was the next step, and here is its result. Table 7.1 displays totals for the dozen best candidates for Dtr, the author of Deuteronomy 5–28. It is extracted from appendix 2, which lists the top forty-seven names.

Table 7.1: Names with Most Coded Groups in Deuteronomy 5–28

Name	Groups	Chapters	All Chapters Have Coded Groups Except:
Micaiah	140	24	None (all chapters coded)
Daniel	138	20	10, 18, 21, 27
Huldah	126	20	10, 17, 19–20
Jacob	122	23	20
Asaiah	110	22	17, 23
Azariah	100	21	10, 23, 26
Ezra	95	22	15, 23
Shephatiah	79	18	10, 17–18, 20, 24, 27
Jonathan	74	21	10, 18, 20
Hushim	73	20	10, 17, 22, 27
Jeremiah	73	20	11, 17, 22–23
Adonijah	66	19	13, 15, 17–18, 20

The table shows that Micaiah's 140 and Daniel's 138 coded spelling groups in the Dtr chapters exceed those of every other person ever named in Scripture. Daniel's 138 total makes its own argument that he was not a figure of legend. Instead, coding tells us that Daniel was an important member of the exilic community and may have been associated with Second Isaiah. There are five other people with 95 or more coded groups in the Dtr chapters. Huldah, Jacob, Asaiah, Azariah, and Ezra score in the range of 126 to 95. After that there is a considerable drop to Shephatiah and others. Huldah the prophet is this book's subject, Jacob was with the Second Isaiah group, Asaiah held the modest title of servant to the

---

5. Compound personal names that exceed eleven letters are not included. Examples of them are Abialbon the Arbathite and Amaziah son of Jehoaddan, both of which contain fifteen Hebrew letters. Also excluded were geographical names in Israel as well as foreign personal and place names. These would have increased the OT and Deuteronomy figures by about 10 percent.

king under Josiah,[6] Azariah was a companion of Daniel, and Ezra was the Priestly Source. As for Micaiah, he was the grandson of Shaphan and Scripture identified him in the year 604 BCE as a young functionary in King Jehoiakim's court (Jer 36:11–25).

Table 7.1 ranks individuals by groups of encodings, but of nearly equal weight should be the number of chapters in which those spellings occur. Experts attribute twenty-four chapters to Dtr.[7] Of the dozen people in the table, only Micaiah has statistically significant coding in every Dtr chapter. However, those listed average twenty-one chapters apiece! If that table were to be expanded to the four dozen highest scorers, average participation would stand at eighteen chapters. Plainly, a large number of experts worked together on Deuteronomy for an extended period—and this new technique allows scholars not only to identify them but to measure their chapter-by-chapter contributions as well.

The figures in table 7.1 come from adding subtotals of coded names. Start with Daniel. The results include significant coding from both Daniel (spelled two different ways) and Belteshazzar, the name given him by the Babylonians. Also yielding strong results were Daniel-son-of-David and Daniel-the-eunuch. Though Scripture comes close, it does not definitely state that Daniel was a son of one of Judah's kings—but it is reasonable to presume that he was.[8] Nebuchadnezzar took him as a hostage to be raised in the court at Babylon. Both logic and the high number of Daniel-son-of-David groups show that he very probably was a son of royalty. Also, the Bible says nothing about whether Daniel was castrated when a youth, though coding supports this.[9] The term Daniel-the-eunuch yields an impressive fifty-five coded groups. Table 7.2 is a breakout of the 138 Daniel groups in the Dtr chapters.

6. Asaiah also was a military leader in the drive during the 570s to take the Promised Land. See Kavanagh, *The Shaphan Group*, 103–4.

7. Deuteronomy 4:44–49 is also attributed to Dtr. For convenience, however, this writer has begun with Deut 5:1.

8. Nebuchadnezzar commanded that his officials "bring some of the Israelites of the royal family and of the nobility" to Babylon to serve in court (Dan 1:3).

9. The term for eunuch also means "official," so an encoded Daniel-the-eunuch could also read Daniel-the-official.

Table 7.2: Source of Daniel Coded Groups in Deuteronomy 5–28

Encoded	Groups
Daniel (two spellings)	21
Daniel-the-Eunuch/Official	55
Daniel-Son-of-David	33
Belteshazzar	21
Belteshazzar-Son-of-David	8
Total Groups	138

Many of Scripture's personal names have several kinds of encoding. Typically, they are "X-son-of-Y," along with "X," plus spelling variations of "X." In the Daniel example, there are six (counting four-letter and five-letter renderings of Daniel). There should be no question about including Belteshazzar under the Daniel category, since that Babylonian name has scriptural authority (Dan 1:7). But Daniel-the-eunuch and Daniel-son-of-David lack such a credential. Without those eighty-eight groups, Daniel would fall from contention as a candidate for Dtr.

Huldah's situation is similar. Two spellings of Huldah and one each of Huldah-the-prophetess and Huldah-wife-of-Shallum come directly from Scripture. Huldah-wife-of-Jehoiakim, Huldah-queen-mother, and Huldah-mother-of-Jehoiachin have been demonstrated in this book's previous chapters. Because Deborah is a creation of the prophetess, it seems proper to catalogue the Deborah coded results with Huldah herself. Think of this coding of an alias as another level of concealment. "Abigail" probably is also interchangeable with "Huldah," though "Abigail," with its fifty groups, could stand alone. Huldah's 126 groups look like this:

Table 7.3: Source of Huldah Coded Groups in Deuteronomy 5–28

Encoded	Groups
Huldah (two spellings)	11
Huldah-the-Prophetess	16
Huldah-Wife-of-Shallum	15
Huldah-Wife-of-Jehoiakim	9
Huldah-the-Queen-Mother	7
Huldah-Mother-of-Jehoiachin	5
Deborah	13
Abigail	50
Total Groups	126

"Jacob," which could have been Second Isaiah's name,[10] ranks fourth in coding in the Dtr chapters among all scriptural persons. Previously, this writer believed Shelomoth was Jacob's father, but Jacob-son-of-Isaac drew fifty groups of significant encodings, and it is difficult to argue with such a large figure. Jacob (17), Jacob-the-prophet (33), and Jacob-the-Levite (25) brought the total of Jacob's groups to 122.[11]

Azariah was a companion of Daniel's, and also bore the Babylonian name of Abednego, which, by itself, had twenty-five groups in the Dtr chapters. In Scripture, seven different fathers had sons named Azariah, so Zadok—the father who recorded the most groups—was selected. Azariah-son-of-Zadok had no fewer than thirty-two significant groups. This makes sense, since the Zadokites were the priestly family that held Jerusalem's temple leadership until the Exile. Azariah, Daniel, and Hananiah (who had forty-six coded groups) were taken from Judah by Nebuchadnezzar in 606 BCE to be raised in Babylon. According to the book of Daniel, they were "Israelites of the royal family and of the nobility," handsome young men "endowed with knowledge and insight, and competent to serve in the king's palace" (Dan 1:3–4).

Asaiah has 110 coded groups and Ezra has 95 within Deuteronomy 5–28, and each name is paired with an alias that contributes substantially to its total. The letters that spell Asaiah are found within the name Joshua, so that every naming of Joshua forms an Asaiah anagram. Coupling Asaiah and Joshua almost doubles the coding groups. As to Ezra, he is the Priestly Source and the letters in his name are an athbash match for those in Aaron. Indeed, Ezra probably introduced the character of Aaron into Scripture.[12] Over half the Ezra total, then, comes from Aaron coded groups.

Clearly, the sorting process does not simply consist of running every possible name through targeted portions of Hebrew Scripture, and then ranking the names in order of groups amassed. Though this is the starting point, adding is often necessary, based on fair-minded scholarly judgment. This makes the absolute number of groups allotted to any name somewhat less important, since scholarly judgment has been known to err. For example, if Daniel was not a prince of Judah, his total groups would stand at 97 rather than 138. Another consideration is that this writer has

10. Kavanagh, *The Exilic Code*, 62–84 ("Second Isaiah's Identity").

11. Though "Israel" can be used interchangeably with "Jacob," its points were not included with Jacob's.

12. Kavanagh, *The Shaphan Group*, 23–44 ("Anagrams Uncover Priestly Source").

worked with Ezra, Jacob, and Daniel for years and acquaintanceship tends to multiply encodings. Daniel-the-eunuch is one example and Jacob-the-Levite another. Scholarship supports these compounds, but this scholar's assumptions are not invariably correct.

Huldah herself has five titles that do not appear in Scripture, starting with Huldah-the-queen-mother. If everything were equal, a name with four variations would tally more groups than one with only two. However, everything in computerized searches is not equal. Those who penned the most Scripture would have developed the most ways to affix their signatures—like Huldah's use of "Abigail" and "Deborah." A conservative screening process assists in weeding out virtually all coincidental spellings. All in all, however, one must admit that some art has been added to this newly fashioned science of selection.

MICAIAH THE DTR

The name Micaiah (or Micah) itself has five different spellings in Scripture, most of which appear within the DH.[13] Second Chronicles uses a four-letter version of the name interchangeably with a six-letter spelling (2 Chr 18:12–14). These variations of Micaiah contribute sixty-three groups, Micaiah-the-scribe accounts for forty-seven, and Micaiah-son-of-Gemariah produces thirty. Coded groups for the Dtr chapters total 140. This ranks Micaiah first among nearly two thousand persons mentioned in Scripture. Daniel is just behind him at 138 groups, followed by Huldah, Jacob, Asaiah, and Azariah. Table 7.4 provides details on Micaiah. Except for the variations of Micaiah and Micah, the spellings and variations are straightforward.

Table 7.4: Source of Micaiah Coded Groups in Deuteronomy 5–28

Encoded	Groups
Micaiah (five spellings)	63
Micaiah-the-scribe	47
Micaiah-son-of-Gemariah	30
Total Groups	140

13. Five variations of Micaiah are מיכיהו (1 Kings 22), מיכיה (2 Kgs 22:12), מיכה (2 Chr 18:14), מיכא (2 Sam 9:12), and מכיהו (Jer 36:11). Second Chronicles 18:8 has another variation, מיכהו, which, for search purposes, is equivalent to מכיהו.

The Bible does not specify that Micaiah was a scribe. However, his father and grandfather held that title, Scripture places him in the king's scribal room, and encodings with forty-seven Micaiah-the-scribe groups strongly support the title.

Jeremiah 36 says this about the young Micaiah: "When Micaiah son of Gemariah son of Shaphan heard all the words of the LORD from the [Jeremiah] scroll, he went down to the king's house, into the secretary's chamber; and all the officials were sitting there: Elishama the secretary, Delaiah son of Shemaiah, Elnathan son of Achbor, Gemariah [Micaiah's father] son of Shaphan, Zedekiah son of Hananiah, and all the officials. And Micaiah told them all the words that he had heard, when Baruch read the [Jeremiah] scroll in the hearing of the people" (Jer 36:11–13). The officials concluded that the king must hear the prophet's words, even though they knew that would place Jeremiah and Baruch in mortal danger. Micaiah was present in the secretary's room of the palace when those officials unanimously decided that Jeremiah and Baruch must hide to avoid King Jehoiakim's wrath. Subsequently, King Jehoiakim ordered that the scroll be read in his presence, and then threw section after section of it into a brazier (anagrams reveals that Huldah, who was then one of the king's wives, witnessed several readings of Jeremiah's scroll).

The phrase "Micaiah told them all the words that he had heard" shows that the youth possessed considerable intelligence. He was repeating the contents of the entire scroll that Baruch had publicly read earlier. Also, to be a grandson of the still-active Shaphan meant that Micaiah had been schooled in the techniques and disciplines of those who were to write no small part of Scripture. Finally, Micaiah would have been reared on the reformist views of his family, views that would have brought the young man into close contact with the older Jeremiah. It is clear that Micaiah helped to protect the prophet, as the passage cited above implies.

A previous book of mine, *The Shaphan Group*, concluded that notables around Shaphan, who was King Josiah's Secretary, had brought together the books of Deuteronomy through Second Kings. This earlier study ranked Micaiah first or tied for first in coded spellings for the books of Deuteronomy, Joshua, and Judges and first overall for the entire DH. That supports the conclusions of this book—conclusions drawn from the more comprehensive approach of examining every Hebrew personal name within Scripture. If a single person is to be nominated for Deuteronomist, let it be Micaiah the scribe—the thinker who placed his mark upon the Hebrew Bible.

Huldah

The other best candidates for Dtr are Daniel, Azariah, Huldah, Jacob, and Asaiah. Remember that a high coding level means that that person either helped to write the coded passage or was its subject. The best way to form opinions on authorship is to read and categorize the thousand or so verses of the DH that contain significant encodings of, say, Daniel. This, however, is a vast undertaking. Instead, this chapter will offer only brief opinions about the roles of Daniel and the rest prior to concentrating on Huldah.

Almost certainly, Daniel received instruction in Jerusalem before Nebuchadnezzar took him in 606 BCE. Quite possibly, his teachers had been of deuteronomistic persuasion, even though 606 was three years into the reign of Jehoiakim, a reactionary monarch. Whether or not the young exile was a royal son of Josiah or Jehoiakim, Daniel must have known both Huldah and Micaiah in the Jerusalem court. Huldah would have been about thirty-five and Micaiah about sixteen—the same age as Daniel— when Daniel left Judah. Once in the Babylonian court, Daniel had to live within a pagan milieu, his Yahweh-oriented education at an end. Despite Daniel's undoubted brilliance, his lack of direct scribal experience might have limited his contribution to the Deuteronomy chapters. Countering this is the fact that a mature Daniel helped to draft the Shema (see below). Clearly, further study of Daniel's contribution to the DH is in order, and the same is true for Daniel's companion Azariah.

As to other candidates, Second Isaiah's famously lyrical style is far too different from the tone of Dtr to support that he was Deuteronomy's architect. One can imagine Jacob—or Daniel— cutting his teeth as part of the composing team, but not framing the whole work. Considering Asaiah, his 110 coding groups probably came more from describing his military prowess than from his own writing skills. The name Joshua conceals an anagram of Asaiah and, in this writer's opinion, the character Joshua was an invention of the Dtr group to mask Asaiah's leadership during the exilic campaign to retake Jerusalem.[14] The Asaiah coding, then, could well have shown more of subject than of authorship. Of necessity, this brief roundup makes assumptions about Daniel, Azariah, Jacob, and Asaiah that are supported more by inference than by facts. What is needed is verse-by-verse analysis of all Dtr-related Scripture. Though the data stands ready, this is too large an order to fit within a biography of Huldah.

14. Kavanagh, *The Shaphan Group*, 103–4.

THE WHERE AND WHEN OF DEUTERONOMY

Where was Deuteronomy written? The coding itself proposes answers to that question. Part of Deuteronomy very likely was written somewhere in Babylonia. Daniel and Azariah were already in residence there, as was another of Daniel's companions—Hananiah, who also was on the list of Israelites with the most coding groups. About 606, Nebuchadnezzar had brought the book-of-Daniel companions east to be raised in the Babylonian court. Then, in 597, Nebuchadnezzar returned to Judah and "carried away all Jerusalem, all the officials, all *the warriors* [H, Jehoiachin], ten thousand captives, all the artisans and the smiths; no one remained, except the poorest people of the land" (2 Kgs 24:14). As anagrams reveal, Huldah and her son King Jehoiachin were exiled, and very likely so were others with high coding totals—Asaiah, Micaiah, and Jacob. To summarize, Daniel's Babylonian contingent and the Micaiah-Huldah group were together in Judah before 606 and then again in Babylon after 597. It is almost certain, however, that Daniel, Azariah, Hananiah, and Micaiah—and probably Jacob, too—were under twenty years of age in 605. At that time, they would have been too unseasoned to have composed (or have been the subjects of) Deuteronomy. These factors place most of the Dtr authors first in Babylonia and then in Egypt rather than Judah. As to where in Babylonia and/or Egypt, we do not yet know. That answer probably will surface when someone addresses coded spelling of place names within Deuteronomy 5–28.

This sixth-century date for Deuteronomy runs counter to the view of most scholars—a view that this writer shared prior to studying the recent results of Deuteronomy's coded spellings. Harvard scholar Bernard Levinson writes that probably "the core of the book was written sometime during the seventh century BCE by educated scribes associated with Jerusalem's royal court." He goes on to note the "very striking similarities between the distinctive . . . requirements of Deuteronomy and the . . . religious reform carried out by King Josiah in 622 B.C.E." Discovery of a scroll of the law triggered the reform, and Levinson concludes that "Scholars have long identified the 'scroll of the Torah' discovered in Josiah's Temple as Deuteronomy, and thus have assigned the book a seventh-century date."[15]

In 597, Nebuchadnezzar cleaned house in Jerusalem and deported Judah's skilled workers, which must have included all of the scribes in the court. On the list of the forty-seven names with the largest coding totals

15. Levinson, "Deuteronomy," 357.

in appendix 2 are at least eleven scribes: Jonathan, Azariah, Shemaiah, Shephatiah, Shaphan, Joshua, Shelemiah, Delaiah, Elishama, and Ezra. These are men who had "the scribe" encoded with their names in the Dtr chapters.[16] In addition, it is certain that Huldah and Jacob—and probably Daniel and Gemariah, too—were sufficiently accomplished to handle scribal duties easily. It seems to be correct that, as Professor Levinson wrote, "the core of the book [of Deuteronomy] . . . was written . . . by educated scribes associated with Jerusalem's royal court." They were indeed associated with Jerusalem's royal court until 597, when Nebuchadnezzar forcibly transferred them from Judah to Babylon. Others in the royal court also made the trip to Mesopotamia. Son-of-David coding helped these princes make a list of top Dtr candidates: Shammua, Adonijah, Daniel, Shephatiah, Nogah, and Elishama.[17] Shephatiah and Elishama are also numbered with the scribes, indicating cross training. Considering the evidence so far, the earliest that the Dtr group could have started on Deuteronomy was during the later 590s in Babylonia.

What is the end date for the Dtr chapters? There are two things that suggest a time boundary for the work. The first deals more with location than with timing. Huldah's biography says that she was in Jerusalem in 586, when the city fell for the second time. If she was in Judah in 586, she could not have been in Babylon at the time working on Deuteronomy. Her absence is suggestive, though the book could have been completed without her.

A second resource for dating the Dtr chapters is Cyrus coding. Fortunately, this book's chapter 4 supplies an approximate timetable for the Cyrus-led campaign to retake Jerusalem. Assume that the Jews recruited young Cyrus in Egypt in about 577. The Israelites left Egypt in about 575, and captured Jerusalem in a year or so. Adding a year for occupation takes things to 573, when disaster struck and either neighbors or the Babylonians retook the city and slaughtered the Israelite defenders. The collapse may have been on April 8, 573—the specific date that Ezekiel used when he outlined plans for a new Jerusalem (Ezek 40:1).

16. The fact that some of these might have been from earlier times should also be kept in mind.

17. See the previous note. Like the scribes, some of the princes may be from eras other than the sixth century.

CYRUS ANAGRAMS ESTABLISH DATES

To provide a mark in time, one must seek out Cyrus *anagrams*, since there is little Cyrus coded spelling within the Dtr chapters. There are forty single-word anagrams distributed across the Dtr chapters. Forty may not seem like many, but all Scripture contains only one short of a thousand. The probability that forty Cyrus anagrams could appear by chance in text the length of Deuteronomy 5–28 is just .0000000017—essentially zero.[18]

In their context, those anagrams are either positive or negative toward Cyrus. Here is an example of a negative anagram from Deuteronomy 20, a chapter about proper conduct in warfare. It instructs Israel to annihilate those living within the Promised Land lest they teach the Jews "all their abominable practices which they have done in the service of their gods, *and so to sin* [Cyrus] against the LORD your God" (Deut 20:18). "To sin" forms a Cyrus anagram and is clearly critical of the Persian. It sounds as though the military campaign is underway in Palestine (c 575), and that Cyrus wants to be more lenient toward defeated neighbors than the writer who formed the anagram. At first glance, the quoted line does appear to be part of a more sizable addition to the chapter, but this writer leaves such determinations to others. Keeping possible ex post facto editing in mind, here is a review of both negative and positive Cyrus anagrams in Deuteronomy 5–28. The balance between the two sides is even—twenty anagrams that are positive about Cyrus and twenty that are negative. Table 7.5 gives details.

18. Forty Cyrus anagrams in the 4,895 Dtr text words compared with 999 in Scripture's 305,496 words yield chi-square proportions of 40 / 959 and 4,895 / 300,601. The probability of coincidence is .0000000017, which is less than one in a half-billion.

Table 7.5: Positive and Negative Cyrus Anagrams
in Deuteronomy 5–28

Chapter	Positive	Negative	Chapter	Positive	Negative
5	4		17		1
6	3		18		
7	1	1	19		
8	1		20		1
9		5	21		
10			22		3
11	4	1	23	1	1
12	1		24		
13		2	25		
14	1		26		
15		1	27	1	
16	2		28	1	4

The two opening chapters—as well as chapters 11 and 16—are more strongly positive toward Cyrus, while 9, 22, and 28 are the most critical of him. About one-third of the chapters contain no Cyrus anagrams at all.

The writers who supported Cyrus frequently relied on a phrase along these lines: "I am the LORD your God, who *brought you out* [Cyrus] of the land of Egypt, out of the house of slavery" (Deut 5:6).[19] The sympathetic author used that verb five times (5:6, 15; 6:12; 8:14; 16:1). However, the unsympathetic writer reversed what it really meant by urging, "Stone them to death for trying to *turn you away* [H] from the LORD your God, who *brought you out* [Cyrus] of the land of Egypt, out of the house *of slavery* [Daniel]" (Deut 13:10 H11). This verse is notable because it is aimed at both Huldah and Cyrus. Moreover, the immediately preceding verse indicted both of them: "But you shall surely kill them; your own hand *shall* [Daniel] *be first* [H, Ezra, Jacob] against them *to execute them* [Cyrus], and afterwards the hand of all *the people* [Ezra]" (Deut 13:9 H10). These same verses also contain anagrams for Jacob, Ezra (two), and Daniel (two). The venture generated plenty of emnity for all. It seems that, at the least, these two verses (and perhaps this whole chapter) were composed after the 573 defeat at Jerusalem.

---

19. The verb הוֹצֵאתִיךָ contains the letters אצי"ך, which is an athbash anagram of Cyrus.

A critic repeats the Cyrus "execute" anagram in another Deuteronomy chapter: "The hands of the witnesses *shall be* [Daniel] *the first* [Ezra] raised against the person *to execute the death penalty* [Cyrus], and afterward [Ezra] the hands of all the people. So you shall purge the evil from your midst" (Deut 17:7). This implies opposition to the Persian captain even before the final battle. The verse also contains one Daniel and two Ezra anagrams. Since Ezra was the P Source, Cyrus apparently had strong support from the priestly faction that was on the scene. The harsh tone of the rest of chapter 17 matches that of the quotation.

The word "sinned" registers the most anti-Cyrus anagrams. This Dtr example from chapter 9 draws on the golden calf story in Exodus and packs four "sin" anagrams together: "Then I saw that *you had indeed sinned* [Cyrus] against the LORD your God, by casting for yourselves an image of a calf . . . Then I *lay prostrate* [Asaiah] before the LORD *as before* [Ezra], forty days and forty nights; I neither ate bread nor drank water, because of all *the sin* [Cyrus] *you had committed* [Cyrus], provoking the LORD by doing what was evil in his sight . . . Then I *took* [Daniel] *the sinful thing* [Cyrus] you had made, the calf, and burned it with fire . . ." (Deut 9:16, 18, 21). Intermixed with these four Cyrus anagrams are others for Asaiah, Daniel, Ezra, Jacob, and Huldah (some of which are not shown)—the core of the leadership of the invasion of Judah. A fifth anagram of the same ilk comes from Deut 20:18: ". . . they may not teach you to do all the abhorrent things that they do for their gods, and *you thus sin* [Cyrus, Ezra] against the LORD." Perhaps these texts come from just after 574, in reaction to forms of newly instituted worship at Jerusalem a year before the catastrophe.

Each side repeated anagram-producing words, setting them in different contexts. "Wine" is an example: "He will love you, *bless you* [Baruch], and *multiply you* [Baruch, Ezra]; *he will bless* [Baruch] the fruit of your womb and the fruit of your ground, your grain and *your wine* [Cyrus] . . ." (Deut 7:13). Deuteronomy 11:14 and 12:17 are similar. This next quote goes out of its way to approve consumption for Cyrus, Huldah, and Baruch: "Spend the money for whatever you desire, oxen, or sheep, or wine *or strong drink* [H, Cyrus, Baruch], whatever your appetite craves . . ." (Deut 14:26). "Elders" rates a double mention and surely involved leaders of the venture: "Moses *and the elders* [H, Cyrus, Baruch] of Israel charged all the people as follows: Keep the entire commandment . . ." and "while the mountain was burning with fire, you approached me, all the heads *of your tribes* [Daniel] *and your elders* [H, Cyrus, Jacob, Baruch, Ezra]" (Deut

27:1, 5:23). Cyrus served with the Israelite elders, who included Huldah, Baruch, Jacob, Ezra, and probably Daniel. "Gates" was another word that supported a Cyrus anagram, as these instances show: "And you shall write them on the doorposts of your house *and on your gates* [H, Cyrus, Baruch, Jehoiachin]" (Deut 6:9; 11:20). The two passages conceal the same four anagrams.

Critics of Cyrus formed anagrams from the verb for "ignore" or "withhold" three times within a few verses to express displeasure with the young Persian commander: "You shall not watch your neighbor's ox or sheep straying away *and ignore them* [Cyrus] . . . you shall do the same with anything else that your neighbor loses . . . You may not *withhold* [Cyrus] your help. You shall not see your neighbor's donkey or ox fallen on the road *and ignore it* [Cyrus] . . . you shall help to lift it up" (Deut 22:1, 3, 4). It seems that Cyrus had failed in some way to come to the aid of the Israelites, perhaps during the campaign of conquest. One can also detect a back and forth between the pro- and anti-Cyrus writers. The most obvious instance is in chapter 28. Deuteronomy 28:5 says, "*Blessed* [Baruch] shall be your basket and *your kneading bowl* [Cyrus]." To which v. 17 answers, "Cursed shall be your basket and *your kneading bowl* [Cyrus]." "Ox" provides another exchange. "The *seventh* [Asaiah] day is a sabbath to the LORD your God; you shall not do any work—you, or your son or your daughter . . . *or your ox* [Cyrus]" (Deut 5:14).[20] This "ox" anagram supports that dictum: "You shall not do work with your firstling *ox* [Cyrus]," but this takes exception: "*Your ox* [Cyrus] shall be butchered before your eyes" (Deut 15:19, 28:31).

A handful of anagrams favorable to Cyrus remain. All of these anagrams very likely were fashioned during the later 570s. The first—"He will give grass in your fields *for your livestock* [Cyrus]" (Deut 11:15)—could refer to the Persian's share of the spoils of combat. Other anagrams promise success in this holy war: "The LORD your God *travels along* [Cyrus] with your camp . . . to hand over your enemies to you," "Every place on which the sole *of your foot* [Cyrus] treads shall be yours," and "*Thrusting out* [Cyrus] all your enemies from before you" (Deut 23:14 H15, 11:24, 6:19). A final favorable anagram could obliquely refer to restraint in slaughtering captives—"If you go into your neighbor's standing grain, you may pluck the ears with your hand, but you shall not put *a sickle* [Cyrus] to your neighbor's standing grain" (Deut 23:25 H26). In years to come, Cyrus was

20. This is interpreted as a positive anagram for Cyrus, though it also might be viewed as a negative one.

to rule over an empire of dozens of nations and become famed for his willing conciliation and generosity of heart.[21]

The last of the negative Cyrus anagrams seems to reach into the final defeat around Jerusalem about 573, though perhaps these only predicted that dismal event: "Your corpses shall be food for every bird of the air *and animal* [Cyrus] of the earth"; "The earth opened its mouth and swallowed them up, along with their households, their tents, and every living being *in their company* [Cyrus]"; "God will send the pestilence against them, until even the survivors *and the fugitives* [Cyrus] are destroyed"; and "She who is the most refined and gentle among you, so gentle and refined that *she does not venture* [Cyrus] to set the sole of her foot on the ground, [during the siege] will begrudge food to the husband whom she embraces . . ." (Deut 28:26; 11:6; 7:20; 28:56). The final quotation, Deut 28:56, is followed by a repulsive image of a woman forced—under duress—to eat the afterbirth of a child, and beneath it is encoded Huldah-wife-of-Shallum. That dates the previous verse, with its Cyrus anagram, at about 573 and indicates that Jerusalem fell only after siege. Moreover, it implies that Huldah had been reunited with Shallum, her first husband, after King Jehoiakim's death.

The forty Cyrus anagrams are highly significant. They show that much—perhaps most—of Deuteronomy was written or added to during the campaign to recapture Jerusalem. Scholars may find that a passage or even a chapter was added later, but this new coding and anagram evidence makes a sixth-century date for the book of Deuteronomy as certain as things can be in biblical studies. Anagrams highlight the running dispute about the role of Cyrus in the holy war to free the Promised Land. These show disagreement about the campaign from its start to its bitter end. Probably the negative Cyrus anagrams originated with the scribal group (perhaps led by Micaiah) that remained in Egypt or—less likely—Babylon. The positive ones, however, must have come from Huldah, Jacob, and others who traveled with the army. The volume of anagrams for Huldah, Baruch, Ezra, Daniel, Jacob, and Asaiah—mixed with those for Cyrus—reinforce the 570s date for Deuteronomy.

A seismic event such as the Cyrus-led expedition to retake the Promised Land also left marks on other Hebrew Scripture. Here is a major example. As the planned invasion of Judah prompted the Dtr group to write, so it may well have inspired Second Isaiah to proclaim, "Comfort, O comfort my people, says your God. Speak tenderly to Jerusalem, and cry to her that she has served her term . . ." (Isa 40:1–2). It also goes far toward

---

21. Xenophon, *Cyropaedia*, I, ii, 1–3; IV, ii, 14.

explaining why God "says of Cyrus, 'He is my shepherd, and he shall carry out all my purpose'; and who says of Jerusalem, 'It shall be rebuilt,' and of the temple, 'Your foundation shall be laid'" (Isa 44:28). The collaboration of Cyrus and Second Isaiah in the 570s offers a different way to understand the date and historical setting of portions of Isa 40–55. Far less tenable "is the position of the vast majority of scholars today" that those chapters "were written in the 540s B.C."[22] Based on this new Cyrus information, the proper composition period could have begun in the 570s BCE.

Even though Deuteronomy incorporates older materials, significantly encoded Micaiah spellings cross at least a quarter of the 623 verses in the Dtr chapters. If verses with coded groups of Daniel, Jacob, Huldah, and other leaders were added, the tally would easily exceed two-thirds of total Dtr verses and might pass the four-fifths mark. Interestingly, overall coding density in this present text is only about half as dense as Scripture as a whole.[23] But fortunately for modern scholars, those who rewrote the DH used anagrams lavishly, with Cyrus anagrams being a prime example. An anagram uses but a single text word, while coded spellings require consecutive strings of them. Anagrams, then, would have been easier to insert into an older text like Deuteronomy. Probably individual words— and less often, newer sections—were carefully woven into older writings. One can tentatively conclude that much of Deuteronomy was reworked. Alternatively, it might simply have been newly written without coded spellings but with anagrams.

The literary setting of the Deuteronomy chapters fits well with the 570s invasion by the Israelites. Moses says to the tribes poised on the east bank of the Jordan, "Now this is the commandment . . . that the LORD your God charged me to teach you to observe in the land that you are about to cross into and occupy . . . so that you and your children and your children's children may fear the LORD your God all the days of your life . . . Hear therefore, O Israel . . . so that you may multiply greatly in a land flowing with milk and honey, as the LORD, the God of your ancestors, has promised you" (Deut 6:1–3). What immediately follows is the great Shema. Jesus said it was "the first" of all commandments (Mark 12:29–30), and rabbinic practice was to recite it daily in the morning and the evening. This single passage may be the high point of Hebrew Scripture: "Hear, O

22. Clifford, "Isaiah (Second Isaiah)," 493.

23. The average of all Scripture is 4.54 groups of coded spellings per text word, while that of Deuteronomy is 2.31. As to the rest of the DH, the four books of Samuel and Kings contain the least dense spellings per text word and Judges ranks ninth from the bottom. Only Joshua is above Scripture's average.

Israel: The LORD is our God, the LORD alone. You shall love the LORD your God with all your heart, and with all your soul, and with all your might" (Deut 6:4–5).

HULDAH AND DANIEL WRITE THE SHEMA

The evidence is that Huldah the prophet helped to write the Shema. First, she is the only one of Deuteronomy's leading authors to be significantly encoded in the initial verses of Dtr's opening chapters—5, 6, 7, and 8 (chapter 5 includes the Ten Commandments and chapter 6 contains the Shema).[24] Using chapter headings like this could be one way that the ancients signed their work. Also, of the leadership group (Asaiah, Azariah, Daniel, Ezra, Huldah, Jacob, and Micaiah), only Huldah and Daniel had coded signatures within the two short Shema verses.[25] It is likely that Huldah and Daniel wrote those verses together. The Shema defined the relationship between Yahweh and Israel. It demanded "that Israel show exclusive loyalty to *our God*, YHVH—but not thereby to deny the existence of other gods!"[26] Imagine that the two most tarred by association with foreign gods (Daniel by those of Babylon, Huldah by the Asherah) wrote Scripture's definitive statement on the supremacy of Yahweh!

Throughout the Dtr chapters, the authors refer to promised territory, routed enemies, and a new start based on Israel's ancient relationship with the Lord. Worship would soon be established at "the place that the LORD your God will choose as a dwelling for his name" (Deut 12:11; 14:23; 16:2, 6, 11; 26:2), which certainly was Jerusalem. In this newly acquired land, deuteronomistic ways would prevail. Paramount was centralized worship, exclusive loyalty to the Lord, and law founded upon the revelations at Horeb/Sinai. What better way to begin the sixth-century invasion of Judah than to identify it with Moses and the original Conquest? If this interpretation of the Dtr chapters is accurate, then the best date for most

---

24. Huldah coded spellings also appear in the opening verses of Deuteronomy 11; 12; 25; and 28.

25. An athbash of דנאל בנדוד, Daniel-son-of-David, is בלשיתל בדב. Taking letters in any sequence, the coded spelling begins at word 6 in v. 4 of Deuteronomy 6 and ends at word 8 in v. 5. The athbash of חלדההגבירה, Huldah-the-queen-mother, is ערלממכיצום. That coded spelling uses letters from ten consecutive text words beginning with word 5–9 of Deuteronomy 6 and ending on word 6-9. Both athbash words have numerous other spellings within Deuteronomy 6.

26. Levinson, "Deuteronomy: Annotation," 380. Italics are Levinson's.

of Deuteronomy's chapters is the 570s, when Huldah and others were recruiting forces in Egypt and then leading them into the Promised Land. If Deuteronomy 5–28 did not exist until the sixth century, what of the temple scroll that triggered Josiah's reforms after 622? Unusual coded spellings of Jeremiah's-book-of-the-law span this Second Chronicles passage: "The priest Hilkiah found the book of the law of the LORD given through Moses. Hilkiah said to the secretary Shaphan, 'I have found the book of the law in the house of the LORD'; and Hilkiah gave the book to Shaphan" (2 Chr 34:14–15). Encoding says that the now-lost scroll was Jeremiah's.[27] And who—more than forty years later—might have been at Micaiah's elbow as he brought together Deuteronomy 5–28? It might have been Jeremiah! Scripture says that the prophet unwillingly made the trip to Egypt after Gedaliah's assassination (Jer 43:6). Also, Jeremiah ranked eleventh in Dtr coding groups and had a presence in twenty of those chapters.

Here is a summary of findings about the DH. The fresh technique of coded spellings has been applied to detect who wrote Deuteronomy 5–28. Close to two thousand names from the Hebrew Bible were run first against Scripture as a whole and then against the Dtr chapters in particular. Conservative probability screens helped to select the highest Dtr scorers—Micaiah, Daniel, Huldah, Jacob, Asaiah, and Azariah—plus about forty others with respectable coding totals. Each of these four dozen persons participated in a number of the twenty-four Dtr chapters. Other studies showed that Micaiah had also led in composing Joshua and Judges. Cyrus anagrams and the identities of the leaders date the Dtr material to the 570s and establish as its context the campaign to retake the Promised Land. Many Second Isaiah chapters share that same context and timeframe. Huldah wrote no small amount of Dtr passages, and she and Daniel probably composed the Shema. Finally, Jeremiah seems to have written the 622 scroll that ignited King Josiah's deuteronomistic reforms. The supposition that Jeremiah aided Micaiah strengthens the possibility that Deuteronomy 5–28 was composed primarily in Egypt, though that matter is far from settled. In this writer's mind what *is* settled is that most of Deuteronomy was written during the 570s under the leadership of Micaiah, Daniel, Huldah, Jacob, Asaiah, Azariah, and Ezra.

---

27. The Hebrew is ספרהתורהלירמיהו. Six spellings take letters from consecutive text words. The starting words are in v. 14, words 8, 9, 13–15; and v. 15, word 1. See Kavanagh, *The Exilic Code,* 153.

8

Huldah Edits Genesis and Exodus

IN TUMULTUOUS TIMES, HULDAH, the author-warrior-prophet-queen, overcame high barriers to women and became a leading author of the Hebrew Bible. She contributed to God's Word a feminine aspect that has inspired numberless believers—men and women alike. Readers of this book may come to agree that Huldah was the foremost feminist in Scripture. This is an initial attempt to award her proper credit for both her achievements and her sufferings. Anagrams and coded spellings, of course, have permitted this writer to trace Huldah's extraordinary life.[1] This is but the start of scholarly application of these new techniques, however. Future analysts will amend and augment this version of Huldah's career, and it is proper that they do so.

Huldah influenced far more of Scripture than this writer has yet credited her for. The Shema, Song of Deborah, Wisdom Woman, Woman of Worth, and the dirge for Saul stand out as more easily recognized blocks of work by or about her. But Huldah's hand shaped many more passages than these favorites. This chapter will concentrate mainly on things in the books of Genesis and Exodus that display Huldah's feminist imprint.

HULDAH AND THE CREATION STORY

The creation story in Genesis is a good place to start. The pattern of coded spellings suggests that Huldah was not an original author but that she lightly edited that book's opening chapters. About two hundred of her

---

1. For example, 2 Kgs 24:14–16 covers the 597 exile to Babylon. Because the passage contains two Huldah anagrams, it seems likely that she also was exiled.

spellings and eight of her anagrams are scattered through the first seven Genesis chapters. Although in total these spellings are not statistically significant, the Huldah anagrams do narrowly qualify. Because of this, one can plainly detect how she modified Scripture's opening chapters. These words came from her: "Then God said, 'Let us make humankind in our image, according to our likeness; and let them have dominion'" over every other creature (Gen 1:26). In the next chapter, Huldah encapsulated the start of human life: "Then the LORD God formed man from the dust of the ground, and breathed into his nostrils the breath of life; and the man became a living being" (Gen 2:7). In the same continuum of coded verses, the prophetess expanded the Garden of Eden story so that the garden contained both the tree of life and the tree of the knowledge of good and evil.

The version of Eve's creation from the rib of Adam bears a Huldah anagram—"The man said, 'This at last is bone of my bones *and flesh* [H] of my flesh; this one shall be called Woman, for out of Man this one was taken'" (Gen 2:23). In that famous verse, the woman is subordinated to Adam, so an opponent may have inserted that anagram to spite Huldah. In contrast, a parallel story in chapter 5 gives the man and the woman equal standing: "When God created humankind, he made them in the likeness of God. Male and female he created them, and he blessed them and named them 'Humankind' when they were created" (Gen 5:1–2).[2] The NRSV gets to the essence of the matter by translating אָדָם as "humankind." These may be the most important words that Huldah ever wrote. Humankind consisted of women as well as men, and each sex, created in God's image, had equal standing before the Lord. Though the work of other biblical writers often fails to display this equality, the portion of Scripture that Huldah wrote does. Recognizing this, we should acknowledge our debt to her.

Additional coding makes it likely that Huldah wrote still more of the early Genesis material. As an example, her coding runs across Gen 3:16–17, which contains God's pronouncement upon the woman that "I will greatly increase your pangs in childbearing; in pain you shall bring forth children." This surely reflects Huldah's own experience. And there is more to the passage. The six Hebrew words at the end of v. 16 say, "Yet your desire shall be for your husband, and he shall rule over you." These words are bare of the Huldah coding that the remainder of vv. 16 and 17 contain.

---

2. Gen 5:1, with its famous image-of-God phrase, lacks Huldah coding. The next verse contains both Huldah and Huldah-wife-of-Shallum spellings. The fifth text word of v. 2 begins a run of חלדהאשתשלם (Huldah-wife-of-Shallum) spellings that runs into v. 5. In all, the chapter contains twenty-nine such encodings.

They could, therefore, have been added by a later editor who wanted to counter Huldah's statement about female equality.[3] This example, added to the conflicting views of women the early Genesis chapters present, suggests an ongoing argument between pro- and anti-Huldah writers. The disagreements may have concerned Asherah worship, the role of women, the Jerusalem fiasco, or several of these together. Further coding work might throw more light on these possibilities.

Huldah as queen mother had served as an Asherah priestess, perhaps even as the chief priestess. As such, she presided over worship in Judah and Egypt, and probably in Babylon, too. In neighboring nations, Asherah was Baal's consort, and Prov 8:30–31 suggests that Asherah also filled that role with Yahweh ("then I was beside him . . . and I was daily his delight, rejoicing before him always, rejoicing in his inhabited world and delighting in the human race"). In Genesis, the symbols of the serpent and the tree could have reminded readers of Huldah's association with Asherah worship.

Huldah encodings come in six forms: Huldah, Huldah-the-queen-mother, Huldah-wife-of-Shallum, Huldah-wife-of-Jehoiakim, Huldah-the-prophetess, and Huldah-mother-of-Jehoiachin. The six register significant coded spellings in nearly ten thousand verses of Hebrew Scripture. What does one do with a new discovery of such large dimension? The first thing is to identify chapters that contain high Huldah densities. This has been done, and the result is 149 chapters, which is 16 percent of Scripture's total. The next order of business is determining whether the coding indicates that Huldah was a subject or an author of the chapter. For instance, Huldah probably composed Genesis 24, the story of Rebekah. It conceals more than four hundred spellings of her name. On the other hand, Leviticus 4 (with over five hundred Huldah spellings) was clearly *about* her rather than *by* her. Since Leviticus 4 deals entirely with sin offerings, detractors of the prophetess must have written it.

PATRIARCHS AND PROMISES

It is simpler to work with entire chapters than with verses, but coded verses can also be rewarding. Consider this set of examples from the Pentateuch.

---

3. The athbash version of Huldah encoded in vv. 16 and 17 is בצ׳ד. Those letters must occur in consecutive text words, but the phrase about a husband ruling over the wife lacks צ. One of the coded spellings ends on the tenth word of v. 16, which is the final word before the possible insertion.

Huldah

The Lord's pledge of the Promised Land in the books of Genesis and Exodus highlights the stories of the patriarchs and of Moses. The writing usually is of the first order, and the phrasemaking often sparkles. The Lord's promises to Abraham, Isaac, Jacob, and Moses are like a string upon which the wanderings of the patriarchs are strung, ever focusing the reader's expectations upon the future settlement of Israel, the land of promise. The first three such encounters with God involve Abram-Abraham and establish the pattern for subsequent promise passages. These emphasize multiplication of Abraham's seed and move from "the land that I will show you" (Gen 12:1–3), to "all the land that you see I will give to you and to your offspring forever" (Gen 13:15–16), to "all the land of Canaan, for a perpetual holding" (Gen 17:4–8). There is no coded evidence that Huldah had a hand in any of these passages, but they establish a precedent for what follows.

Table 8.1 lays out Huldah coding in the promise passages of Genesis, Exodus, and Leviticus, including the three earlier Genesis accounts. The right-hand column gives this writer's opinion on whether Huldah was a co-author.

Table 8.1: Huldah Coding in Pentateuch's Promise Passages

Passage	Coded Groups	God Speaks to	Key Phrase	By Huldah?
Gen 12:2–3	0	Abram	make you great nation	No
Gen 13:15–16	0	Abram	dust of the earth	No
Gen 17:4–7	0	Abraham	father of nations	No
Gen 22:17–18	2	Abraham	sand on seashore	Yes
Gen 26:3–5	2	Isaac	stars of heaven	Yes
Gen 28:13–14	2	Jacob	dust of the earth	Yes
Gen 35:10–12	1	Jacob	Jacob becomes Israel	Probably
Exod 3:8	1	Moses	milk and honey	Yes
Exod 3:16–18	3	Moses	milk and honey	Yes
Exod 6:1–8	6	Moses	milk and honey	Yes
Exod 13:5, 11	1	Moses	milk and honey	Possibly
Exod 33:1–3	1	Moses	milk and honey	Possibly
Lev 20:24	0	Moses	milk and honey	No

These passages always are addressed to one of the patriarchs, usually name Canaan as the land of promise, and contain an eye-catching reference to numerous descendants. Covenant may or may not be included. And often God pledged that reservation of the land was to benefit all the nations of the earth. Excerpts most likely to have been written by Huldah follow.

God said to Abraham, "'I will indeed bless you, and I will make your offspring as numerous as the stars of heaven and as the sand that is on the seashore. And your offspring shall possess the gate of their enemies, and by your offspring shall all the nations of the earth gain blessing for themselves'" (Gen 22:17–18). In this writing, Diaspora readers receive two vivid images—descendants as numerous as heaven's stars and as the seashore's sand. It sounds like vintage Huldah. Also, note the martial air. Not only will Israel possess their enemies' gates, but this action over a longer period will benefit the earth's nations. Does this hint at an end to Babylon's sway? Perhaps when this was written the venture to free the Jerusalem was gathering momentum. Two significant groups of coded Huldah spellings say that the passage was by or about her.

In this next example, the Lord invited Isaac, "'Reside in this land as an alien, and I will be with you, and will bless you; for to you and to your descendants I will give all these lands, and I will fulfill the oath that I swore to your father Abraham. I will make your offspring as numerous as the stars of heaven, and will give to your offspring all these lands; and all the nations of the earth shall gain blessing for themselves through your offspring'" (Gen 26:3–4). Here is "stars of heaven" again and the blessing that Isaac will convey to his descendants and to the earth's nations. Verses 4–5 conceal two groups of Huldah-queen-mother.

Now it is Jacob's turn. The Lord, after identifying himself as the God of Abraham and Isaac, says, "'The land on which you lie [Bethel] I will give to you and to your offspring; and your offspring shall be like the dust of the earth, and you shall spread abroad to the west and to the east and to the north and to the south; and all the families of the earth shall be blessed in you and in your offspring'" (Gen 28:13–14). Again, mark the picturesque images—the four directions and offspring "like the dust of the earth." Two different groups totaling eight coded spellings of Huldah-wife-of-Shallum run beneath the text.

Next, the Lord instructs Jacob, "'I am God Almighty [El Shaddai]: be fruitful and multiply; a nation and a company of nations shall come from you, and kings shall spring from you. The land that I gave to Abraham and Isaac I will give to you, and I will give the land to your offspring after you'" (Gen 35:11–12). This is one of the few instances in which

Huldah

Yahweh is called El Shaddai, and in the previous verse God changed Jacob's name to Israel. Also, in another promise passage, Abram's name becomes Abraham. Perhaps Huldah had something to do with these surprising changes. In the same vein, immediately preceding the El Shaddai promise verse was the report that Rebekah, Deborah's nurse, had died. That name pairing was not coincidental, since both Deborah and Rebekah were Huldah's literary inventions. This insertion might even have been an announcement of Huldah's own death. The nearby spelling of Huldah-prophetess coding completes the argument that she or her followers helped to compose this section of Genesis 35.

Now Huldah attaches Moses to the Abraham-Isaac-Jacob chain. In Exod 3:8, the Lord proclaims, "'I have come down to deliver them from the Egyptians, and to bring them up out of that land to a good and broad land, a land flowing with milk and honey, to the country of the Canaanites, the Hittites, the Amorites, the Perizzites, the Hivites, and the Jebusites.'" In these coded lines, Huldah introduces the striking word picture "a land flowing with milk and honey." She and others were to repeat it more than a score of times. The site of the revelation has shifted from Canaan to Egypt, so one can say with reasonable confidence that Huldah, probably acting with others, penned this during her Egyptian period, 586–575 BCE. The task was to be twofold: to escape from Egypt and to defeat the specified nations then occupying the Promised Land. Again, Huldah-prophetess was the chosen coded spelling.

Exodus 3:16–18 repeats the features of God's prior promise of deliverance in v. 8. The text, however, includes for the first time Israel's elders: "'I will bring you up out of the misery of Egypt, to the land of the Canaanites, the Hittites, the Amorites, the Perizzites, the Hivites, and the Jebusites, a land flowing with milk and honey. They will listen to your voice; and you *and the elders* [H, Baruch, Cyrus] of Israel shall go to the king of Egypt . . .'" Anagrams within "and the elders" date this promise passage in the earlier 570s—after Cyrus had been hired but before the Israelites had escaped from Egypt.[4] Huldah and her assistants are placing the Lord's imprimatur upon their own campaign to retake the Promised Land. Numerous encodings of Huldah-the-prophetess undergird these verses.

The opening verses of Exodus 6 offer yet another promise passage—one that lays particular emphasis upon redemption from Pharaoh:

4. "And the elders" is וזקני. The athbash anagram of Huldah is יונה, of Baruch is יונב, and of Cyrus is קונה.

"I appeared to Abraham, Isaac, and Jacob as God Almighty [El Shaddai], but by my name 'The LORD' [Yahweh] I did not make myself known to them. I also *established* [Jacob] my covenant with them, to give them the land of Canaan, the land in which they resided as aliens . . . Say therefore to the Israelites, 'I am the LORD, and I will free you from the burdens of the Egyptians and deliver you *from slavery* [Daniel] to them . . . *I will take you* [Daniel] as my people, and I will be your God [Elohim]. You shall know that I am the LORD your God, who has freed you from the burdens of the Egyptians. I will bring you into the land that I swore to give to Abraham, Isaac, and Jacob; I will give it to you for a possession.'" (Exod 6:3–4, 6–8)

Huldah coding in these verses is especially strong, which means that authorship is probably hers. Under her hand, God's ancient covenant with the patriarchs becomes the basis for divine intervention against Pharaoh. Interestingly, Huldah uses three names for God—Yahweh, Elohim, and El Shaddai. A check of Huldah coding in the thirty-one verses of Scripture that contain El Shaddai produces no proof that Huldah introduced that name.

The "milk and honey" phrase was good enough to repeat, but most other passages that did this lacked sufficient coding to support Huldah's authorship. Exodus 33:1–3 and Lev 20:24 are two examples. A third example, Exod 13:5, had both "land of the Canaanites" and "milk and honey" but no coded Huldah spellings. It says: "When the LORD brings you into the land of the Canaanites, the Hittites, the Amorites, the Hivites, *and the Jebusites* [Baruch, Daniel], which he swore to your ancestors to give you, a land flowing with milk and honey, you shall keep this observance . . ." (Exod 13:5). The rest of the Pentateuch has verses that use the "milk and honey" phrase but lack a promise from the Lord or, in Deuteronomy, come instead from the mouth of Moses.[5] Of these, only one probably originated with Huldah. It reads, ". . . that you may be strong, and go in and take possession of the land which you are going over to possess, and that you may live long in the land which the LORD swore to your fathers to give to them and *to their descendants* [H], a land flowing with milk and honey" (Deut 11:8–9). Coded names and a Huldah anagram validate the queen mother's authorship. Like the rest of the Dtr work, Deut 11 was written in the 570s.

---

5. Num 13:27; 14:8; Deut 6:3; 11:9; 26:9, 15; 27:3.

Huldah

HULDAH'S FEMINIST TOUCH

The best of the promise passages show that Huldah the prophetess was deeply involved in composing or editing the Genesis-Exodus stories of Israel's beginnings. These generally track the visions of the patriarchs, combining Huldah coding with the Promised Land theme. Of course, where the coding is less concentrated, conclusions about authorship (or more likely joint authorship) must be tentative. But there also are chapters that stand by themselves in density of Huldah coding, and Genesis and Exodus contain a number of these. Genesis 18 is one. It concerns the visit to Abraham by three strangers who announce that his wife, Sarah, will conceive and bear a son. Sarah, listening at the tent door, overhears and laughs, for she thinks that she is well past the age of childbearing. (Only a woman could have written this. Now we know that the author was Huldah.) Four groups of concealed spellings crisscross this account—Huldah-wife-of-Jehoiachin, Huldah-the-queen-mother, and two versions of Huldah-the-prophetess. The chapter as a whole contains 142 spellings. The probability that so many encodings could appear coincidentally in a chapter this size has ten zeroes to the right of the decimal point.

Genesis 18 also has the tale of Abraham bargaining with God as to how few righteous people Sodom and Gomorrah needed to have before God stayed his destruction of the cities (Gen 18:25–33). Abraham started at fifty and worked God down to ten before the Lord went his way, figuratively shaking his head. In view of Huldah's business acumen, this section, too, is entirely in keeping with Huldah's authorship. She would have been a formidable negotiator. Two other Genesis chapters, 38 and 39, also contain significant totals of Huldah spellings. The first tells of Tamar posing as a harlot to secure from Judah her right to remarry after the death of her own husband, who was Judah's brother. The second chapter relates the story of a righteous Joseph evading the advances of Potiphar's wife. Both are tales that involve women, and statistics announce that Huldah wrote— or at minimum collaborated on—both chapters. Elsewhere, six chapters in the book of Exodus with high levels of Huldah coding are technical in nature.[6] They concern the design, framing, and contents of the tabernacle as well as details of Aaron's ordination. It sounds as though the tabernacle was made during the sixth-century march on the Promised Land rather than some six centuries earlier in the time of the Moses-led exodus.

6. Exodus chapters 26–27, 29, 36, 38, and 40 are technical in nature.

Continuing with the study of Huldah's feminist influence within individual passages of the Pentateuch, here are some specific examples that carry Huldah coding. It is quite possible that the prophetess composed the Garden of Eden interplay between the woman, the snake, the man, and God—with all its subtlety and insight. Here are a few verses that have significantly coded Huldah signatures beneath them:

> The woman said to the serpent, "We may eat of the fruit of the trees in the garden" . . . So when the woman saw that the tree was good for food, and that it was a delight to the eyes, and that the tree was to be desired to make one wise, she took of its fruit and ate; and she also gave some to her husband, who was with her, and he ate . . . They heard the sound of the LORD God walking in the garden at the time of the evening breeze, and the man and his wife hid themselves from the presence of the LORD God among the trees of the garden. (Gen 3:2, 6, 8)

In addition, Huldah retouched or composed the Cain story: "Now Adam knew Eve his wife, and she conceived and bore Cain, saying, 'I have gotten [a play on Cain] a man with the help of the LORD.' And again, she bore his brother Abel. Now Abel was a keeper of sheep, and Cain a tiller of the ground" (Gen 4:1–2). In the Noah story, Huldah coding appears in the summary about the animals loaded on the ark: "And those that entered, male and female of all flesh, went in as God had commanded" (Gen 7:16). Huldah coding also accompanies the brief account of the bareness of Sarei (to be Sarah) and the family's emigration from Ur to Haran in upper Mesopotamia (Gen 11:31–32). Coding also attributes to Huldah the verses about Lot's wife becoming a pillar of salt during the destruction of Sodom and Gomorrah (Gen 19:25–26).

The prophetess used anagrams along with coding to identify herself in the birth story of Isaac: "Sarah conceived and bore Abraham a son *in his old age* [H, Baruch, Cyrus] . . . Abraham gave the name Isaac to his son" (Gen 21:2–3). Somewhat later, Huldah used the same text word to produce the same anagrams: "Who would have said to Abraham that Sarah would suckle children? Yet I have borne him a son *in his old age* [H, Baruch, Cyrus]" (Gen 21:7). Huldah-the-prophetess coding underlies both passages. The Cyrus anagrams, of course, date this segment after 575 BCE. Coding in this same chapter suggests that Huldah may also have written the account of God's rescue of the slave girl Hagar and her child from the desert (Gen 21:17–21).

Huldah

A generous number of coded spellings verify that Huldah originated the tale of the reconciliation between a fearful Jacob and his brother Esau (Gen 33:4–12). The scriptural picture is one of groups of mothers with their children, a procession staged by Jacob to blunt Esau's justifiable anger. "Jacob looked up and saw Esau coming, and four hundred men with him. So he divided the children among Leah and Rachel and the two maids. He put the maids with their children in front, then Leah with her children, and Rachel and Joseph last of all. He himself went on ahead of them, bowing himself to the ground seven times, until he came near his brother." Then Huldah caps her story by writing, "But Esau ran to meet him, and embraced him, and fell on his neck and kissed him, and they wept." The ominous threat of "and four hundred men with him" is balanced by the small parade of women and children, and then unexpected forgiveness and reconciliation win the day. No man could have written this better than Huldah.

In Genesis 34, only four verses contain significant Huldah coding, but they all concern women. Here are two of them: "Make marriages with us; give your daughters to us, and take our daughters for yourselves"; and "The other sons of Jacob came upon the slain, and plundered the city, because their sister had been defiled" (Gen 34:9, 27).

Rachel, who died in childbirth, was the wife of the patriarch Jacob, and Genesis chapter 35 contains a brief description of her gravesite: "Jacob set up a pillar at her grave; it is the pillar of Rachel's tomb, which is there to this day. Israel [Jacob] journeyed on, and pitched his tent . . ." (Gen 35:20–21). Beneath these two verses runs an unusual athbash coding of Huldah-wife-of-Shallum.[7] Throughout her career, the prophetess freely encoded both Huldah-wife-of-Shallum and Huldah-wife-of-Jehoiakim. It may be that Huldah's first husband, Shallum, survived her marriage to King Jehoiakim and that she and Shallum came together again after the Babylonians executed Jehoiakim. The chapter's final two verses, which are encoded with Huldah-prophetess, relate the death (at a biblical age of 180) of Isaac (Gen 35:28–29).

Moving now to the book of Exodus, this chapter will continue to select the passages with high proportions of Huldah coding that show particular sympathy toward women. Of necessity, this bypasses the bulk of spellings and those entire chapters that contain statistically significant coding. In Exodus, for example, six whole chapters of highest significance

---

7. The athbash spelling of Huldah-wife-of-Shallum begins at v. 20, word 5. Using one letter per text word, the sequence is ‫מ.ייהדחקהצאן‬.

have over eleven hundred hidden Huldah spellings. They are Exodus 26–27; 29; 36; 38; and 40, which deal with details of the tabernacle and with Aaron's ordination. Comment on these will come later. The second chapter of Exodus has significant Huldah coding in only three verses. The first two concern the rearing of Moses: "Pharaoh's daughter said to her [the child's mother], 'Take this child and nurse it for me, and I will give you your wages.' So the woman took the child and nursed it. When the child grew up, she brought him to Pharaoh's daughter, and she took him as her son. She named him Moses" (Exod 2:9–10). In the other verse (Exod 2:15), an adult Moses flees to Midian, where he is soon to meet his future wife. It appears that Huldah has lightly retouched the traditional story about Moses by inserting these verses. Further on, Huldah coding shows that she added information about the antecedents of Moses and of Aaron, to give more credit to wives and mothers: "Amram married Jochebed his father's sister and she bore him Aaron and Moses . . . Aaron married Elisheba, daughter of Amminadab and sister of Nahshon, and she bore him Nadab, Abihu, Eleazar, and Ithamar" (Exod 6:20, 23).

Huldah coding is heavy in an Exodus text about a contest of the serpents between Moses and Aaron on one side and Pharaoh's magicians on the other (Exod 7:9–13). Perhaps Huldah the priestess of Asherah penned this to show that serpents sided with the Israelites. At the same time, another part of this passage uses a Huldah anagram to state that she is a sorceress. Exodus 7:11 says, "Then Pharaoh summoned the wise men and the sorcerers; and they also, the magicians of Egypt, did the same *by their secret arts* [H]." Editors from both sides apparently were having their say. In the same chapter, Huldah probably is the one who countered this calumny with anagrams of her own. She uses numerous Huldah-queen-mother encodings to show that she had not acted alone against Pharaoh. In a marvel of anagrams, Huldah lists no fewer than six other prominent leaders—most of them twice—who participated in the plot to flee Egypt and retake Jerusalem. The text says that "I will plague your whole country *with frogs* [H, Ezra, Jacob, Daniel] . . . [Frogs would swarm] *into your ovens* [Jehoiachin, Baruch, Daniel] *and your kneading bowls* [H, Daniel, Baruch, Cyrus] . . . *The frogs* [Ezra, Jacob] shall come up on you . . ." (Exod 7:27–29 H8:2–4).

Coding shows that the prophetess played a leading role in listing the plagues inflicted upon Pharaoh. These included turning the Nile's water into blood (Exod 7:17–22); the aforementioned frogs (H7:27–29 E8:2–4); lice and flies (H8:11–18 and 20–27 E14–21 and 23–30); and hail, thunder, and rain (9:26–29). Each of these verses contains significant Huldah coded spellings. Finally, there was the plague upon the firstborn. At the Lord's direction, Moses told Pharaoh, "Every firstborn in the land of Egypt shall die, from the firstborn of Pharaoh who sits on his throne to the firstborn of the female slave who is behind the handmill, and all the firstborn of the livestock" (Exod 11:5). Of all the plagues, the death of a nation's firstborn would perhaps have seemed even more horrific to women than to men. This book makes no attempt to unravel the real story of the Israelites' sixth-century struggle to leave Egypt.[8] It seems to have been difficult and lengthy. That story awaits the attention of those scholars who have, among other things, mastered anagrams and coded spelling.

As keepers of their households, women in the Exile would have had to prepare for Judean feast days. Huldah neatly summarizes these in two heavily coded verses. The Lord speaks: "You shall observe the festival of unleavened bread; as I commanded you, you shall eat unleavened bread for seven days at the appointed time in the month of Abib [March/April], for in it you came out of Egypt . . . You shall observe the festival of harvest, of the first fruits of your labor, of what you sow in the field. You shall observe the festival of ingathering at the end of the year, when you gather in from the field the fruit of your labor" (Exod 23:15–16). The heavy Huldah coding, a nearby Cyrus anagram, and the reference to coming out of Egypt help to date this as after 575 BCE but before Huldah's death in 564. This also tells analysts that the Jews in Egypt launched their campaign against Jerusalem in the spring of the year, probably in 575.

HULDAH FINANCES TABERNACLE

Massive Huldah coding in Exodus 26 offers strong evidence that Huldah was a principal author of the chapter. It describes at some length the design of the tabernacle's curtains, frames, and screens along with its fabrics and woods. One suspects that the queen mother was lovingly involved with designing and constructing an actual tabernacle—perhaps in Egypt. It could even have been used during the Israelites' trek northwards towards the Promised Land. Exodus 26 contains over two hundred spellings within twenty groups of Huldah variations. Huldah also helped to

8. Some scholars think there was more than one exodus of Jews from Egypt. See Shanks, "When Did Israel Begin?" 62, 67. This view accords with this writer's opinion that the present Genesis-Exodus story contains at least elements of the departures of the patriarchs and of the sixth-century Jews.

compose Exodus 27, 29, and 36. These, too, are devoted in good part to the tabernacle. In addition, Exodus 35 barely misses statistical significance, and its final eleven verses have several Huldah earmarks. First, they house a cluster of Huldah anagrams. Next, those verses contain about forty coded spellings of Huldah, Huldah-queen-mother, and Huldah-wife-of-Shallum. And third, these verses feature a large group of women laboring joyfully at work they do well. An excerpt from that text follows.

> All the skillful women spun with their hands, and brought what they had spun in blue *and purple* [Ezra] and crimson yarns and fine linen; all the women whose hearts moved them to use their skill spun the goats' hair. And the leaders brought onyx stones and gems to be set *in the ephod* [Asaiah] and the breastpiece, and spices and oil for the light, and for the anointing oil, and for the fragrant *incense* [Daniel]. All the Israelite men and women whose hearts made them willing to bring anything for the work that the LORD had commanded by Moses to be done, brought it as a freewill offering to the LORD. (Exod 35:25–29)

One can almost hear the excited buzz of the women as they worked.

Two of the closing chapters of Exodus (38 and 40) have large numbers of Huldah coded spellings that far exceed coincidental occurrence. These deal with making the altar to fit inside the tent-like tabernacle, and though they contain several hundred Huldah spellings they make no mention of anything feminine. The coding, however, ensures that Huldah is either the subject or the author of Exodus 38 and 40. A possibility is that the wealth devoted to the altar, the tabernacle, and its furnishings came from Huldah's private fortune. Chapter 38 is precise about the weight of gold, silver, and bronze that went into the construction of the sanctuary—down to the last shekel. For gold, it was twenty-nine talents and 730 shekels; for silver, one hundred talents and 1,775 shekels; and for bronze, seventy talents and 2,400 shekels (Exod 38:24–25, 29). Such precision demonstrates established controls and careful accounting over a prolonged period. It also necessitates sources of considerable wealth.

The text says the funds were contributed by those numbered by a census, a total of 603,550 men twenty years old and upward, but this figure is far too large for the sixth-century male Judean residents of Egypt. Instead, the total has been invented to provide text words necessary to spell Huldah-the-queen-mother and three variations of Jehoiachin. Probably only these two in the entire exilic community in Egypt had the resources to furnish that much gold, silver, and bronze. In English, the text of Exod

38:26 is "a beka a head (that is, half a shekel, measured by the sanctuary shekel), for everyone who was counted in the census, from twenty years old and upward, for six hundred three thousand, five hundred fifty men." The original text contains twenty-two Hebrew words. A rare athbash spelling of Huldah-the-queen-mother starts at word 1 and ends on word 10 of v. 26, using one letter per text word to complete the spelling.[9] How unusual is this coded athbash version? *There are only ten other such spellings in all of Hebrew Scripture.* The odds against an occurrence in this especially apt location are about twenty-eight thousand to one. This coded spelling alone goes far toward verifying that Scripture used coding and athbash, that this is an exilic passage, and that Huldah is the funding source. It also shows that exilic authors were not above rigging text to accommodate coded spellings.

The Huldah encoding uses the verse's first ten text words. In addition, words 14 through 19 support three separate Jehoiachin athbash encodings—though each is much more commonly found in Scripture than the Huldah coding.[10] Previous work has shown that Jehoiachin and his mother used trading to become wealthy. It follows that this enabled them to finance construction of the altar and the tabernacle in the 570s. Huldah was even more than a poet, prophet, warrior, merchant, and queen. She was a devoted believer and a philanthropist as well.

Exodus 38:21 uses the phrase "the tabernacle of the covenant," which, according to the NRSV, establishes that the sanctuary contained the ark and the Ten Commandments.[11] This makes it possible that the ark and the Ten Commandments that it contained were carried to the Promised Land, only to be destroyed at the subsequent battle of Jerusalem c 574 BCE.

THE DAUGHTERS OF ZELOPHEHAD

There is a segment of the book of Numbers that adds luster to Huldah as a defender of feminine principles, even despite the limits that tradition had previously imposed. In the culture of the times, women were not allowed

---

9. The true spelling of Huldah-the-queen-mother is חלדהההגבירה. The athbash version of it is תדצקקפפעבלק. The sequence of that athbash spelling, from words 1 through 10 of v. 26 of Exodus 38, is קתצקקדל בעף.

10. The athbash spellings of Jehoiachin are פשע, עמפתש, and פעשמפת. Spellings all begin at word 14 of v. 26 and end at words 17, 18, and 19, respectively. The true spellings are יוכן, בניהו, and יכוניה.

11. The phrase is used in the note to Exod 38:21.

to inherit property. In Numbers 27, the daughters of Zelophehad asked Moses that they be allowed to inherit after the death of their father, who had had no sons. Moses brought their case "before the LORD," who ruled that if a man died without surviving male issue then daughters should inherit (Num 27:1–11). The heart of the case is stated in the first seven verses and all but one of them conceal coding of Huldah spellings—Huldah, Huldah-mother-of-Jehoiachin, and Huldah-the-queen-mother. Verses 8–11 are by someone else, a traditionalist who enumerated three other situations in which men would inherit if the deceased had no daughters.

In the final chapter of Numbers, Moses supplements the earlier decision about the daughters of Zelophehad by announcing the following: "'Let them marry whom they think best; only it must be into a clan of their father's tribe that they are married, so that no inheritance of the Israelites shall be transferred from one tribe to another'" (Num 36:6–7). This short chapter conceals so many Huldah spellings that coding in the entire text cannot be coincidental. In chapter 27, Huldah won for women the right to inherit if they had no living brothers. In chapter 36, by yielding the point that land should not transferred outside the tribe, she wins for the daughters of Zelophehad the right to choose their own husbands—even though that choice was narrowed somewhat. Not only did the daughters avoid arranged marriages but they also generated their own dowries. Numbers 27:1–7 and Numbers 36 represent breakthroughs for women, and it is highly likely that Huldah wrote both texts.

A question remains about the separation within Num 27:1–11 and Numbers 36. Coding sheds light upon this. First, Huldah composed Num 27:1–5, winning the right of Zelophehad's daughters to inherit. Next, within that same chapter, a traditionalist tacked on several verses that preserved for men their rights to inherit when the deceased man died childless. Time must have passed—though not much of it, because the book of Numbers has much material about ordering the tribes for occupation of the Promised Land. Also, Huldah coding is statistically significant in over a quarter of the book's chapters.[12] She would have written those in Egypt or perhaps a few on the march towards Judah (585–575 BCE). Chapter 36, which is an addition to an addition, would then have been added in the years before her death in 564.

Several keys for unlocking the mystery of Huldah's place in Scripture lie within the book of Proverbs. Not only is Proverbs important to

---

12. Numbers 1–4, 7, 16, 26, 28–29, and 36 contain significant amounts of Huldah coding.

Huldah

understanding her, but it seems likely that Huldah will greatly expand one's grasp of why and when the book of Proverbs was written. Also, it is one of the books in Scripture with inordinately high Huldah coding. Proverbs is of such importance that the next chapter will be devoted entirely to analyzing Huldah's place within that book.

9

Huldah in the Book of Proverbs

PROVERBS, OF ALL SCRIPTURE's books, contains the richest characterizations of Huldah. Probabilities say that almost three-quarters of the chapters in Proverbs are by or about the sixth-century prophet, and not all of them favorably so. Though chapters are easier to visualize than verses, coded verses may be an even better measure of the density of Huldah coding. On average, no fewer than six out of ten verses will contain Huldah coded spellings. The book of Proverbs features women characters, both good ones and bad ones. In previous scholarly works, your writer understood this as an assault upon and defense of Jacob's wife.[1] Apologies are in order. It will soon be apparent that the woman involved was not Jacob's wife. Instead, it was Jacob's colleague, Huldah.

HULDAH ANAGRAMS SHOW POLARIZATION
IN PROVERBS

Anagrams offer a quick snapshot of the polarization within Proverbs of Huldah-related sentiments. All twenty-two of Huldah's own anagrams plus some of those from other notables follow.[2] After a discourse on wisdom, chapter 2 warns about those "whose *paths* [Cyrus] are crooked, and who are *devious* [H] in their ways. You will be saved from the loose woman, from the adulteress with her smooth words" (Prov 2:15–16). The

---

1. Kavanagh, *The Exilic Code*, 144–48 and *The Shaphan Group*, 104–9.

2. Proverbs contains only twenty-two Huldah anagrams, which is half as many as one would expect. More than sixty would be required to meet the .001 standard of significance.

word "loose" can also be translated as "foreign" or "harlot." Remember that Huldah probably was of Moabite origin and had been married at least twice. The anagram for Cyrus helps to date this as during or after the 570s. Further along, the text reads "*the treacherous* [H] will be rooted out of" the land (Prov 2:22). A milder voice is heard two chapters later. The author's words are "healing to all *their flesh* [H]. Keep your heart with all vigilance . . ." (Prov 4:22–23). The next chapter contains two Cyrus anagrams (not shown) and is sexually disparaging to Huldah: "Drink water from *your own cistern* [Baruch], *flowing water* [H] from your own well. Should your springs be scattered abroad . . .?" (Prov 5:15–16). Hiring the foreigner Cyrus must have been Huldah's offense. Note that Baruch also stands accused. The next chapter continues the anti-Huldah pattern. The word "steal" houses one Huldah anagram and "Can fire be carried in the bosom without burning *one's clothes* [H]?" contains another (Prov 6:27).

At chapter 8, in a moving passage on wisdom, a champion for Huldah steps forward—a champion who supports Cyrus, Jehoiachin, and Baruch, too. "I, wisdom, live with prudence, and I attain knowledge and discretion . . . perverted speech I hate . . . I have *strength* [Jehoiachin]. By me kings reign, *and rulers* [H] decree what is just . . . I love those who love me, and those who *seek me diligently* [Cyrus] *find me* [Baruch]" (Prov 8:12–15, 17). From the wording, one might even conjecture that young Cyrus was near to conversion to Yahweh—though this is much to hang upon a single Hebrew text word. Because of its personification of Woman Wisdom, Proverbs 8 is a famous chapter. Suddenly, after several thousand years, we can understand that its context is the mid-Exilic revolt. It sounds as if Cyrus was on the scene, which would date Proverbs 8 between 579 and about 572 BCE. Woman Wisdom might or might not be Huldah—more on that later. "By me kings reign" is preceded with a Jehoiachin anagram, which probably means that he has been confirmed as Judah's monarch-in-exile.

The next Proverbs chapter returns to criticism of Huldah. A foolish woman calls to those "going straight *on their way* [Cyrus] . . . to him who is without sense she says, 'Stolen [H] water is sweet, and bread eaten in secret is pleasant.' But they do not know . . . that her guests are in the depths of Sheol" (Prov 9:15, 17–18).

Continuing this study of Huldah anagrams, chapters 10–22 comprise a second major division of the book of Proverbs. Chapter 11 starts with a barrage of anti-Huldah anagrams. The Hebrew root for "righteousness" can contain the letters spelling a Huldah anagram. See how critics turn this fact against her. "The integrity of the upright guides them, but the crookedness of *the treacherous* [H] destroys them. Riches do not profit in the day of wrath, but righteousness delivers from death. *The righteousness* [H] of the blameless keeps their ways straight, but the wicked fall *by their own wickedness* [H, Jehoiachin]. *The righteousness* [H] of the upright saves them, but the treacherous are taken captive by their schemes" (Prov 11:3–6). The last anagram in that same chapter attacks Huldah and Jehoiachin for their wealth: "Those who trust *in their riches* [H, Jehoiachin] will wither, but the righteous will flourish like green leaves" (Prov 11:28). This repeats the thought already quoted: "Riches do not profit in the day of wrath..." (Prov 11:4). Huldah's enemies turned the affluence of the queen mother and her royal son against them. Looking ahead, chapter 27 also censures the wealth of Huldah and Jehoiachin. That text cautions, "Give attention *to your herds* [H]; for riches do not last forever, nor a crown for all generations" (Prov 27:23). Because "herds" surely refers to the subjects governed, chapter 27 could well refer either to the Egyptian period (585–574) or to the later 570s—the time when the Jews briefly controlled Jerusalem.

Other Huldah anagrams, though scattered, are easy to categorize as hostile or supportive. Here are two examples: "Diverse *weights* [H] are an abomination to the LORD," which answers a positive anagram four chapters back—"Honest *balances* [H] and scales are the LORD's" (Prov 20:23 and 16:11). An interesting anagram blames Cyrus and excuses Huldah. Note that it associates Huldah with the wise woman of Proverbs: "The wise woman builds her house, but the foolish *tears it down* [Cyrus] with her own hands. Those who walk *uprightly* [H] fear the LORD" (Prov 14:1–2). This next is especially venomous: "For a prostitute is a deep pit; an adulteress is a narrow well. She lies in wait like a robber and increases the number of *the faithless* [H] ... At the last it bites like a serpent, and stings *like an adder* [H, Jehoiachin]" (Prov 23:27–28, 32).[3]

In this same chapter 23 Jehoiachin fares especially badly. The authors form anagrams for his name not only from "*adder*," but from "*vomit*" and "*despise*" as well (Prov 23:32, 8, 9). The chapter ends in this way: "'*They struck me* [Jehoiachin],' you will say, 'but I was not hurt; they beat me, but I did not feel it. When shall I awake? I will seek another drink'" (Prov 23:35). This presents Jehoiachin as an alcoholic, which he may have been. Alternatively, the words might be announcing that Jehoiachin had been taken at the final battle, deprived of water, and put to torture. Possibly both are true—alcoholic Jehoiachin may have been captured and tortured. If

---

3. The Huldah anagram formed within "adder" is נצרי, which is rare. Scripture contains only twelve of them.

Jehoiachin was a true alcoholic, his drinking would have created the most serious problems for the exiles. He was, after all, the last link in a chain of kings that led back to King David. Those in the modern world who have known alcoholics are familiar with the emotional, physical, and fiscal damage they can do. If Jehoiachin was unfit to rule, the hope of restoring the Davidic line became even less plausible. Another passage intimates that both Jehoiachin and Huldah had drinking problems. Chapter 31 says, "It is not for kings to drink wine, *or for rulers* [H] to desire strong drink; or else they will drink and forget what has been decreed" (Prov 31:4–5).

The next-to-last chapter in Proverbs makes a Huldah anagram within the word "steal" (Prov 30:9). That plaint could be among Huldah's final words. "Two things I ask of you; do not deny them to me before I die: Remove far from me falsehood and lying; give me neither poverty nor riches; feed me with the food that I need, or I shall be full, and deny you, and say, 'Who is the LORD?' or I shall be poor, *and steal* [H], and profane the name of my God" (Prov 30:7–9). The very last Huldah anagram in Proverbs lies in the center of the famous poem to a Woman of Worth. That tribute starts with Prov 31:10 and runs through v. 31, which is the book's concluding verse. Proverbs 31:19 says, "She puts her hands *to the distaff* [H, Cyrus, Baruch], and her hands hold the spindle."

The trails of Huldah, Cyrus, and Jehoiachin anagrams give context to the book of Proverbs. Huldah is both criticized and defended—even while the campaign to retake Jerusalem is underway. If this interpretation is sound, then much of Proverbs dates during the 570s. Chapters 1–9, 17–20, and 23–26 contain almost all the Cyrus anagrams, which dates their compositions after 575. Proverbs has far more anti-Huldah anagrams than ones that support her, which leads us to assume that Huldah's critics wrote most of the book. These inferences are based upon scanty data, however. One-fourth of the Proverbs chapters lack Cyrus or Huldah anagrams. What are these about? The shortage of anagrams tells us something important—Proverbs is not primarily about Huldah. Instead, it may well relate what was going on in Judah and in the Diaspora settlements during the middle of the Exile. In form, the individual proverbs were composed to instruct young men. Undoubtedly, the book was subsequently used for that, but Proverbs was originally written to argue policy and to convey information. So far as this writer knows, no other analyst has argued this. To fill our information gap about the Exile, scholars might test the book's chapters for each and every possible anagram of each and every possible name in Scripture. One hopes that this will happen sooner rather than later.

WOMAN WISDOM IS HULDAH

In addition to anagrams, there is coded writing. Proverbs ranks third in percentage of chapters with significant Huldah coding. Table 9.1, seen previously, places the importance of Proverbs in context.

Table 9.1: Books with High Percentages of Significant Huldah Coding

Books	Significant Chapters	% Significant Chapters
Daniel	10	83%
Ezra-Nehemiah	17	74
Proverbs	22	71
Joshua	10	41
Chronicles	24	37
Psalms	55	37
Numbers	13	33
Ezekiel	16	33
Rest of OT	118	22%
All	286	31%

The table shows that Proverbs has twenty-two chapters in which Huldah's name is significantly encoded. In six of them, either she or her critics achieve this in her own name. In the rest, she significantly participated with other members of the Shaphan group in coding texts.[4] This widespread encoding by exilic figures supports the conclusion that Proverbs carries a sixth-century date. Scholarly estimates run from the end of the monarchy (late seventh century) to the fifth or fourth century BCE.[5]

Proverbs is rich in female characterizations—both favorable and unfavorable to Huldah. Principally, they are Woman of Worth, Woman Wisdom, and Foreign Woman.[6] The opening of the book inveighs against

4. Significantly coded Proverbs chapters with only Huldah's name are 10, 17–18, and 31. Those with significant coding where Huldah is part of the Shaphan group are 1–2, 7–21, 26–29, and 31. After eliminating overlaps, twenty-two Proverbs chapters contain significant Huldah coding. This table has higher percentages of Huldah coding than table 6.1 due to the inclusion of Shaphan group chapters in which Huldah participated.

5. Scott, "Proverbs," 1273; Blank, "Proverbs," 940.

6. Woman Wisdom is used by Fontaine, "Proverbs," 153. She also uses Strange Woman, for whom this writer substitutes Foreign Woman.

those who lie in wait to rob innocents. It has heavy Huldah coding. After this, Woman Wisdom makes her first appearance, and this too contains hidden Huldah spellings. Huldah was a prophet, and as the NRSV notes, Woman Wisdom's words ring with the words of a prophet.[7] She said, "Wisdom cries out in the street; in the squares she raises her voice . . . Because I have called and you refused, have stretched out my hand and no one heeded . . . when panic strikes you like a storm, and your calamity comes like a whirlwind . . . For waywardness kills the simple, and the complacency of fools destroys them; but those who listen to me will be secure and will live at ease, without dread of disaster" (Prov 1:20, 24, 26, 33–34). Beneath this prophecy lie significant coded spellings of Huldah-queen-mother, Huldah-wife-of-Shallum, and two versions of Huldah. It appears that Huldah is the long-sought Woman Wisdom of Proverbs 1.

The eighth chapter of Proverbs in its entirety is another portrayal of Woman Wisdom. Huldah's coding extends from vv. 1 through 10 and from vv. 16 through 25. While plentiful, the coded spellings are not sufficient to gain statistical significance for her alone. Instead, Proverbs 8 is one of the chapters in which she joined with other Shaphan-group members to win significance. Chapter 8 opens with: "Does not wisdom call, and does not understanding raise her voice . . . 'All the words of my mouth are righteous; there is nothing twisted or crooked in them. They are all straight to one who understands'" (Prov 8:1, 8–9). One half-dozen significantly coded spellings of Huldah-the-prophet and Huldah-wife-of-Shallum underlie this chapter's first ten verses. In them, Huldah rejects the charges by her opponents that she is a liar and a schemer. Instead, she says, "I have good advice and sound wisdom; I have insight, I have *strength* [Jehoiachin]" (Prov 8:14). By using the word translated as "strength," Huldah does two things. First, she reminds readers of her valor in the past, displayed perhaps during several sieges of Jerusalem. Second, because "strength" contains a Jehoiachin anagram, Huldah reinforces her son's claim to be king of Judah in absentia and invokes her own authority as queen mother—exile or no exile.

Speaking as Woman Wisdom, Huldah continues, "By me kings reign, *and rulers* [H] decree what is just; by me rulers rule, and nobles, all who govern rightly" (Prov 8:15–16). Verse 15 lacks coded spelling but includes a Huldah anagram, while her words bespeak sovereignty. A Cyrus anagram in the next line helps to date this in the 570s: "I love those who

---

7. "Wisdom personified as a prophet" reads the NRSV's note to Prov 1:20–33.

love me, *and those who seek me* [Cyrus] diligently find me" (Prov 8:17). Is Huldah tutoring Cyrus in Yahweh?

Coding beneath these next several verses includes Huldah-the-prophet and two different versions of Huldah-wife-of-Jehoiakim. There are eleven spellings, certainly enough to advise informed readers as to whom the words refer. "Riches and honor are with me, enduring wealth and prosperity. My fruit is better than gold, even fine gold, and my yield than choice silver. I walk in the way of righteousness, along the paths of justice, endowing with wealth those who love me, and filling their treasuries" (Prov 8:18–21). Huldah was wealthy and at the same time generous. Certainly, she helped to finance the Cyrus-led army and to support some of the exiles in Egypt. Beneath "Riches and honor are with me, enduring wealth and prosperity" are nine spellings of two different athbash versions of Huldah-wife-of-Jehoiakim. When Huldah was writing these words in Egypt, her former husband King Jehoiakim had been dead for twenty years and Huldah had reached her early sixties. However, age had not dimmed the honor attached to royalty. As to wealth, trade and war seem to have swelled her riches. There is no mention of the privations of siege and exile, of spousal deaths and conquerors' abuses. This is Huldah personified as a goddess, and goddesses do not suffer human ills and failings.

The concluding portion of chapter 8 says, "Ages ago I was set up, at the first, before the beginning of the earth . . . Before the mountains had been shaped, before the hills, I was brought forth . . .When he established the heavens, I was there . . . when he marked out the foundations of the earth, then I was beside him, like a master workman; and I was daily his delight, rejoicing before him always" (Prov 8:23, 25, 27, 29–30). Woman Wisdom had been Yahweh's constant companion. She was beside God when he established the heavens and set the bounds of earth. She acted with God "as the source of truth, righteousness, instruction, and knowledge."[8]

Woman Wisdom does not claim direct participation in creation, much less equality with God. Instead, according to Huldah and her fellow authors, Woman Wisdom was God's companion. She advised Yahweh "like a master workman" and was "daily his delight." Huldah as queen mother probably had presided over Asherah worship in Jerusalem and perhaps also in Babylon. Once in Egypt, Huldah apparently took leadership of queen-of-heaven worship, and likely debated Jeremiah about the practice (Jeremiah 44). Also, much in Proverbs 8 is supported by parallels

8. Meyers, *Discovering Eve*, 152.

with Egyptian goddesses.[9] What may surprise us in Proverbs 8 about Woman Wisdom's companionship with God would not have shocked a sixth-century Judean exile—though members of the Deuteronomistic school apparently took strong offense. To sum up, Huldah was the model for the Woman Wisdom of Proverbs, and much of the book was composed during her stay in Egypt.

FOREIGN WOMAN TO DETRACTORS

If Huldah was Woman Wisdom to her supporters, she also was Foreign Woman to her detractors. As mentioned above, chapter 2 warns about those "whose *paths* [Cyrus] are crooked, and who are *devious* [H] in their ways. You will be saved from the loose woman, from the adulteress with her smooth words" (Prov 2:15–16). The word "loose" can also be translated as "foreign," and this book will use Foreign Woman, to remind readers of Huldah's Moabite origins. In addition to the "devious" anagram, no fewer than three different sets of significantly coded spellings traverse the text—Huldah-prophetess, Huldah-wife-of-Shallum, and Huldah-mother-of-Jehoiachin. The coding sets contain five, three, and five spellings, respectively, of each combination. Those who understood the coding technique would quickly have recognized that Huldah was the devious, adulterous Foreign Woman.

Proverbs devotes an entire chapter to the Foreign Woman. Proverbs 5:3–5 reads, "For the lips of a loose [foreign] woman drip honey, and her speech is smoother than oil; but in the end she is bitter as wormwood, sharp as a two-edged sword. Her feet go down to death; her steps follow the path to Sheol." Huldah's opponents were masters of the coded insult, and these twenty Hebrew text words shelter four different Huldah groups—Huldah, Huldah-wife-of-Jehoiakim, Huldah-wife-of-Shallum, and Huldah-mother-of-Jehoiachin. Further down are these words: "Why should you be intoxicated, my son, by another [foreign] woman and embrace the bosom of an adventuress?" (Prov 5:20). Also, sets of Huldah and Huldah-wife-of-Jehoiakim encodings cross this Foreign Woman citation.

Another reference to Foreign Woman is in Proverbs 7, where a man instructs his son, "Say to wisdom, 'You are my sister,' and call insight your intimate friend, that they may keep you from the loose [foreign] woman, from the adulteress with her smooth words. For at the window of my house I looked out through *my lattice* . . ." (Prov 7:4–6, italics

9. Fontaine, "Proverbs," 156.

added). This passage has neither Huldah coding nor anagrams. Lacking them, how did the authors announce to their sixth-century readers that Huldah was the Foreign Woman? A single word supplies the linkage. "Lattice" makes only two appearances in Hebrew Scripture. Proverbs 7:6 is one, and the Song of Deborah is the other. In the period of the judges, Israel under Deborah's leadership defeated an army of Canaanites. Their general Sisera lay dead, slain by a woman who drove a tent-peg through his skull. The Song pictures the vigil of Sisera's mother awaiting her son's return: "Out of the window she peered, the mother of Sisera gazed through *the lattice*: 'Why is his chariot so long in coming? Why tarry the hoofbeats of his chariots?'" (Judg 5:28, italics added). Huldah herself wrote this superb dramatic poem, which must have preceded the Foreign Woman chapter in Proverbs 7. Scholars can and should assume that Huldah was indeed the author. Seven different groups of Huldah-related encodings cross beneath Judg 5:28, which is the lattice verse. In addition, the chapter as a whole contains eight Huldah anagrams and 108 coded spellings. This gives the Song of Deborah statistically significant probabilities in both anagrams and spellings—a rare double occurrence.[10] The Song was by Huldah. All her contemporaries who understood coding would have known it. Most would also have spotted the Proverbs-Judges connection, and understood that the use of "lattice" meant Huldah was the Foreign Woman of Proverbs 7.

The final Foreign Woman passage in Proverbs is this: "The mouth of a loose [foreign] woman is a deep pit; he with whom the LORD is angry will fall into it" (Prov 22:14). This also is underscored with significant encodings of Huldah and Huldah-queen-mother. In summary, five locations in chapters 2, 5, 7, and 22 have Foreign Woman verses linked directly to Huldah the prophet. But there is more. A trio of passages also speaks derogatorily about women, and these too take aim at Huldah: "Then a woman comes toward him, decked out like a prostitute, wily of heart"; "The foolish woman is loud; she is ignorant and knows nothing"; and "Like a gold ring in a pig's snout is a beautiful woman without good sense" (Prov 7:10, 9:13, 11:22). Each of these has significantly encoded Huldah spellings under or next to the quoted verse.

10. Significant groups of spelling that run below Judg 5:28 include three Huldah and two Huldah-wife-of-Shallum variations, and single versions of Huldah-mother-of-Jehoiachin and Huldah-the-prophetess. The Song of Deborah as a whole contains both significant Huldah anagrams ($P = 6.1 \times 10^{-5}$) and encodings ($P = 6.7 \times 10^{-7}$).

Huldah

HULDAH IS THE WOMAN OF WORTH

Proverbs 31, the book's final chapter, is justly famous for its praise of the Woman of Worth. It is an acrostic poem of twenty-two lines. That is, each line starts with a different letter and those starting letters follow the order of the Hebrew alphabet. Not surprisingly, the subject of the poem is Huldah. Knowing her biography, one can identify many of Huldah's characteristics in the verses. However, the best reason that Prov 31:10–31 pertains to Huldah is the dense spelling coded within the text. There are sixteen different groups spelling Huldah's name or office, almost invariably inserted multiple times. For example, the fourteen letters of one of the passage's athbash versions produce Huldah-wife-of-Jehoiakim. It has eight separate spellings. In all, the text of Prov 31:10–31 conceals over sixty spellings of half a dozen different compound names.[11] It could be called a coding landslide. Table 9.2 on the facing page shows how the authors of the text arranged their Huldah encodings.

The left-hand column lists the poem's verses—twenty-two of them, labeled 10 through 31. An "x" to the right of the verse number means that one of the spellings starts in, crosses, or ends on that verse. The total number of x's opposite any verse number measures the Huldah coding activity. Clearly, the author inserted his Huldah coding in two clumps: the first in vv. 13 through 18 and the second in vv. 23 through 27. Verses 16 and 17 have the highest amount of Huldah coding activity, though the totals for 25–27 are more than respectable. Plainly, this coding is purposeful rather than random—the two clumps could hardly have been coincidental. Indeed, they suggest that different individuals worked on different portions of the text. Readers should bear in mind, though, that when the full story is told, the Woman of Worth passage will reveal several dozen—possibly a hundred—significantly coded names, things, and places in addition to the Huldah spellings.

---

11. The coded names are Huldah (3), Huldah-wife-of-Jehoiakim (3), Huldah-wife-of-Shallum (1), Huldah-mother-of-Jehoiachin (5), Huldah-the-prophetess (2), and Huldah-the-queen-mother (1). Numbers within parentheses give athbash variations of that word. Each variation makes a coding group.

136

Table 9.2: Verses Used by 15 Significant Huldah Coding Groups in
Proverbs 31:10–31

Verse							
10							
11							
12							
13	X	X					
14	X	X	X				
15	X	X	X	X			
16	X	X	X	X	X	X	X
17	X	X	X	X	X	X	
18	X	X	X	X			
19							
20							
21							
22							
23	X	X	X				
24	X	X	X				
25	X	X	X	X	X		
26	X	X	X	X	X		
27	X	X	X	X	X		
28							
29							
30							
31							

As a whole, the Huldah coding within the passage is statistically highly significant and cannot be coincidental.[12] Huldah herself may have put her hand to this, but it is more likely that someone else composed it. The fifteen-member Shaphan group weighs in heavily on this text. The encoding of their names, too, has a near-zero probability of coincidence.[13]

12. The chi-square proportions for Prov 31:10–31 are 43 / 24,137 and 151 / 305,345. The first shows Huldah encodings in the passage and in the rest of Scripture; the second gives text words for both categories. The probability of coincidence for the 43 encodings is 2.27×10^{-15}.

13. Kavanagh, *The Shaphan Group*, 121.

The woman is presented from her husband's point of view, and Carole Fontaine writes that the Woman of Worth "is the living embodiment of Woman Wisdom's teachings and attributes."[14] Moreover, coding and anagrams show that Woman of Worth and Woman Wisdom are both embodiments of Huldah herself. Several excerpts from that final Proverbs chapter follow.

- "A capable wife who can find? She is far more precious than jewels" (Prov 31:10). "Wife" is the word for "woman" and "capable" can also mean valorous—which fits Huldah well. She may at this point have been single and like her creation, Deborah, a leader in war.

- "She is like the ships of the merchant, she brings her food from far away" (Prov 31:14). Huldah's wealth supplied Israel's army. In Egypt, she probably used ships on the Nile, the Red Sea, and the Mediterranean to stock the Jerusalem expedition.

- "She girds herself with strength, and makes her arms strong" (Prov 31:17). This is Huldah the warrior. Also, six different coded spellings underlie this verse.

- "She perceives that her merchandise is profitable. Her lamp does not go out at night" (Prov 31:18). Trade again, but the author is also pushing back against the slander that Huldah sold herself for profit and kept her lamp lit all night to do so.

- "She puts her hands *to the distaff* [H, Cyrus, Baruch], and her hands hold the spindle. She opens her hand to the poor, and reaches out her hands to the needy" (Prov 31:19-20). "Distaff" houses Huldah, Cyrus, and Baruch anagrams. This helps to date Prov 31 as somewhat after 575. Even Huldah's enemies acknowledged her openhanded generosity.

- "Her husband is known in the city *gates* [Jehoiachin], taking his seat among the elders of the land" (Prov 31:23). This is poetic license because Jehoiachin was Huldah's son, not her husband. Strong evidence from other anagrams says that both mother and son served as elders in Egypt.

- "She opens her mouth with wisdom, and the teaching of kindness is on her tongue" (Prov 31:26). "Wisdom" alludes to Woman Wisdom, one of Huldah's personifications in Proverbs. Also, coded spellings of

14. Fontaine, "Proverbs," 160.

Huldah, Huldah-mother-of-Jehoiachin, and two versions of Huldah-the-prophetess cross this verse.

- "'Many women have done excellently, but you surpass them all.' Charm is deceitful, and beauty is vain, but a woman who fears the LORD is to be praised" (Prov 31:29–30). The fear of the Lord was at Huldah's core.

Huldah's supporters could have composed this closing poem when the Cyrus revolt was afoot and Huldah was in her sixties. Therefore, Prov 31:10–31 is retrospective, because it shows Huldah at the height of her powers as a woman and as a wife.[15]

Coded spellings in Proverbs 31 show that the human Huldah is the model for the Woman of Worth and, most famously, for Woman Wisdom of Proverbs 8, who was said to be present when the Lord created the heavens and the earth. She also is the woman whom most of the book's Huldah anagrams attack. As a personification, Huldah the prophet is the basis for the evil Foreign Woman. While the book of Proverbs is about Huldah, it is not *all* about her. Perhaps only one-tenth of its verses feature her. However, that lesser proportion is widely distributed and unusually well written. The Huldah sections give purpose and context to the entire book, and also should help scholars in assigning dates to the other 90 percent of Proverbs. Because the Huldah passages are so dispersed and commonly date from the middle of the Exile, it seems likely that the remainder were also created during that period—likely, but not certain. Future work with the coding and anagrams for other names is in order and likely to help.

HULDAH AND WISDOM LITERATURE

A major branch of Hebrew Scripture is called wisdom literature. Wisdom literature includes Job, Proverbs, and Ecclesiastes, though most agree that it also reaches into other OT books. It uses the terms "wise" and "wisdom" extensively and stresses day-to-day right thinking and acting rather than God's salvation history. However, "biblical wisdom is basically religious, not secular," writes one expert, grounding his opinion in Scripture.[16] Proverbs 1:7 says, "The fear of the LORD is the beginning of knowledge," a thought that Prov 9:10 and Job 28:28 echo. Significantly, Huldah coded spellings underlie Prov 1:7 and the verse from Job. It is likely that she wrote

15. Fontaine, "Proverbs," 160.
16. Murphy, "Wisdom," 922.

or inspired them both. Therefore, the beginnings of scholarly knowledge about wisdom literature must involve Huldah. In addition to being warrior, prophet, author, and queen mother, she is the embodiment of Woman Wisdom. While in Judah, as queen mother she could have served as high priestess of the Asherah; during her decade in Egypt, she probably debated Jeremiah about queen of heaven worship. At a stroke, Huldah provides connections to two centers that may have originated the thought and literature of biblical wisdom—Egypt and the court school at Jerusalem.[17]

There is more. As the Israelites in Egypt in the 570s gathered themselves to invade Judah, there appears to have been a hot dispute about whether Jehoiachin was fit to rule in a recaptured Jerusalem. We know that Jeremiah had strongly opposed him earlier (Jer 22:24–27) and that, among other things, Jehoiachin seems to have been an alcoholic. First Kings 1 relates how the queen mother Bathsheba gained the throne for her son Solomon. Recall that the chapter teems with Huldah and Jehoiachin coded spellings, which indicates that "Bathsheba" is, in truth, Huldah and that "Solomon" is actually Jehoiachin. Finally, in some spellings, the word for "wisdom" is itself an athbash of "messiah," and "messiah" can conceal an anagram of Jehoiachin.[18] In simpler form:

- Bathsheba stands for Huldah.
- Solomon stands for Jehoiachin.
- Wisdom stands for messiah.
- Messiah stands for Jehoiachin.

Therefore, when wisdom was associated with something derogatory, the biblical author meant it as an insult to Huldah and/or her son King Jehoiachin. Here are several examples of such comments. The first is from Jeremiah: "Thus says the LORD: Do not let the wise boast in *their wisdom* [messiah], do not let *the mighty* [Jehoiachin] boast *in their might* [Jehoiachin], do not let the wealthy boast *in their wealth* [H, Jehoiachin]" (Jer 9:23). Ezekiel said, "*By your wisdom* [messiah] and *your understanding* [Daniel] you have amassed wealth for yourself, and have gathered gold and silver *into your treasuries* [Cyrus, Baruch]. By your great *wisdom* [messiah] in trade you have increased your wealth, and your heart *has become proud* [H] in your wealth" (Ezek 28:4–5). Jeremiah and Ezekiel

17. Ibid., 921.

18. Wisdom, חכמה, contains the letters חתכב, which is an athbash for משיח, messiah.

condemned Huldah and Jehoiachin through "wisdom-messiah" and separately they used "wealth" anagrams to get at Huldah and "might" anagrams to disparage Jehoiachin. The Ezekiel quote is especially interesting because it confirms that Daniel was involved in the Cyrus revolt. Moreover, this explains why Ezekiel inserted his famous reference to Daniel in the preceding verse: "You are indeed wiser than Daniel; no secret is hidden from you" (Ezek 28:3).

The author of Job contributed in the same negative vein: "'Let days speak, and many years teach *wisdom* [messiah]' . . . It is not *the old* [H, Cyrus] that are wise, nor the aged that understand what is right" (Job 32:7, 9). When Huldah and Cyrus made common cause, the prophet was in her sixties, which explains the "old" references. And also, "Who has *the wisdom* [messiah] to number the clouds? . . . when the dust runs into a mass *and the clods* [H, Jehoiachin] cling together?" (Job 38:37–38).[19] In another example (1 Kgs 2:5–6), David on his deathbed charges Solomon to settle an old score. Joab, David's military commander, had put "'innocent blood upon *the girdle* [Jehoiachin] about my loins, and upon the sandals *on my feet* [H, Jehoiachin]. Act therefore *according to your wisdom* [messiah] . . .'" This sounds like blame for the innocent blood shed at the battle of Jerusalem.

Proverbs 11 delivers another negative wisdom connection against Huldah and Jehoiachin: "*Wisdom* [messiah] is with the humble . . . the crookedness *of the treacherous* [H] destroys them. Riches do not profit in the day of wrath . . . The *righteousness* [H] of the blameless keeps their ways straight, but *the wicked* [H, Jehoiachin] fall by their own wickedness" (Prov 11:2–5). Balancing this is Proverb's notable wisdom chapter. Proverbs 8 says, "'I, *wisdom* [messiah], live with prudence, and I attain knowledge and discretion . . . perverted speech I hate . . . I have insight, I *have strength* [Jehoiachin]. By me kings reign, *and rulers* [H] decree what is just . . .'" (Prov 8:12, 14–15). Further, a passage from the book of Daniel may signal Cyrus' agreement that Jehoiachin should rule in a liberated Judah: "Daniel said: 'Blessed be the name of God from age to age, *for wisdom* [messiah, Cyrus, Jehoiachin] and power are his. He changes times *and seasons* [H], deposes kings and sets up kings; he gives *wisdom* [messiah, Cyrus] to the wise and knowledge to those who have understanding'" (Dan 2:20–21).

This concludes a chapter devoted to Proverbs, to wisdom, and to Huldah. Within the book of Proverbs, Huldah was both the Woman of Worth

---

19. For another anti-Jehoiachin, anti-Huldah wisdom passage, see Job 28:20–22.

and Woman Wisdom. At the very same time, her detractors charged that she was Foreign Woman. Though Proverbs seems to be about many things other than Huldah, this newly discovered attention given to the prophet helps to date the book as sixth-century exilic.

The chapter to come will do further—though far from full—justice to this extraordinary genius. It will discuss Huldah's very large contribution to the book of Psalms. Measured by coding, she appears to have had her hand in over 20 percent of the Psalter. *20 percent!* If you are ready, please turn the page and start this final chapter.

10

Huldah the Psalmist

HULDAH THE PROPHET LIVED an extraordinary life during an extraordinary time—the period that saw the formation of much of the Hebrew Bible. Huldah herself wrote and edited appreciable amounts of Scripture, much of which has been highlighted in the preceding chapters. Her inspired writing has been treasured by generations of believers—Jews and Christians alike. Among the Scripture to which Huldah contributed are the eighteen psalms listed in table 10.1. Each of these conceals statistically significant numbers of Huldah names and/or titles, though one (Psalm 116) is hostile to her and another (Psalm 143) makes her a subject instead of an author. Psalm 71 makes the list because it hides a significant number of Huldah anagrams rather than coded spellings. With the exceptions of Psalms 116 and 143, she probably wrote substantial portions of each of these psalms. Measured by number, Huldah authored one-tenth of the Psalter. But because Huldah's psalms on average were longer, she actually participated in about one-fifth of the Psalter's words.

"Participate" is a good term to use when discussing biblical authorship. After considering coded spellings, anagrams, athbash, and Word Links (word associations), one has to conclude that individuals did not compose biblical texts by themselves. The number of concealed names within any passage probably will run into the hundreds. Nevertheless, in exploring Psalms, I have concentrated on three names—Huldah, Cyrus, and Jehoiachin—and used chi-square probabilities to measure their involvement. For the psalms charted below, participation shades down into authorship. When categorizing texts, probability guides. Though young, and perhaps still frail, this method for determining biblical authorship seems superior to any other yet devised.

Huldah

Table 10.1: Psalms with Significant Huldah Coding

Psalm	Text Words	Coded Groups/ Word	Cyrus Coding	Likely BCE Date
2	92	23	Yes	574
17	124	45	Yes	574–573
18	397	8	Yes	575–574
31	220	19	Yes	564
51	153	50	Yes	570
54	62	12		573–572
61	68	17		574
65	109	38	Yes	564
71	203	17	Yes	570–564
77	154	21	Yes	569
78	530	13	Yes[1]	573
80	141	26	Yes[1]	570
89	384	13		569
106	330	16	Yes	568
107	278	12	Yes	574
119	1064	12	Yes[1]	576
126	50	17		570
143	117	17		570–569

Chapters 3 and 4 of this book constructed a chronological biography of Huldah. She began her prophetic ministry in 622 BCE, when emissaries from King Josiah consulted her on the newly found temple scroll, and she died in about 564. Except for memoirs from her opponents or followers, then, every psalm with statistically significant Huldah coding can be dated between 622 and 564. The Cyrus-led expedition to free the Promised Land began approximately 576–575 and ended several years afterward, in about 573. Much later—in 539—Cyrus completed his conquest of Babylon and was crowned king of that empire. Cyrus died in 530. Thus, any psalm with significant Cyrus coding probably bears a date between 576 and 530. By using established dates for both Huldah and Cyrus, one can date thirteen psalms, which range between 576 and 564. To this writer's knowledge, no analyst has ever fixed the date of even one psalm. Table 10.1 lists thirteen.

1. Psalms 78, 80, and 119 contain significant numbers of both Cyrus and Jehoiachin coded spellings.

The other five psalms—54, 61, 89, 126, and 143—lack Cyrus coding. This means that they date either from before 575, when young Cyrus came to Egypt, or after 570, when he had departed. This is the broader framework. More narrowly, the composition dates of the eighteen Huldah psalms seem to fall between 576 and 564 BCE.

For two millennia, experts have tried to match the characteristics of psalms by their arrangement in the Psalter. Now we have a group of psalms from a common period by or about a common author. What are their differences and similarities? First, while a few Huldah psalms fall into such traditional categories as laments, praise, royal, wisdom, and the like, at least half of the eighteen psalms fit no category. Next, there is no particular concentration of Huldah psalms in any of the Psalter's five collections, with the minor exception that five of the eighteen psalms in collection 3 originated with the prophetess. Also, these Huldah psalms have the same proportion of David superscriptions as the other 132 psalms.

There are, however, three standout differences between all psalms and the Huldah batch. The first is length. The five psalms with the most text words are all by Huldah. In descending order, these are Psalms 119, 78, 18, 89, and 106. At 1,064 words, Psalm 119 is the longest chapter in all of Scripture. The prophetess had a penchant for length, which she exercised in Psalms and also elsewhere in the Bible. Another standout difference is that, to a greater extent in her own psalms, Huldah encoded information about Cyrus. A third major difference is that Huldah used the Psalter to showcase her extraordinary facility in encoding. Psalms 17, 51, and 65 pack more coded spellings per text word than any other chapters in all Scripture. Ranked by coding density, those three psalms outdo every one of the Bible's 926 other chapters. A discussion follows of the eighteen psalms in which Huldah played a leading role.

PSALM 2: CYRUS ANOINTED

Psalm 2 is a so-called royal psalm—that is, it concerns a king of the Davidic monarchy. Verse 2 in part reads, "The kings of the earth set themselves, *and the rulers* [H] take counsel together, against the LORD and his anointed." Subsequent verses say God will "terrify them in his fury, saying, 'I have set my king on Zion, my holy hill.' I will tell of the decree of the LORD: He said to me, 'You are my son; today I have begotten you. Ask of me, and I will make the nations your heritage, and the ends of the earth your possession. You shall break them with a rod of iron . . . Now therefore, O kings, be wise; be warned, O rulers of the earth'" (Ps 2:2, 5–10).

This short psalm conceals multiple spellings of different versions of Huldah: Huldah-the-prophetess, Huldah-mother-of-Jehoiachin, Huldah-wife-of-Jehoiakim, and Huldah-wife-of-Shallum. Also, v. 2 contains a Huldah anagram. It is very likely that she was the principal author. Her authorship sets the date between 622 and 564, though one can considerably narrow that.

The name Jehoiachin is heavily encoded starting at v. 8, which says, "Ask of me, and I will make the nations your heritage, and the ends of the earth your possession." An earlier verse has the Lord setting his king on Zion. Jehoiachin would have ruled from Zion twice. The first time was in 597, when he reigned for three months before being deported to Babylon. The second time was about 574, when the Cyrus-led Israelites retook Jerusalem. The fact that Psalm 2 also contains significant Cyrus coding ensures that the date of this psalm is not 597 but 574 BCE, give or take a year, depending upon when the invasion of the Promised Land began. Verse 7 of the psalm says, "He [the Lord] said to me, 'You are my son.'" If the son in the psalm is Jehoiachin, then "me" probably referred to Huldah herself, Jehoiachin's mother.

For Jehoiachin, making "the nations your heritage, and the ends of the earth your possession" is extreme, even allowing for the hyperbole that a newly restored king and an under-construction Jerusalem might permit. But it would not have been extreme to apply such words to the man who came to be known as Cyrus the Great. And as it happens, unusual Cyrus coding is beneath this part of the psalm. A rare athbash version of Cyrus-king-of-Anshan runs across vv. 8, 9, and 10.[2] Though this coded spelling occurs in Scripture only seventeen times, no fewer than four of them are under vv. 8–10 in Psalm 2. In addition, Cyrus-the-Mede (once) and Cyrus-the-Persian (eight times) also underlie the text words of vv. 8–10. To complete the inventory, different versions of Cyrus-the-Mede and Cyrus-the-Persian begin in the first verse and end in the second within a few words of "the LORD and his anointed" (Ps 2:2).

By itself, the psalm is unclear as to whether Cyrus or Jehoiachin became an anointed one. But Isa 45:1 answers this handily: "Thus says the LORD to his anointed, to Cyrus, whose right hand I have grasped to subdue nations before him . . ." Cyrus had become an anointed one of the Lord

2. The unusual athbash of Cyrus-king-of-Anshan, יסאאהתתיטירזחז, occurs four times in Ps 2.

more than three decades before the Persian brought down Babylon![3] That occurred in 539, though his anointing took place about 574. But this Huldah psalm contained a proviso for young Cyrus. Verse 8 instructs, "Ask of me . . ." Cyrus must first ask the Lord to make the following possible: "I will make the nations your heritage, and the ends of the earth your possession. You shall break them with a rod of iron" (Ps 2:8–9). Presumably, Cyrus did ask of the Lord, though God delayed his answer for thirty-five years. It was to arrive in God's rather than man's time. Huldah also writes, "I have set my king on Zion, my holy hill" (Ps 2:6), and for good reason she leaves it at that. She mentions no temple or palace because in 574 they were in ruins. With Jerusalem destroyed, she reverted to Mount Zion itself. Jehoiachin resumed his interrupted reign amidst the rubble.

What was the purpose of Psalm 2? The psalm is packed with news— Jerusalem retaken, Jehoiachin reinstalled, a threatening alliance gathering, Cyrus anointed. Surely the psalm was circulated around the Diaspora to convey that confidential information. Throughout the Fertile Crescent, from Lower Egypt to southern Babylonia, trained interpreters would have teased out the psalm's concealed meanings and used word of mouth to pass them to their exiled countrymen.

PSALM 17: HULDAH SURROUNDED BY ENEMIES

Psalm 17 is another text with statistically significant coded spellings of Huldah and of Cyrus. That combination limits the time of composition to shortly before 575, when the Cyrus-led rebellion commenced, to a few years later when the two fled Jerusalem at the close of a siege. The psalm has urgency, as if enemies are closing in. "Guard me as the apple of the eye, hide me in the shadow of your wings." Huldah asks, "from the wicked who despoil me, my deadly enemies who surround me" (Ps 17:8–9). Who were these enemies? By measuring coded foreign names, that answer is easily found.

Although Psalm 17, at just 124 words, is short, let it serve as an example. Computers tested the psalm for hidden spellings—athbash and normal—of every proper name in Scripture. Most, of course, were the names of Israelites, but the names of foreigners mentioned in the Bible were also tested. The harvest was 5,539 *groups* of coded names that met the strict standard of less than a .001 probability of coincidence (a group

3. Scholars should consider whether Isa 45 was written in 574 instead of around 539, when Babylon fell.

averages up to one dozen individual hidden spellings of identical coded words within a chapter). The next step was tallying foreign states and leaders. Doing so made the "deadly enemies" of the psalm apparent. It was Babylon that led with fifty-four groups. The authors—probably Huldah and her assistants—encoded the names of various nations and also Babylon, Babylon-Nimrod, Babylon-Shinar, Nebuchadnezzar, Nebuzaradan, Nebosarsechim, Chief-Guardsman, and Captain-of-the-Guard, all of which were associated with Babylon. Table 10.2 shows the ranking among Israel's possible enemies.

Table 10.2: Encoded Groups and Spellings of Foreign Nations in Psalm 17

Nation	Groups	Spellings
Babylon	54	222
Egypt	14	44
Lydia	11	26
Ammon	10	28
Aram	7	21
Moab	6	14
6 others	12	36

Babylon has almost four times as many groups as the next, which is Egypt. However, with Nebuchadnezzar armed and in the west, one doubts that Pharaoh would be pursuing the Israelites into Palestine. Of the others, Lydia was in Asia Minor, Ammon and Moab were across the Jordan from Israel, and the Arameans were in modern Syria. Possibly, many of these marched with Babylon against the Israelites. Of the six others (in the table's last line), five were desert tribes. For comparison with Babylon's fifty-four groups, Cyrus had seventeen groups and Huldah fourteen.

Psalm 17 makes "my deadly enemies who surround me" sound like personal, well-known opponents: "They close their hearts to pity; with their mouths they speak arrogantly. They track me down; now they surround me" (Ps 17:10–11). Huldah may well have personally known the Babylonian leaders—the king, the chief guardsman, and the captain of the guard. After her exile, she had spent part of the post-597 years in Babylonia, with at least some of that period at the court of Nebuchadnezzar. It is even possible that Babylonian authorities allowed Huldah to return to Judah sometime after the 597 exile to keep an eye upon the unreliable King Zedekiah. At any rate, she was in Jerusalem during the Babylonian siege of 586. At its conclusion, the high official Nebuzaradan permitted her to remain in Judah (with Jeremiah) rather than deporting her again to Babylonia.

As to the date of Psalm 17, Cyrus is on the scene, fighting has begun ("Rise up, O LORD, confront them . . . By your sword deliver my life . . ." Ps 17:13), famine is implied ("May their bellies be filled . . . may their children have more than enough" Ps 17:14), and it seems that a siege is underway. A good estimate would be 574 or 573.

PSALM 18: NEARLY IDENTICAL TO SECOND SAMUEL 22

Psalm 18, the third longest in the Psalter, is similar to Psalms 2 and 17 in its numerous Huldah and Cyrus coded spellings. Psalm 18 is also a virtual word-for-word duplicate of 2 Sam 22. Coding offers clues as to how the two came to be in Scripture. To begin, experts say that "Linguistic and stylistic evidence" in Psalm 18 makes it "one of the oldest psalms in the Psalter, dating most likely from the tenth century B.C.E."[4] But how can this be so, considering that both the psalm and 2 Sam 22 contain significant sixth-century coding? With Jehoiachin coding groups included, about 85 percent of the verses of each chapter carry this later coding. The answer seems to be that both things could be true: some of the language and style is ancient, while at the same time coding from a much later period has been imposed upon the older writing.

To judge soundly the coding in Psalm 18, one should compare it with the rest of Scripture. The mean of coded groups per text word for the whole of Hebrew Scripture is 4.2, while Psalm 18, at 6.1 groups per text word, is somewhat above that average. However, Psalm 18 is far, far below the average of the rest of Huldah's psalms in table 10.1 (the densities are shown in the middle column of the table). And how does the coding density of her psalms compare to the rest of Scripture? The Huldah psalms do extraordinarily well. Psalms 51, 17, and 65 have the three highest coding densities among *all* 929 chapters in Scripture. Overall, the mean of the Huldah psalms was in the ninety-seventh percentile of Scripture's chapters.[5] Her average was 17.2 groups per text word, but the figure for Psalm

---

4. Berlin and Brettler, "Psalms," 1299.

5. Coding density was established by testing 2,741 words with their 22 athbash variations against all 929 chapters of Scripture. This produced 3.4 million groups of coded spellings in 305,496 text words. The average density per text word was 11.1 groups. Psalms 51, 17, and 65 had densities of 40.5, 36.4, and 31.6, respectively.

18 was only about one-third of that. By Huldah's standards, the coding in the 2 Sam 22/Psalm 18 twins is light. Given the experts' opinion about the antiquity of the language, the best explanation is that Huldah converted an older text to her use.

One difference between the Samuel text and Psalm 18 must be important, though it is not clear why. Second Samuel 22 contains five Huldah anagrams and Psalm 18 has only three. The reason for the difference is that Second Samuel uses the feminine form of "righteousness," while Psalm 18 substitutes the masculine version.[6] In 2 Sam 22, the feminine version adds a *taw*, the letter needed to complete the Huldah anagram. To us it may seem a minor difference, but to the person who finally compiled the Psalter that difference was of great importance. Huldah anagrams would not have been lightly voided. This cancellation could be read as a signal that Huldah originally did her coding work on 2 Sam 22 and that someone else—probably a man—dropped the *taw*s and brought the Samuel chapter into the Psalter. Malice seems likely.

One can estimate when Huldah reworked 2 Sam 22. The date was after 575—the year the Jews in Egypt recruited Cyrus. The psalm itself first speaks of encirclement and danger, then "He delivered me from my strong enemy," next "He trains my hands for war," and finally "You delivered me from strife with the peoples; you made me head of the nations; people whom I had not known served me" (Ps 18:17, 34, 43). Huldah could be speaking of herself, of Cyrus, or of them both. The psalm could celebrate Israelite victories over Pharaoh or over the peoples who fought to prevent the Israelites from reoccupying the Promised Land. These combinations suggest a timing of between 575 and 573 BCE. But there is no reference to a crushing defeat such as the one that Israel suffered about 573 at Jerusalem. Therefore, Huldah must have altered the 2 Sam 22/Psalm 18 texts prior to that event.

PSALM 31: HULDAH'S FINAL WORDS

Psalm 31 is the next psalm with significant Huldah and Cyrus coding. As a previous chapter in this book stated, the words of this psalm are among the last she ever wrote. When Huldah penned them, she was sorrowful, shunned, and ill. "Into your hand I commit my spirit," she said—as did Jesus on the cross (Ps 31:5 H6; see Luke 23:46). Then she pleaded, "Be

---

6. "Righteousness" appears in vv. 21 and 25 of both 2 Sam 22 and Ps 18. In all four verses, the NRSV translates the word as "according to my righteousness."

gracious to me, O LORD, for I am in distress; my eye wastes away from grief, my soul and body also. For my life is spent *with sorrow* [H], and my years with sighing; my strength fails because of my misery, and my bones waste away. I am the scorn of all my adversaries, a horror to my neighbors, an object of dread to my acquaintances; those who see me in the street flee from me . . . they plot to take my life" (Ps 31:9–11, 13 H10–12, 14). A Huldah anagram in v. 10 confirms the coding evidence that Huldah wrote the psalm. The estimate is that the year was 564 BCE—Huldah's last—and that she was then seventy-six years of age. It has taken twenty-seven hundred years to associate Huldah the prophet with these, her own last words.

PSALM 51: SCRIPTURE'S DENSEST CODING

Psalm 51 is the classic penitential psalm. In its 153 text words, it packs over seven thousand six hundred coded *groups*—not spellings—and with fifty groups per text word, Psalm 51 is more densely coded than any chapter in the Bible. A prior book discussed the Shaphan group, that band of craftsman-patriots who wrote much of Scripture during the last years of the monarchy and the first half of the Exile.[7] Huldah herself was a member, and she and each of the other fourteen Shaphan-group participants had significant coding in important psalms like this one. The broad support for the venture that Huldah, Jacob, Cyrus, and the rest enjoyed is reflected in the plethora of coding within Psalm 51. Clearly, it was written after the catastrophic defeat of Israelite forces at Jerusalem. Given what the slaughter must have been like, "Save me from bloodguilt" (Ps 51:16 H17) was entirely appropriate. That defeat also explains why the temple was unavailable and the walls of Jerusalem destroyed (51:20 H21). A date after 573 is required. Make it about 570.

PSALM 54: HULDAH BETRAYED

Psalm 54 is short and contains high coding for Huldah but none for Cyrus. The lack of Cyrus coding makes it harder to place this text within Huldah's biography. However, there are several clues. The psalm's subscript reads in part, ". . . when the Ziphites went and told Saul, 'David is in hiding among us'" (Ps 54:1). This intimates that Huldah's hiding place has been

---

7. Kavanagh, *The Shaphan Group*, 116–20. Psalms in which all fifteen Shaphan-group members had significant coded groups were 17, 18, 44, 48, 51, 68, 77, 78, 80, 89, 107, and 119.

betrayed. Also, one of the opening verses says, "Insolent men have risen against me, *ruthless* [Zoar anagram] men seek my life; they do not set God before them" (Ps 54:3 H4). As chapter 4 relates, when Jerusalem fell in 573, Huldah and others fled southward to the Moabite city of Zoar, which, until its destruction in an earthquake, stood on the southeastern shore of the Dead Sea. Daniel and perhaps others also sought refuge in Zoar and, fortuitously, they also have anagrams in the psalm. In addition, Zoar itself is spelled out in Psalm 54 within the word for "ruthless."[8]

The single verse 54:3 holds still more information. It contains two unusual athbash spellings of "Jerushah." Like Huldah, Jerushah was a queen mother, and the two verses in which Jerushah appears—2 Kgs 15:33 and 2 Chr 27:1—both contain Huldah anagrams.[9] This modest find can have important implications for biblical research. Huldah uses *coded* words to point her readers to *text* words located elsewhere. This appears to be a highly sophisticated Word Link.[10]

So far, Huldah has told readers of her psalm that she and Zoar were involved. However, she has not yet revealed the identity of the ruthless men seeking her life. The answer was the Edomites. The same v. 5 of Psalm 54 that holds the other secret information also encodes alternate spellings of Edomites.[11] They ruled the area south of the Dead Sea and were traditional enemies of the Israelites. During the Exile, the Edomites annexed part of southern Judah, and the Israelite forces may well have fought Edom on their way north to recapture the Promised Land. Probably the Edomites acted as an agent or junior partner of the Babylonians. In view of these things, the likely date that Huldah and perhaps others composed Psalm 54 was 573 or 572 BCE.

---

8. The word for "ruthless," ועריצים, contains an anagram for Zoar, צוער.

9. The two unusual coded athbash spellings for Jerushah, ירושא, are זקבצע and גסזנל. The coded spellings start at words 1 and 11 of v. 5, respectively, using one letter from the next four text words.

10. A Word Link connects two passages that have in their texts the same unique batch of words. The author uses this form of word association to transfer the reader's attention from one passage to another. See Kavanagh, *Secrets*, 54–76.

11. The two spellings of Edomites are אדמיים and אדומים. The rare athbash versions are זיקעעק and זייל קעק. Both spellings start encoding at words 5–1 and 5–2 (H4–1 and 4–2). That is, both versions have two consecutive coded spellings.

PSALM 61: ENTHRONEMENT AT ISSUE

Psalm 61 is short in length and has above-average coding density when compared with Huldah's other psalms. The initial verses have a militant aspect—"You have been . . . a tower of strength against the enemy" (Ps 61:3 H4)—while the concluding ones praise an unidentified king: "Prolong the life of the king . . . May he be enthroned forever before God" (Ps 61:6–7 H7–8). In this psalm's thousand or so coded groups, there is no distinct concentration to ease the task of identification. However, because there are many names from the time of David and Solomon, this might, like Psalm 18, be an ancient text that Huldah reworked. Whether or not this is so, she inserted five groups of Cyrus encodings. Two of them are Cyrus-king-of-Babylon and one is Cyrus-anointed. However, the Cyrus spellings fall just short of the usual statistical standard for qualification. The phrase "you have been a tower of strength against the enemy" tilts Psalm 61 in the direction of Cyrus as its subject, but readers should have reservation. Other coding within the psalm suggests that Daniel and Ezra worked with Huldah on it. A date of 574 BCE is possible.

PSALM 65: HULDAH, CYRUS, AND NEBUCHADNEZZAR

Psalm 65 teems with encodings. Its hundred-plus words conceal an average of thirty-two coded groups, which places the chapter third in density among 929 OT chapters. Because of this plentitude of coding, it is challenging to determine the psalm's setting proper and its approximate time. A reasonable approach is to test for repetition of different athbash forms of the same true spelling. However, only twelve true spellings have eight or more groups. Among the leaders of that dozen are Huldah, with seventeen groups, and Cyrus the Persian, with fifteen. This makes Psalm 65 another of the Huldah-Cyrus psalms and puts its date of composition between 575 and 564 (Cyrus appeared in Egypt around 575 and Huldah died about 564). Nebuchadnezzar's score of fourteen groups supports that this was the correct time period for Psalm 65, since he reigned in Babylon until 562.

At eighteen groups, Daniel tops all others, though the gap between him and Huldah is but a single group. Since Daniel and Huldah co-authored Deuteronomy's Shema, one might recognize them as co-authors of Psalm 65. Micaiah and Ezra (the P Source), however, each have at least ten groups and, given the complexity of fashioning four thousand groups

Huldah

within Psalm 65's 109 text words, it is reasonable to stretch authorship to include those two. Micaiah's son Achbor may also belong in that company. Achbor and Achbor-son-of-Micaiah registered a total of eight encoded groups. A new name from this same era is Shephatiah son of Mattan. Shephatiah was an official of Judah's King Zedekiah and had been a sworn enemy of Jeremiah. Including coding from Shephatiah-the-scribe, he earned fourteen groups.

Daniel, Huldah, Ezra, Micaiah, Achbor, Shephatiah, Cyrus, and Nebuchadnezzar are easily associated in time, but a few others with solid coding are not. Foremost among them is Shimea son of David and Bathsheba. Shimea's coding might be left over from a far earlier time, in which case Psalm 65—like Psalms 18 and 61—might be a reworked Solomon-era text. This seems doubtful, however, given the density of coding in Psalm 65.

Two other encoding sets also tie the psalm to Huldah. Psalm 65 has four groups of Jerushah-daughter-of-Zadok. Like Psalm 54, this psalm uses Jerushah coding to direct readers to 2 Kgs 15:33, which contains a Huldah anagram and says that Jerushah was a queen mother. In addition, Psalm 65 also contains no fewer than eight Bethel-Oak-of-Weeping concentrations. Earlier, text in chapter 3 of this book had associated the oak in Bethel with the burial site of Huldah the prophet (see also Gen 35:7–8). Perhaps others were buried there, but Huldah is the most likely candidate. Making this assumption—even in the face of some Cyrus coding—a date of 564, the approximate year of Huldah's death, seems in order for Psalm 65.

PSALM 71: HULDAH'S OLD AGE

Psalm 71 has heavy Huldah and Cyrus coding and, according to the text, Huldah is in her final years. Verses 9 and 18 say, "Do not cast me off in the time of old age," and "So even to old age and gray hairs, O God, do not forsake me." If the prophet was in her seventies, then the date of Psalm 71 would be between 570 and 564 BCE. Enemies are talking against her, which makes this psalm much like Psalm 31 in tone. Both are psalms of her old age. But in Psalm 71, Huldah also mentions her whole lifespan, from womb to old age. "Upon you I have leaned from my birth; it was you who took me from my mother's womb" (Ps 71:6). This could refer to her own call that, until now, had been attributed to her fellow prophet Jeremiah (Jer 1:5). Daniel and Belteshazzar—Daniel's Babylonian name—have some twenty coding groups within Psalm 71. This suggests that Daniel might have been its leading author. Finally, the psalm carries five Huldah anagrams, a large though not quite statistically significant number.

PSALM 77: HAS GOD FORGOTTEN TO BE GRACIOUS?

The opening phrase of Psalm 77 is a plea for help that contains a Huldah anagram: "I cry aloud to God, aloud to God, that *he may hear me* [H]. In the day of my trouble . . ." (Ps 77:1 H2). The first section asks rhetorically, "'Has God forgotten to be gracious? Has he in anger shut up his compassion?'" (Ps 77:9 H10). Huldah, the psalmist, is in deep trouble. She leads every other person in all Scripture in the psalm's coding groups. Included in her encodings are four Nehushta groups, which catch one's attention. Also in Psalm 77's mix are groups of statistically significant Cyrus encodings. The dark mood of the psalm plus the combination of densely coded Huldah and Cyrus spellings place the psalm's composition date after the Jerusalem defeat of 573. Probably, Huldah was indeed recalling happier times when she was both queen mother and high priestess Nehushta, and when she rode north with Cyrus to win back the Promised Land.

In the psalm's second half, remembrance takes a different course. The author's exalted language portrays the Lord's triumph over chaos as he leads Israel through storm and flood. If it sounds like Second Isaiah, there is a reason—it *is* Second Isaiah who has penned this "paean of praise."[12] Daniel is well represented, while Jacob's name is in v. 16 and two anagrams of that prophet close the final verses.[13] Psalm 77 was a joint venture between Huldah, Jacob, and Daniel (who was second in coding density only to Huldah). Achbor, who was a scribe and the son of Micaiah, also contributed. The date is not difficult to fix. A time in the early 560s, say 569 BCE, would fit well. Huldah by then would have settled in Bethel and it appears that the other leaders were also with her. These included Jacob; Daniel, with seventeen groups; Azariah, with eight; and Ezra, with eight groups plus an anagram. These anagrams and coded spellings witness that a good part of the Israelite leadership survived the Jerusalem defeat, though Jehoiachin is notably absent.

12. The phrase is from the JSB's note to Ps 77.

13. The most spectacular anagram is "yet your footprints," וְעִקְּבוֹתֶיךָ, which contains the letters for יַעֲקֹב, "Jacob," in Ps 77:19 H20.

PSALM 78: COINCIDENCE EIGHTY ZEROS AWAY

Psalm 78 is the second-longest psalm in the Psalter. Like the other psalms reviewed here, Psalm 78 has a plentitude of Huldah coding and, like many others, it also contains numerous Cyrus spellings. Statistically, the concealed spellings of both names are at the extreme end of coincidence. That is, the probability that they occur by chance alone has at least eighty zeroes to the right of the decimal point. The encodings of each are broadly spread across this long psalm, touching more than four-fifths of its verses. This means that both Huldah and Cyrus had much to do with the events that Psalm 78 describes and that the Hebrew female prophet aided in its composition.

The psalm itself has been described as a "lengthy review of Israel's history, focusing on the wilderness period" of the Exodus.[14] Given the Huldah and Cyrus coding, however, it is far more likely to be a cloaked account of the sixth-century struggle to leave Egypt and of the march north to retake the Promised Land. Though the Cyrus and Huldah coding is broadly spread, it peaks twice in the psalm. The first concentration is vv. 47–49, which read in part: "He let loose on them [the Egyptians] his fierce anger, wrath, indignation, and distress, a company of destroying angels" (Ps 78:49). Excerpts from the other concentration, vv. 56–59, read: "They tested the Most High God, and rebelled against him . . . and were faithless like their ancestors . . . For they provoked him to anger with their high places; they moved him to jealousy with their idols" (Ps 78:56–59). These verses could be an attack upon Huldah and her Asherah practices. The coding evidence seems to be that she was simultaneously a subject and an author of the psalm.

Jacob—who, with Daniel, may have been Second Isaiah—has the most coding groups in Psalm 78, and the superb styling surely is due mainly to him. In addition, Jacob left four signatures in the text itself—three Jacob-Israel parallels (in vv. 5, 21, and 71) and a single Holy One of Israel (in v. 41).[15] Nebuchadnezzar and Daniel were close behind Jacob and Huldah in encodings, and Cyrus the Persian also had heavy representation.

When was Psalm 78 written? Cyrus arrived on the scene about 575 and departed within three years. Huldah died about 564 and Nebuchadnezzar's death in 562 is well documented. Jacob the prophet was one of Huldah's companions in Egypt in the 570s and outlived her by some years.

---

14. NRSV note to Ps 78.

15. Kavanagh, *The Exilic Code*, 71–72.

The closing half-dozen verses speak of Judah, Zion, a restored sanctuary, and David. Addressing this diversity, a preliminary answer as to date of composition is during the 570s, after the expedition retook Jerusalem, but before the catastrophic defeat of about 573. With poetic imagination, this could fit the narrow window of 575–573 in Israel, which allows time for reestablishing worship at the site of the temple. Also arguing for this is the mention of David, which presumably was Jehoiachin. Let 573 be Psalm 78's composition date pending evidence to the contrary.

PSALM 80: THREE THOUSAND CODED GROUPS

Psalm 80 is the next psalm by Huldah. Though phrased as if it mourned the loss of the northern kingdom, the psalm actually applies to Judah and the disastrous result of the Israelites' 570s campaign. Since Psalm 80 has significant Jehoiachin and Cyrus coding, it would have been written during the decade between Jerusalem's fall and Huldah's death. A reasonable approximation is the year 570. The psalm's high coding density—three thousand coded groups rank it thirteenth out of 929 chapters—shows that its authors worked with skill and care. The psalm, as it closes, says, "Let your hand be upon the one at your right hand, the one whom you made strong for yourself" (Ps 80:17 H18). Understandably, commentators have thought that these words referred to the king of Judah, but this is not the case. While no Jehoiachin groups cross this verse, two Cyrus groups do—encodings of Cyrus-the-Persian and of Cyrus-king-of-Babylon. This shows that, even after the resounding defeat of the Cyrus-led forces, those who wrote the psalm (and probably most other exiles) wished Cyrus well.

PSALM 89: RESTORING THE DYNASTY

Psalm 89 is a long plea to the Lord to restore the Davidic dynasty, with insignificant coding of either Cyrus or Jehoiachin. The psalm makes no mention of the temple or even of Zion. The date, then, must be after the 573 battle for Jerusalem, at a time when Cyrus had departed to return to his homeland and King Jehoiachin likely had been captured. The Babylonians subsequently executed him as a substitute king in 562 (Second Kings 25:27–30 uses carefully worded language to reveal this).[16] A composition date of 569 will be close to the mark.

16. Kavanagh, *The Exilic Code*, 53–61.

Huldah

The lack of Jehoiachin coding in Psalm 89 hints that the authors no longer considered it possible for Huldah's son to regain David's throne. However, the psalm's language is clear that a candidate is at hand: "Our shield belongs to the LORD, our king to the Holy One of Israel . . . 'I have set the crown on one who is mighty, I have exalted one chosen from the people. I have found my servant David; with my holy oil I have anointed him'" (Ps 89:18–20 H19–21). "Holy One of Israel" is a signature of the prophet Jacob, while Huldah the prophet had no fewer than five different coding groups running beneath these verses. Undoubtedly, both prophets had much to do with composing Psalm 89's text. Who was to succeed Jehoiachin? Underneath the very words about anointing David is encoded an extremely rare spelling of Shenazzar-son-of-Jehoiachin, who was Huldah's grandson (1 Chr 3:18).[17] This athbash spelling appears only twice in all of Scripture. The rarity and placement make one suspect this was a deep secret shared in extreme confidence with other exiles. However, this is but one of some five thousand coded groups within Psalm 89, and it might mean nothing.

A name with many coded groups is Shephatiah, son of Mattan. Counting Shephatiah-son-of-David, Shephatiah-the-scribe, and Shephatiah itself, the total is twenty-seven groups, which is the highest in the psalm. Jeremiah 38:4 calls Shephatiah שׂר, a term that could be translated as "ruler" or even "prince." If Shephatiah was in fact a prince, then a dozen of the twenty-seven coding groups most certainly belonged to him. If not, subtract the twelve and reduce Shephatiah's total number of groups to fifteen. Perhaps Shephatiah was to step into the Davidic line in the interim until Shenazzar could be spirited from Babylon. Admittedly, however, this is far more supposition than history.

PSALM 106: TARGETING HULDAH AND CYRUS

Psalm 106 is the fourth-longest in the Psalter and, like Psalms 18, 78, and 119, it contains significant numbers of encodings of both Huldah and Cyrus. But unlike those others, Psalm 106 is not a text that counts Huldah as a principal author. Instead, the psalm's composer made Huldah and Cyrus major targets. The *Jewish Study Bible* summarizes Psalm 106 as "a history of . . . sins that polluted the land of Israel and led to the

---

17. The athbash spelling of Shenazzar-son-of-Jehoiachin takes one letter per word from v. 19, word 3 (ג), through v. 20, word 7 (ו). The sequence is גקיבזרזסאתה.

destruction and exile."[18] At the same time, Huldah-coded spellings reach across two-thirds of the psalm's four dozen verses. It is not difficult to determine whether she was a subject or an author of the work. Three Huldah anagrams decide this: God swore that he "would make them fall in the wilderness, and would disperse their descendants *among the nations* [H]"; "They did not destroy the peoples, as the LORD commanded them, but they mingled *with the nations* [H]"; and "Thus they became unclean by their acts, and *prostituted themselves* [H] in their doings" (Ps 106:26–27, 34–35, 39).

Who composed this text? Based on total encoding groups, Daniel is the leading candidate. Psalm 106 houses two dozen groups of Daniel, Daniel-the-eunuch, Daniel-son-of-David, and the like. For comparison, Huldah has nineteen groups. Both are among the leaders in a text that contains some five thousand groups. Daniel, who grew to manhood in Nebuchadnezzar's court, would have been in close contact with those who later would suffer most from the attempt by Huldah and her colleagues to win back the Promised Land—namely the Judean exiles in Babylon. Recall that the prophetess and Daniel co-authored the Shema, so Daniel had come west with Jehoiachin to join Huldah, Jacob, and others in Egypt for the attempt against Jerusalem. So far, any Daniel-Huldah split is but a possibility, one that scholars should test as they become more familiar with coded spellings. On the other hand, the as-yet unidentified author of Psalm 106 might have been attacking Daniel along with Huldah. One hopes that time will tell.

The next-to-last verse helps to date the psalm because it appeals to God for an end to exile. Within that lengthier period, the following suggests that the psalmists wrote after the defeat at Jerusalem: "They were rebellious in their purposes, and were brought low through their iniquity" (Ps 106:43). Nebuchadnezzar had fifteen groups to go with Huldah's nineteen. Both, then, were still alive. A date in the early 560s for Psalm 106 would serve—that is, 568 or so.

PSALM 107: JACOB, DANIEL, AND HULDAH

Scholars assign a post-exilic date to Psalm 107, but its coding indicates that it belongs with the rest of the Huldah psalms—in the period from 575 to 565. Jacob leads all others in coding groups with twenty-two, Cyrus has seventeen, and Huldah and Daniel contribute sixteen apiece.

18. Berlin and Brettler, "Psalms," 1401.

The three principal authors, then, would have been Jacob, Daniel, and Huldah (her encodings span all but two of the psalm's forty-three verses). The writing is of first quality, and a major section of Psalm 107 describes a tortuous period in prison: "Some sat in darkness and in gloom, prisoners in misery and in irons, for they had rebelled against the words of God . . . Then they cried to the LORD in their trouble, and . . . he brought them out of darkness and gloom, and broke their bonds asunder" (Ps 107:10, 13-14). Interestingly, these verses and others nearby contain Jehoiachin coded spellings, which help to flesh out his biography.

Assuming that Jehoiachin was imprisoned sometime after his first deportation, what was his offense? They "rebelled against the words of God," said the psalm and "Their hearts *were bowed down* [Jehoiachin anagram] with hard labor" (Ps 107:11-12). Possibly this was related to the rebellious prophets Ahab and Zedekiah, who as early as 597 were stirring the hopes of the exiles in Babylon (Jer 29:20-23). Any opposition to the Babylonians could have gathered around the young exiled king, Jehoiachin. And Psalm 107 said further, "Some were sick through *their sinful ways* [Jehoiachin], and because of their iniquities endured affliction; they loathed any kind of food, and they drew near to the gates of death" (Ps 107:17-18). This sounds like a hunger strike among the prisoners—similar to the one that an older Jehoiachin resorted to before his execution in 562.[19] Whatever the offense, Jehoiachin and others received scant sympathy from the authors of Psalm 107.

Another section of this sizable psalm begins, "Some went down to the sea in ships, doing business on the mighty waters" (Ps 107:23). Jehoiachin coding also reaches these words, reminding readers that he and Huldah became wealthy in Egypt through trade—wealth that helped to finance the expedition against the Promised Land. The heavy Cyrus coding and the lack of recognition of his defeat at Jerusalem lead one to date Psalm 107 at 574 BCE.

PSALM 119: THE HUGE BILLBOARD

Psalm 119 is a scriptural giant. It contains more words and verses than any other chapter in the Hebrew Bible; is twice the length of any other psalm; and is filled with such synonyms for law as commandments,

---

19. For Jehoiachin's hunger strike, see Kavanagh, *The Exilic Code*, 49–53.

statutes, precepts, and decrees. Experts consider it to be post-exilic,[20] but it was written during the Exile by Huldah and perhaps others. The coding evidence for this authorship is overwhelming—probably stronger than for any other text that ever came from her hand. She uses versions of Huldah, Huldah-wife-of-Jehoiakim, Huldah-wife-of-Shallum, Huldah-the-mother-of-Jehoiachin, Huldah-the-queen-mother, and Huldah-the-prophetess to engulf the psalm with encodings. Psalm 119 has 176 verses and 173 of these contain at least one coded spelling of those signatures. The computer counts no fewer than 702 individual Huldah encoded spellings. Huldah accomplishes this by first choosing athbash versions spelled with commonly used letters and then weaving a multitude of those versions into the Hebrew text.[21] Because of the way that she piles on these common spellings, they easily pass pre-established probability standards, however rigorous.

Impressive as Huldah's coding is in Psalm 119, Cyrus coding matches it. His name also is ciphered in 173 of the psalm's 176 verses. Moreover, Huldah's son Jehoiachin rang up coding in at least 162 verses. But Daniel outdoes them all. He records more than twice the number of groups and concealed spellings that Huldah does, using Daniel-the-eunuch, Daniel-son-of-David, Daniel-son-of-the-king, and Daniel itself to sign his name. Daniel's average spellings per group were at the same high level as Huldah's, which shows that he used the same technique as she did—frequent repetition.

The Huldah, Cyrus, Jehoiachin, and Daniel hidden signatures make Psalm 119 a coding masterpiece, though they do little to support the ostensible theme of the psalm, which describes the different aspects of torah. The resounding coding evidence makes the psalm's surface wording appear to resemble a billboard constructed to convey secrets to those who know how to read the hidden message. And what was that message? Perhaps that Daniel, the prodigy reared in Babylon's court, and Huldah, the queen mother, were in Egypt together and had co-authored the giant psalm. Further, that Jehoiachin was to reign again in Jerusalem, and that Cyrus the Persian had agreed to lead the effort to retake the Promised Land. Given these assumptions, date Psalm 119 at about 576 BCE.

20. NRSV 880; Berlin and Brettler, "Psalms," 1415.

21. Here is the best example among twenty-five groups: the compound word for Huldah-wife-of-Jehoiakim is חלדדהאשתיהויקים. Used 183 times, it has encodings in 113 of the psalm's 176 verses. Though the coding is common elsewhere in Scripture, Huldah's use of it in Ps 119 is so frequent that its chance of being coincidental is zero.

Huldah

PSALM 126: "ASSENTS" IS A CYRUS ANAGRAM

Psalm 119 is very long and the next text by Huldah, Psalm 126, is very short. It has just fifty words. Psalm 126 bears the title "A Song of Assents," and "assents" is a Cyrus anagram.[22] Further along, another text word contains a Huldah anagram. More importantly, however, eight Huldah coded spellings within the text are statistically significant. The Daniel coding is also prominent. The brief text of Psalm 126 also has two sections that support the account of Jerusalem's situation as this book has presented it. "When the LORD restored the fortunes of Zion, we were like those who dream. Then our mouth was filled with laughter . . ." (Ps 126:1–2). That is, the Cyrus-led Israelites had initially recaptured Jerusalem. The crushing defeat, however, came next. It evoked the plea: "Restore our fortunes, O LORD . . . May those who sow in tears reap with shouts of joy" (Ps 126:4–5). The psalm's two conflicting sections have puzzled interpreters, but once the *Sitz im Leben* of the 570s is clear, the psalm makes good sense. As to date, make it 570 BCE, a few years after Nebuchadnezzar retook Jerusalem. The authors were Huldah and Daniel, with coding help from Micaiah the scribe, Gemariah son of Shaphan, and perhaps others.

PSALM 143: HULDAH NOT AUTHOR BUT SUBJECT

Psalm 143 is the final Huldah psalm. It is not unlike Psalm 31—Huldah's despairing lament when she was close to death. Psalm 143 says, for example, "My spirit fails. Do not hide your face from me, or I shall be like those who go down to the Pit" (Ps 143:7). The problem in interpreting Psalm 143 is the diversity of coding information that it yields. Jacob leads all with fourteen coding groups, while Nebuchadnezzar has ten and Huldah nine. Jehoiachin and "tabernacle" have eight apiece. Sorting through almost two thousand other groups, one set seems of particular interest—"court-of-the-guard" in Jerusalem, which has five separate coding groups.

What set of historical circumstances produced such a mixture? Here is one possibility. The battle of Jerusalem is over (no significant Cyrus coding) and the Babylonians (Nebuchadnezzar) still are pursuing Huldah. She says, "Save me, O LORD, from my enemies; I have fled to you for refuge" (Ps 143:9). Although Huldah has evaded capture, her son Jehoiachin has

22. "Assents," המעלות, includes the letters תחמל, which is a Cyrus anagram. Psalms 120 and 122–34 each have this title, suggesting that all fourteen psalms are related to Cyrus.

been taken and is being held in the same jail that once housed Jeremiah, the court of the guard in Jerusalem: "The enemy has pursued me, crushing my life to the ground, making me sit in darkness like those long dead" (Ps 143:3). Significant Jehoiachin coding lends support to this theory. We know that a decade later Jehoiachin emerged from a Babylonian prison (2 Kgs 25:27). Next, Jacob's fourteen coding groups suggest that he himself wrote Psalm 143, perhaps in collaboration with Huldah. However, it could also be that Jacob spoke for both Huldah and her son. That is, Huldah was a *subject* rather than an *author*. As to the encodings of "tabernacle," the psalm could be announcing that the tabernacle was captured or destroyed during the fighting. An appropriate date would be a year or two after Jerusalem fell and after Huldah had reached Bethel. Make it 570 or 569.

In conclusion, Huldah's work as a psalmist is summarized below. Coding indicates that Huldah led or participated in composing sixteen of the eighteen psalms listed in table 10.1. Daniel and Jacob were frequent co-authors. Although Psalm 106 also has high Huldah coding, it is hostile to her and may have been authored by Daniel. Psalm 143 is more likely to have originated with Jacob than with Huldah. These eighteen psalms bear likely dates that fall between 576 and 564 BCE. Characteristics common to this batch of psalms are that often they are lengthy (five are exceptionally so) and that many (a dozen) contain significant Cyrus coding. Their content invariably bears upon the Cyrus-led revolt and its abortive aftermath. Another frequent theme is the future of the Davidic line. Jehoiachin is often cited, and in Psalm 89, Shenazzar and—possibly—Shephatiah are royal candidates. Nebuchadnezzar was often coded as being the personal enemy of Huldah. Psalm 2 discloses that as early as the mid-570s Cyrus was anointed to conquer the known world. The Lord tells him, "I will make the nations your heritage, and the ends of the earth your possession" (Ps 2:8). Also worth special mention is the discovery that Huldah and Daniel wrote Psalm 119, the longest chapter in Scripture. This writer has worked for years on that identification. Measured by length of text, Huldah participated as author or subject in almost a quarter of the Psalter. Finally, three of Huldah's psalms rank one-two-three in coding density among the 929 chapters of Hebrew Scripture. Huldah the prophet probably was more skillful at coding than any other biblical author.

APPENDIX 1

Location of Huldah Anagrams

USING HEBREW VERSE NUMBERING, this appendix lists the 1,773 Huldah anagrams in Scripture. Italics within the list indicate the verse contains a second or a third anagram. The sixteen Hebrew words below are athbash spellings of חלדה, "Huldah." Numbers associated with each athbash version give total occurrences within Scripture. Single Roman letters, at the end of each verse in the list immediately below, correspond to the athbash word in the list of anagrams.

אקהד A 1, בורש B 620, דחתא D 1, חלדה H 19, האטח h 90, מצפע M 5, נציכ N 12, פמשר P 72, רבעפ R 27, שפגב S 3, תדצק T 88, טהמל t 141, ערלמ U 99, ויבג W 367; ינוז Y 227, זגבי Z 1.

Gen 2:12H	Gen 17:11U	Gen 29:14B
Gen 2:23B	Gen 17:23U	Gen 30:33T
Gen 7:18W	Gen 19:17t	Gen 30:35t
Gen 7:24W	*Gen 19:17t*	Gen 30:42M
Gen 8:13B	Gen 19:19t	Gen 31:20W
Gen 10:5W	Gen 19:20t	Gen 31:27B
Gen 10:20W	Gen 19:22t	Gen 31:39W
Gen 10:32W	Gen 20:9h	*Gen 31:39h*
Gen 14:1U	Gen 21:2Y	Gen 36:39t
Gen 14:2B	Gen 21:7Y	Gen 37:27B
Gen 14:4U	Gen 23:8R	Gen 37:29W
Gen 14:5U	Gen 24:53W	Gen 38:24Y
Gen 14:9U	Gen 25:34Y	Gen 40:14Y
Gen 14:17U	Gen 27:27W	Gen 41:56B

Appendix 1

Gen 42:2B	Exod 29:29W	Lev 6:18h
Gen 42:38W	Exod 29:31B	*Lev 6:18h*
Gen 43:2B	Exod 31:2t	Lev 6:19h
Gen 43:4B	Exod 31:5B	Lev 7:15B
Gen 44:2B	*Exod 31:5B*	Lev 7:19B
Gen 44:25B	Exod 31:6t	*Lev 7:19B*
Gen 44:31W	Exod 32:13U	Lev 8:2h
Gen 47:21U	Exod 32:19B	Lev 8:14h
Gen 49:8R	Exod 32:21h	*Lev 8:14h*
Gen 50:9P	Exod 32:30h	Lev 8:17B
Exod 3:18Y	Exod 32:31h	Lev 8:30W
Exod 4:4t	Exod 32:21h	*Lev 8:30W*
Exod 4:7B	Exod 32:30h	Lev 9:1Y
Exod 7:11t	Exod 32:31h	Lev 9:8h
Exod 7:22t	Exod 34:7h	Lev 9:10h
Exod 7:27R	Exod 34:13B	Lev 9:15h
Exod 7:28B	Exod 35:21W	*Lev 9:15h*
Exod 8:3t	Exod 35:30t	Lev 9:22h
Exod 8:14t	Exod 35:33B	Lev 10:6W
Exod 10:9Y	*Exod 35:33B*	Lev 10:16h
Exod 12:46B	Exod 35:34t	Lev 10:17h
Exod 14:4R	Exod 36:29t	Lev 11:25W
Exod 14:17R	Exod 38:4t	Lev 11:28W
Exod 14:17B	Exod 38:22t	Lev 11:29H
Exod 14:18R	Exod 38:23t	Lev 11:33B
Exod 14:18B	Exod 39:20t	Lev 11:40W
Exod 14:28P	Lev 4:8h	*Lev 11:40W*
Exod 15:14Y	Lev 4:11B	Lev 13:2B
Exod 15:19B	Lev 4:14h	*Lev 13:2B*
Exod 21:28B	Lev 4:20h	Lev 13:3B
Exod 22:13B	Lev 4:25h	Lev 13:4B
Exod 22:14B	Lev 4:29h	Lev 13:6W
Exod 22:30B	*Lev 4:29h*	Lev 13:11B
Exod 23:24B	Lev 4:33h	Lev 13:13B
Exod 26:24t	Lev 4:34h	Lev 13:18B
Exod 27:5t	Lev 5:9h	Lev 13:34W
Exod 28:27t	Lev 5:15h	Lev 13:44B
Exod 29:21W	Lev 5:24B	Lev 13:45W
Exod 29:21W	Lev 6:3B	Lev 14:4t
Exod 29:21W	Lev 6:4W	Lev 14:8W

Lev 14:9B	Lev 17:13R	Num 5:7B
Lev 14:9W	Lev 17:15W	Num 7:12t
Lev 14:13h	Lev 17:16B	Num 8:7t
Lev 14:19h	Lev 18:6B	Num 8:21t
Lev 14:47W	Lev 18:20t	Num 9:5B
Lev 14:47W	Lev 18:23t	Num 9:12B
Lev 15:2B	Lev 19:23U	Num 10:10B
Lev 15:3B	*Lev 19:23U*	Num 11:5h
Lev 15:3B	Lev 19:31t	Num 11:7H
Lev 15:5W	Lev 19:35B	Num 11:30Y
Lev 15:6W	Lev 20:25t	Num 12:12B
Lev 15:7W	Lev 21:5B	Num 13:2t
Lev 15:8W	Lev 21:10W	Num 13:4t
Lev 15:10W	Lev 22:2Y	Num 13:5t
Lev 15:11W	Lev 22:6B	Num 13:6t
Lev 15:13W	Lev 22:8t	Num 13:7t
Lev 15:13B	Lev 22:22B	Num 13:8t
Lev 15:16B	Lev 23:27B	Num 13:9t
Lev 15:21W	Lev 24:11t	Num 13:10t
Lev 15:22W	Lev 25:9B	Num 13:11t
Lev 15:27W	Lev 25:49B	*Num 13:11t*
Lev 15:32t	Lev 26:13B	Num 13:12t
Lev 16:4B	Lev 26:19B	Num 13:13t
Lev 16:4B	Lev 26:29B	Num 13:14t
Lev 16:6h	Lev 26:33W	Num 13:15t
Lev 16:11h	Lev 26:38W	Num 14:33Y
Lev 16:11h	Num 1:4t	Num 15:28h
Lev 16:15h	Num 1:21t	Num 17:3h
Lev 16:24W	Num 1:23t	Num 17:4P
Lev 16:24B	Num 1:25t	Num 18:18B
Lev 16:25h	Num 1:27t	Num 19:7B
Lev 16:26W	Num 1:29t	*Num 19:7W*
Lev 16:26B	Num 1:31t	Num 19:8B
Lev 16:27h	Num 1:33t	*Num 19:8W*
Lev 16:27h	Num 1:35t	Num 19:10W
Lev 16:27P	Num 1:37t	Num 19:17h
Lev 16:28W	Num 1:39t	Num 19:19W
Lev 16:28B	Num 1:41t	Num 19:21W
Lev 16:29B	Num 1:43t	Num 20:26W
Lev 17:7U	Num 1:47t	Num 20:28W

Appendix 1

Num 21:6P	Deut 11:9U	Josh 8:10Y
Num 22:7Y	Deut 11:20B	Josh 8:33Y
Num 22:7Y	Deut 12:3B	Josh 9:10B
Num 23:9W	Deut 12:27B	Josh 9:11Y
Num 26:27Y	Deut 13:6H	Josh 10:4Y
Num 26:59U	Deut 13:10B	Josh 10:7W
Num 28:11B	Deut 13:11H	Josh 11:8P
Num 29:7B	Deut 14:12Y	Josh 11:13P
Num 31:4t	Deut 14:26B	Josh 11:23t
Num 31:4t	Deut 15:6W	Josh 12:4B
Num 31:5t	Deut 17:13Y	Josh 13:6P
Num 31:6t	Deut 22:10B	Josh 13:12B
Num 32:35W	Deut 25:18Y	Josh 13:15t
Num 34:19t	Deut 27:1Y	Josh 13:24t
Num 34:20t	Deut 28:13t	Josh 15:1t
Num 34:21t	Deut 28:65W	Josh 15:21t
Num 34:22t	Deut 29:3Y	Josh 15:63B
Num 34:23t	Deut 29:18B	Josh 17:1t
Num 34:24t	Deut 31:16Y	Josh 17:10B
Num 34:25t	Deut 32:1Y	*Josh 17:10B*
Num 34:26t	Deut 32:21W	Josh 17:11B
Num 34:27t	Deut 33:5B	Josh 18:9U
Num 34:28t	Deut 33:21T	Josh 18:20W
Num 35:2U	Josh 1 14W	Josh 18:21t
Num 35:6t	Josh 2:19B	Josh 19:1t
Num 36:9t	*Josh 2:19B*	Josh 19:11U
Deut 1:8U	Josh 4:19B	Josh 19:24t
Deut 2:6B	Josh 5:7U	Josh 19:26B
Deut 2:12B	Josh 6:2W	Josh 19:27W
Deut 4:27W	Josh 6:4B	Josh 19:34B
Deut 5:23Y	Josh 6:8B	Josh 19:40t
Deut 6:9B	Josh 6:9B	Josh 19:49W
Deut 6:22R	Josh 6:13B	Josh 20:2t
Deut 7:5B	*Josh 6:13B*	Josh 22:27Y
Deut 9:4B	Josh 6:16B	Josh 23:2Y
Deut 9:4T	Josh 6:20B	Josh 23:7W
Deut 9:5T	Josh 7:1t	Josh 24:6P
Deut 9:5B	Josh 7:6Y	*Josh 24:6B*
Deut 9:6T	Josh 7:18t	Judg 1:3W
Deut 9:17B	Josh 8:3W	Judg 1:8B

Judg 1:21B	Judg 14:20U	1 Sam 30:5W
Judg 3:27B	Judg 15:2U	1 Sam 30:9B
Judg 4:10W	Judg 15:6U	1 Sam 30:10B
Judg 4:15W	Judg 15:18U	1 Sam 30:13Y
Judg 4:17W	Judg 16:28Y	1 Sam 30:21B
Judg 5:2R	Judg 19:25W	1 Sam 31:4U
Judg 5:3Y	Judg 19:25S	2 Sam 1:2W
Judg 5:11U	Judg 19:29W	2 Sam 1:6P
Judg 5:11T	Judg 19:29S	2 Sam 1:19W
Judg 5:11T	Judg 20:6S	2 Sam 1:20U
Judg 5:13W	Ruth 1:16B	*2 Sam 1:20B*
Judg 5:15W	Ruth 4:11Y	2 Sam 1:21W
Judg 5:23W	1 Sam 1:11Y	2 Sam 1:22W
Judg 6:11R	1 Sam 3:11Y	2 Sam 1:27W
Judg 6:24R	1 Sam 4:9U	2 Sam 2:2W
Judg 6:34B	1 Sam 4:18B	2 Sam 2:18W
Judg 7:8P	1 Sam 5:6W	2 Sam 2:28B
Judg 7:15B	1 Sam 8:8Y	2 Sam 4:4U
Judg 7:18B	1 Sam 8:11B	2 Sam 5:1B
Judg 7:18B	1 Sam 10:23W	2 Sam 5:5B
Judg 7:19B	1 Sam 12:7T	2 Sam 5:14B
Judg 7:20B	1 Sam 13:3B	2 Sam 6:5B
Judg 7:20B	1 Sam 13:5P	2 Sam 7:10B
Judg 8:11W	1 Sam 14:6U	2 Sam 7:14W
Judg 8:26W	1 Sam 14:38h	2 Sam 7:17Y
Judg 8:27R	1 Sam 15:18h	2 Sam 7:22Y
Judg 8:27Y	1 Sam 18:27U	2 Sam 8:4P
Judg 8:32R	1 Sam 19:24W	2 Sam 9:13B
Judg 8:33Y	1 Sam 20:20t	2 Sam 10:18P
Judg 9:2B	1 Sam 20:29t	2 Sam 11:1B
Judg 9:9H	1 Sam 25:5U	2 Sam 11:12B
Judg 9:11H	1 Sam 25:14W	2 Sam 11:16B
Judg 9:13H	1 Sam 25:18W	2 Sam 13:22U
Judg 9:23W	1 Sam 25:27U	*2 Sam 13:22U*
Judg 11:35W	1 Sam 25:39B	2 Sam 13:31W
Judg 12:11Y	1 Sam 25:43U	2 Sam 14:28B
Judg 12:12Y	1 Sam 26:23T	2 Sam 15:4T
Judg 12:15R	1 Sam 27:1t	2 Sam 15:6W
Judg 14:3U	1 Sam 27:3W	2 Sam 15:8B
Judg 14:8W	1 Sam 27:9W	2 Sam 15:14B

169

Appendix 1

2 Sam 15:16W	1 Kgs 6:15B	1 Kgs 16:13h
2 Sam 15:17W	1 Kgs 6:34B	1 Kgs 16:19h
2 Sam 16:3B	1 Kgs 7:33W	1 Kgs 16:26h
2 Sam 16:13R	1 Kgs 7:35B	1 Kgs 16:28B
2 Sam 18:12Y	1 Kgs 8:7P	1 Kgs 16:29B
2 Sam 18:19B	1 Kgs 8:12R	1 Kgs 16:32B
2 Sam 18:20B	1 Kgs 8:32T	1 Kgs 16:34W
2 Sam 18:22B	*1 Kgs 8:32B*	1 Kgs 17:6B
2 Sam 18:25B	1 Kgs 8:57Y	*1 Kgs 17:6B*
2 Sam 18:27B	1 Kgs 9:4B	1 Kgs 18:2B
2 Sam 19:4W	1 Kgs 9:11B	1 Kgs 19:11B
2 Sam 19:6t	1 Kgs 9:19B	1 Kgs 19:17t
2 Sam 19:13B	*1 Kgs 9:19P*	*1 Kgs 19:17t*
2 Sam 19:14B	1 Kgs 10:26P	1 Kgs 20:20P
2 Sam 19:25W	*1 Kgs 10:26P*	1 Kgs 20:23B
2 Sam 19:34B	*1 Kgs 10:26B*	1 Kgs 20:25B
2 Sam 20:22B	1 Kgs 10:27B	1 Kgs 20:31B
2 Sam 21:2W	1 Kgs 11:31U	1 Kgs 20:34B
2 Sam 22:7Y	1 Kgs 11:33Y	1 Kgs 21:18B
2 Sam 22:21T	1 Kgs 11:36B	1 Kgs 21:27B
2 Sam 22:25T	1 Kgs 11:42B	*1 Kgs 21:27W*
2 Sam 22:40Y	1 Kgs 12:21U	1 Kgs 22:37B
2 Sam 22:50W	1 Kgs 12:27B	1 Kgs 22:42B
1 Kgs 1:5P	1 Kgs 13:26B	1 Kgs 22:52B
1 Kgs 1:8W	1 Kgs 13:34H	1 Kgs 22:53h
1 Kgs 1:10W	1 Kgs 14:7U	2 Kgs 1:2B
1 Kgs 1:15W	1 Kgs 14:10U	2 Kgs 2:12W
1 Kgs 1:34B	1 Kgs 14:11U	2 Kgs 3:1B
1 Kgs 1:39B	1 Kgs 14:13U	2 Kgs 3:3h
1 Kgs 2:5W	1 Kgs 14:16h	2 Kgs 4:27W
1 Kgs 2:11B	1 Kgs 14:21B	2 Kgs 5:3B
1 Kgs 2:33B	1 Kgs 15:2B	2 Kgs 5:7W
1 Kgs 2:36B	1 Kgs 15:4B	2 Kgs 5:8W
1 Kgs 2:38B	1 Kgs 15:9U	2 Kgs 5:14B
1 Kgs 3:6B	1 Kgs 15:10B	2 Kgs 6:25B
1 Kgs 5:6P	1 Kgs 15:18Y	2 Kgs 6:30B
1 Kgs 5:20N	1 Kgs 15:26h	*2 Kgs 6:30W*
1 Kgs 5:22B	1 Kgs 15:29U	2 Kgs 6:32Y
1 Kgs 5:24B	1 Kgs 15:30h	2 Kgs 7:8W
1 Kgs 5:32W	1 Kgs 15:34h	2 Kgs 8:17B

2 Kgs 8:26B	2 Kgs 15:27B	2 Kgs 24:18B
2 Kgs 9:13B	2 Kgs 15:28h	2 Kgs 24:20B
2 Kgs 9:22Y	2 Kgs 15:33B	2 Kgs 25:1B
2 Kgs 10:1B	2 Kgs 16:2B	2 Kgs 25:12W
2 Kgs 10:5Y	2 Kgs 17:1B	2 Kgs 25:13B
2 Kgs 10:17B	2 Kgs 17:21h	2 Kgs 25:23Y
2 Kgs 10:29h	*2 Kgs 17:21h*	1 Chr 1:50t
2 Kgs 10:31h	2 Kgs 7:31P	1 Chr 2:16W
2 Kgs 10:35B	2 Kgs 18:2B	1 Chr 2:17W
2 Kgs 10:36B	2 Kgs 18:4B	1 Chr 2:28B
2 Kgs 11:10t	2 Kgs 18:8W	1 Chr 2:29B
2 Kgs 11:18B	2 Kgs 18:22B	1 Chr 3:4B
2 Kgs 12:2B	2 Kgs 18:24P	1 Chr 3:5B
2 Kgs 13:1B	2 Kgs 19:1W	1 Chr 4:10W
2 Kgs 13:2h	2 Kgs 19:23B	1 Chr 4:30W
2 Kgs 13:6B	2 Kgs 19:30t	1 Chr 4:31B
2 Kgs 13:7P	2 Kgs 21:1B	1 Chr 5:24W
2 Kgs 13:9B	2 Kgs 21:4B	1 Chr 5:25Y
2 Kgs 13:10B	2 Kgs 21:7B	1 Chr 5:36B
2 Kgs 13:11h	2 Kgs 21:11W	1 Chr 6:17B
2 Kgs 13:13B	2 Kgs 21:12Y	1 Chr 6:42t
2 Kgs 14:2B	2 Kgs 21:16h	1 Chr 6:52t
2 Kgs 14:16B	2 Kgs 21:19B	1 Chr 7:2W
2 Kgs 14:19B	2 Kgs 22:1B	1 Chr 7:5W
2 Kgs 14:20B	2 Kgs 22:11W	1 Chr 7:7W
2 Kgs 14:23B	2 Kgs 22:14H	1 Chr 7:9W
2 Kgs 14:24h	*2 Kgs 22:14B*	1 Chr 7:10Y
2 Kgs 15:1U	2 Kgs 22:17Y	1 Chr 7:11W
2 Kgs 15:2B	2 Kgs 23:4P	1 Chr 7:28U
2 Kgs 15:8B	2 Kgs 23:9B	1 Chr 7:40W
2 Kgs 15:9h	2 Kgs 23:14B	1 Chr 8:28B
2 Kgs 15:13B	2 Kgs 23:15h	1 Chr 8:32B
2 Kgs 15:14B	2 Kgs 23:23B	1 Chr 9:3B
2 Kgs 15:16W	2 Kgs 23:24B	1 Chr 9:13W
2 Kgs 15:17B	2 Kgs 23:31B	1 Chr 9:22U
2 Kgs 15:18h	2 Kgs 23:33B	1 Chr 9:34B
2 Kgs 15:20W	2 Kgs 23:36B	1 Chr 9:38B
2 Kgs 15:23B	2 Kgs 24:8B	1 Chr 10:4U
2 Kgs 15:24h	2 Kgs 24:14W	1 Chr 11:1B
2 Kgs 15:25B	2 Kgs 24:16W	1 Chr 11:6B

Appendix 1

1 *Chr 11:6B*

1 Chr 11:10W

1 Chr 11:19W

1 Chr 11:26W

1 Chr 11:34Y

1 Chr 12:1W

1 Chr 12:4W

1 Chr 12:16U

1 Chr 12:20B

1 Chr 12:22W

1 Chr 12:26W

1 Chr 12:31W

1 Chr 12:41W

1 Chr 13:8B

1 Chr 14:3B

1 Chr 14:4B

1 Chr 15:13B

1 Chr 15:25Y

1 Chr 16:23B

1 Chr 16:24W

1 Chr 16:31W

1 Chr 16:38U

1 Chr 17:9B

1 Chr 17:20Y

1 Chr 18:4P

1 Chr 19:6P

1 Chr 19:8W

1 Chr 20:1B

1 Chr 21:16Y

1 Chr 23:25B

1 Chr 24:8U

1 Chr 25:27U

1 Chr 26:1U

1 Chr 26:6W

1 Chr 26:16U

1 Chr 26:18U

1 Chr 26:23U

1 Chr 26:31W

1 Chr 27:23t

1 Chr 27:29B

1 Chr 28:1W

1 Chr 28:8Y

1 Chr 28:11Y

1 *Chr 28:11Z*

1 Chr 28:18P

1 Chr 29:24W

1 Chr 29:27B

2 Chr 1:4B

2 Chr 1:14B

2 Chr 1:14P

2 *Chr 1:14P*

2 Chr 1:15B

2 Chr 2:6B

2 Chr 2:7B

2 Chr 3:1B

2 Chr 3:5B

2 Chr 3:13P

2 Chr 3:16B

2 Chr 4:20U

2 Chr 5:8P

2 Chr 6:1R

2 Chr 6:6B

2 Chr 6:23T

2 *Chr 6:23B*

2 Chr 6:40Y

2 Chr 7:15Y

2 Chr 8:6P

2 *Chr 8:6B*

2 Chr 9:1B

2 Chr 9:25P

2 *Chr 9:25B*

2 Chr 9:27B

2 Chr 9:30B

2 Chr 11:1U

2 Chr 11:5B

2 Chr 11:15U

2 Chr 12:3P

2 Chr 12:7B

2 Chr 12:13B

2 *Chr 12:13B*

2 Chr 13:2B

2 Chr 13:3W

2 Chr 14:2B

2 Chr 14:7W

2 Chr 14:12B

2 Chr 15:6W

2 Chr 15:14B

2 Chr 16:8P

2 Chr 16:12W

2 Chr 16:14Y

2 Chr 17:6W

2 Chr 17:13W

2 Chr 17:13B

2 Chr 17:14W

2 Chr 19:4B

2 Chr 19:8B

2 Chr 20:31B

2 Chr 20:37B

2 Chr 21:5B

2 Chr 21:11Y

2 Chr 21:20B

2 Chr 22:2B

2 Chr 22:9B

2 Chr 23:9t

2 Chr 23:17B

2 Chr 23:18B

2 Chr 24:1B

2 Chr 24:9B

2 Chr 24:15Y

2 Chr 24:19Y

2 Chr 25:1B

2 Chr 25:27B

2 Chr 26:3B

2 Chr 26:9B

2 Chr 26:10B

2 Chr 26:12W

2 Chr 26:15B

2 Chr 27:1B

2 Chr 27:4B

2 Chr 27:8B

2 Chr 28:1B	2 Chr 36:11B	Ezra 9:9B
2 Chr 28:23Y	2 Chr 36:14B	Ezra 9:13t
2 Chr 28:24B	2 Chr 36:23B	Ezra 10:8Y
2 Chr 28:27B	Ezra 1:2B	Neh 2:9P
2 Chr 29:1B	Ezra 1:3B	Neh 2:20B
2 Chr 29:23h	Ezra 1:4B	Neh 3:7t
2 Chr 29:24h	*Ezra 1:4B*	Neh 4:2B
2 Chr 30:1B	Ezra 1:5B	Neh 4:12B
2 Chr 30:2B	Ezra 1:6B	Neh 4:17W
2 Chr 30:5B	Ezra 2:2W	Neh 5:5B
2 Chr 30:14B	Ezra 2:14W	Neh 6:6W
2 Chr 30:21B	Ezra 2:68B	Neh 6:7B
2 Chr 30:26B	Ezra 4:18P	Neh 6:10t
2 Chr 30:26B	Ezra 4:22Y	Neh 7:3B
2 Chr 31:1B	Ezra 4:24B	Neh 7:5B
2 Chr 31:1U	Ezra 5:1B	Neh 7:7W
2 Chr 31:16B	Ezra 5:2B	Neh 7:19W
2 Chr 31:17B	Ezra 5:3Y	Neh 8:3Y
2 Chr 32:3W	Ezra 5:6Y	Neh 8:7B
2 Chr 32:9B	Ezra 5:14B	Neh 8:8P
2 Chr 32:10B	Ezra 5:15B	Neh 8:15B
2 Chr 32:30t	Ezra 5:16B	Neh 9:2h
2 Chr 33:1B	Ezra 5:17B	Neh 9:10R
2 Chr 33:4B	Ezra 6:3B	Neh 9:15U
2 Chr 33:7B	Ezra 6:5B	Neh 9:30Y
2 Chr 33:14W	*Ezra 6:5B*	Neh 10:17W
2 Chr 33:15B	Ezra 6:6Y	Neh 11:1B
2 Chr 33:21B	Ezra 6:9B	*Neh 11:1B*
2 Chr 34:1B	Ezra 6:12B	Neh 11:2B
2 Chr 34:19W	Ezra 6:13Y	Neh 11:3B
2 Chr 34:22B	Ezra 6:18B	Neh 11:4B
2 Chr 34:22H	Ezra 7:15B	Neh 11:6B
2 Chr 34:25Y	Ezra 7:16B	Neh 11:14W
2 Chr 34:32B	Ezra 7:17B	Neh 11:22B
2 Chr 35:1B	Ezra 7:27B	Neh 12:27B
2 Chr 36:1B	Ezra 8:14W	Neh 12:44U
2 Chr 36:2B	Ezra 8:18B	Neh 13:6B
2 Chr 36:3B	Ezra 8:22P	Neh 13:14B
2 Chr 36:5B	Ezra 8:29B	Neh 13:16B
2 Chr 36:9B	Ezra 9:3Y	Neh 13:26W

Neh 13:26h	Job 19:26B	Ps 10:9B
Esth 1:18Y	Job 20:8Y	Ps 11:7T
Esth 2:12W	Job 22:3T	Ps 17:5W
Esth 2:15W	Job 22:6W	Ps 17:14N
Esth 4:1W	Job 23:11B	Ps 18:7Y
Esth 4:13t	Job 24:5U	Ps 18:40Y
Esth 6:8B	Job 24:20B	Ps 18:50W
Esth 8:9P	Job 27:6T	Ps 22:29W
Esth 9:1B	Job 28:18W	Ps 22:32T
Esth 9:3P	Job 28:22Y	Ps 25:3W
Esth 9:9P	Job 29:17B	Ps 26:12B
Job 1:15t	Job 30:16Y	Ps 27:10Y
Job 1:16t	Job 30:31W	Ps 28:7Y
Job 1:17t	Job 31:31B	Ps 29:5B
Job 1:19t	Job 32:9Y	Ps 30:12Y
Job 2:5B	Job 33:12T	Ps 31:2T
Job 4:13Y	Job 33:15Y	Ps 31:11W
Job 4:19R	Job 33:21B	Ps 32:1h
Job 5:7W	Job 33:25B	Ps 34:16Y
Job 7:14Y	Job 33:26T	Ps 36:7T
Job 7:18U	Job 34:2Y	Ps 36:11T
Job 9:15T	Job 34:5T	Ps 37:33Y
Job 9:27W	Job 35:7T	Ps 39:14W
Job 10:11B	Job 35:8T	Ps 40:7h
Job 10:15T	Job 36:7W	Ps 40:11T
Job 10:20W	Job 36:9W	Ps 41:2t
Job 14:8R	Job 36:29P	Ps 42:8N
Job 14:13Y	Job 38:8W	Ps 44:2Y
Job 14:22B	Job 38:10B	Ps 44:12Y
Job 15:12Y	Job 38:26t	*Ps 44:12W*
Job 15:21Y	Job 38:38W	Ps 44:15W
Job 16:6H	Job 39:30B	Ps 46:11W
Job 16:12t	Job 40:8T	Ps 49:2Y
Job 16:12R	Job 40:13R	Ps 51:6T
Job 16:15R	Job 41:15B	Ps 51:16T
Job 18:8W	Ps 2:2Y	Ps 57:5t
Job 18:19W	Ps 4:1W	Ps 62:5H
Job 19:20t	Ps 5:9T	Ps 63:7B
Job 19:20B	Ps 6:1W	Ps 66:7W
Job 19:22B	Ps 7:17B	Ps 68:7B

Ps 68:12B	Ps 109:24B	Prov 16:11Y
Ps 69:28T	Ps 110:6W	Prov 20:23Y
Ps 71:2T	Ps 111:3T	Prov 23:28W
Ps 71:15T	Ps 112:3T	Prov 23:32N
Ps 71:16T	Ps 112:9T	Prov 27:23U
Ps 71:19T	Ps 116:4t	Prov 30:9W
Ps 71:24T	Ps 119:40T	Prov 31:4Y
Ps 72:1T	Ps 119:142T	Prov 31:19B
Ps 75:5U	Ps 124:5Y	Eccl 1:1B
Ps 77:2Y	Ps 124:7t	Eccl 1:12B
Ps 78:16Y	Ps 126:2W	Eccl 2:7B
Ps 78:44Y	Ps 135:9R	Eccl 2:9B
Ps 78:48P	Ps 135:17Y	Eccl 2:14B
Ps 78:57W	Ps 139:10Y	Eccl 2:21B
Ps 78:71B	Ps 143:1T	Eccl 3:21t
Ps 81:13B	Ps 143:11T	Eccl 4:5B
Ps 83:4N	Ps 144:13Y	Eccl 5:7W
Ps 84:3B	Ps 145:4W	Eccl 9:11W
Ps 88:13T	Ps 145:7T	Eccl 12:6B
Ps 89:17T	Ps 145:12W	Song 2:14W
Ps 89:33W	Ps 145:15B	Song 4:4W
Ps 92:12B	Ps 146:5B	Song 4:9N
Ps 96:2B	Ps 146:7U	Song 4:15Y
Ps 96:3W	Ps 147:3B	Song 7:7W
Ps 96:10W	Ps 149:7W	Isa 1:2Y
Ps 98:2T	Ps 150:2W	Isa 1:9U
Ps 102:22B	Prov 2:15Y	Isa 1:10Y
Ps 103:6T	Prov 2:22W	Isa 1:15P
Ps 103:17T	Prov 4:22B	*Isa 1:15B*
Ps 104:7Y	Prov 5:15Y	Isa 1:28B
Ps 104:11B	Prov 6:27W	Isa 2:10R
Ps 104:17B	Prov 6:30W	Isa 2:20M
Ps 104:27B	Prov 8:15Y	Isa 3:16W
Ps 105:22Y	Prov 9:17W	Isa 3:21Y
Ps 105:33B	Prov 11:3W	Isa 3:22M
Ps 106:27W	Prov 11:5B	Isa 4:3B
Ps 106:35W	*Prov 11:5T*	*Isa 4:3B*
Ps 106:39Y	Prov 11:6T	Isa 5:16W
Ps 107:41W	Prov 11:28B	Isa 5:18h
Ps 109:7h	Prov 14:2B	Isa 5:22W

Appendix 1

Isa 5:23T	Isa 27:3U	Isa 51:6T
Isa 5:30R	Isa 27:13B	Isa 51:8T
Isa 6:2P	*Isa 27:13B*	Isa 51:19B
Isa 6:6P	Isa 28:7B	Isa 51:23U
Isa 6:10Y	Isa 28:13B	Isa 54:17T
Isa 6:10Y	Isa 28:14B	Isa 55:1B
Isa 8:9Y	Isa 28:15B	*Isa 55:1B*
Isa 8:15B	Isa 28:23Y	Isa 55:13B
Isa 9:10W	Isa 29:6B	Isa 56:1T
Isa 10:6W	Isa 30:14B	Isa 57:12T
Isa 10:12B	Isa 30:19B	Isa 57:21U
Isa 10:33W	Isa 30:21Y	Isa 58:7B
Isa 11:3Y	Isa 31:1P	Isa 59:16T
Isa 11:4B	Isa 31:5t	Isa 59:17B
Isa 13:3W	Isa 31:9B	Isa 60:6B
Isa 13:8Y	Isa 32:3Y	Isa 60:13B
Isa 13:9h	Isa 33:1W	Isa 60:14N
Isa 14:8B	Isa 33:12P	Isa 60:18B
Isa 17:2U	Isa 33:15T	*Isa 60:18W*
Isa 17:4B	Isa 35:5Y	Isa 61:9W
Isa 17:14Y	Isa 36:9P	Isa 63:2W
Isa 19:6Y	Isa 37:1W	Isa 63:18U
Isa 19:23B	Isa 37:24B	Isa 64:3Y
Isa 20:4Y	Isa 37:31t	Isa 64:5T
Isa 21:3Y	Isa 38:18B	Isa 65:12B
Isa 21:4H	Isa 40:2h	Isa 65:14B
Isa 21:7P	Isa 40:23Y	Isa 65:19B
Isa 21:9P	Isa 41:3W	Isa 65:20h
Isa 21:17W	Isa 41:19B	Isa 66:4B
Isa 22:1Y	Isa 42:3B	Isa 66:7t
Isa 22:3N	Isa 43:8Y	Isa 66:13B
Isa 22:3N	Isa 43:26T	Isa 66:19W
Isa 22:5Y	Isa 44:3Y	Jer 1:16Y
Isa 22:6P	Isa 44:23B	Jer 3:2Y
Isa 22:7P	Isa 45:24T	Jer 3:6Y
Isa 22:18N	Isa 46:13T	Jer 4:5B
Isa 24:16W	Isa 47:14P	Jer 4:6B
Isa 24:23B	Isa 48:18T	Jer 5:5B
Isa 24:23Y	Isa 48:22U	Jer 5:7Y
Isa 26:11Y	Isa 51:4Y	Jer 5:9W

Jer 5:10B	Jer 31:37t	Jer 51:54B
Jer 5:16W	Jer 32:20B	Jer 51:56W
Jer 5:29W	Jer 34:5P	Jer 51:57W
Jer 6:1B	Jer 34:6B	Jer 52:1B
Jer 6:24Y	Jer 34:8B	Jer 52:3B
Jer 7:12B	Jer 35:11B	Jer 52:4B
Jer 7:24B	Jer 36:9B	Jer 52:12B
Jer 9:8W	*Jer 36:9B*	*Jer 52:12B*
Jer 9:15W	Jer 36:15Y	Jer 52:16W
Jer 9:22B	Jer 36:21Y	Jer 52:17B
Jer 9:25U	Jer 39:10W	Lam 1:1W
Jer 11:8B	Jer 40:8Y	Lam 1:3W
Jer 11:15B	Jer 42:1Y	Lam 1:8h
Jer 13:10B	Jer 43:12P	Lam 1:19Y
Jer 13:15Y	Jer 43:13B	Lam 2:9B
Jer 13:18W	Jer 46:4P	*Lam 2:9W*
Jer 15:4B	Jer 46:5W	Lam 2:12M
Jer 15:13W	Jer 46:9W	Lam 2:19M
Jer 16:21W	Jer 48:3B	Lam 3:29R
Jer 17:3W	Jer 48:14W	Lam 3:47B
Jer 17:11Y	Jer 48:19t	Lam 4:15W
Jer 17:18B	Jer 48:41W	Lam 4:16t
Jer 18:13W	Jer 49:14W	Lam 4:20W
Jer 18:14Y	Jer 49:15W	Ezek 1:8U
Jer 18:16B	Jer 49:16W	Ezek 1:10U
Jer 19:1Y	Jer 49:22W	Ezek 1:18W
Jer 19:1Y	Jer 50:2W	Ezek 1:27t
Jer 19:3Y	Jer 50:14h	Ezek 3:10Y
Jer 19:10B	Jer 50:22B	Ezek 3:20T
Jer 22:20B	Jer 50:23B	Ezek 3:27H
Jer 23:17B	*Jer 50:23W*	Ezek 4:11B
Jer 25:31W	Jer 50:36W	Ezek 4:16B
Jer 26:21W	Jer 50:46W	Ezek 4:13W
Jer 27:18B	Jer 51:8B	Ezek 4:16B
Jer 28:7Y	Jer 51:10T	Ezek 5:14W
Jer 28:10B	Jer 51:11t	Ezek 5:16B
Jer 28:12B	Jer 51:27W	Ezek 6:4B
Jer 29:2W	Jer 51:30B	Ezek 6:6B
Jer 29:25B	Jer 51:30W	Ezek 6:8W
Jer 31:13Y	Jer 51:41W	Ezek 6:9W

Appendix 1

Ezek 7:11t	Ezek 18:24T	Ezek 27:14P
Ezek 7:16t	Ezek 18:26T	*Ezek 27:14Y*
Ezek 8:1Y	Ezek 20:1B	Ezek 27:16Y
Ezek 8:2t	Ezek 20:7W	Ezek 27:19Y
Ezek 8:11Y	Ezek 20:18W	Ezek 27:22Y
Ezek 10:10U	Ezek 20:23W	Ezek 27:24W
Ezek 10:12U	Ezek 20:39W	*Ezek 27:24W*
Ezek 11:16W	Ezek 21:11B	*Ezek 27:24Y*
Ezek 12:10B	Ezek 21:16t	Ezek 27:27Y
Ezek 12:15W	Ezek 21:21D	Ezek 27:33Y
Ezek 12:16W	Ezek 21:25B	Ezek 28:5W
Ezek 14:5W	Ezek 22:3t	Ezek 28:10U
Ezek 14:7Y	Ezek 22:4W	Ezek 29:12W
Ezek 14:13B	Ezek 22:15W	Ezek 29:15W
Ezek 14:14T	Ezek 23:3Y	Ezek 29:17B
Ezek 14:20T	Ezek 23:6P	Ezek 30:8B
Ezek 16:14W	Ezek 23:7Y	Ezek 30:9H
Ezek 16:15Y	Ezek 23:8Y	Ezek 30:20B
Ezek 16:15Y	Ezek 23:11Y	Ezek 30:22B
Ezek 16:16Y	*Ezek 23:11Y*	Ezek 30:23W
Ezek 16:17Y	Ezek 23:12P	Ezek 30:24B
Ezek 16:22Y	Ezek 23:14Y	Ezek 30:26W
Ezek 16:26Y	Ezek 23:18Y	Ezek 31:8B
Ezek 16:28Y	Ezek 23:19Y	Ezek 31:12B
Ezek 16:28Y	Ezek 23:25Y	Ezek 31:14W
Ezek 16:33Y	Ezek 23:29Y	Ezek 31:18U
Ezek 16:34Y	*Ezek 23:29Y*	Ezek 32:9W
Ezek 16:36Y	Ezek 23:30W	Ezek 32:10U
Ezek 16:50W	Ezek 23:35Y	Ezek 32:12W
Ezek 16:51T	Ezek 24:1B	Ezek 32:19U
Ezek 16:51h	Ezek 25:10W	Ezek 32:21U
Ezek 16:52T	Ezek 26:7B	*Ezek 32:21W*
Ezek 16:52T	*Ezek 26:7P*	Ezek 32:24U
Ezek 17:15t	Ezek 26:16U	Ezek 32:25U
Ezek 17:19B	Ezek 27:4W	Ezek 32:26U
Ezek 18:4h	Ezek 27:5B	Ezek 32:27W
Ezek 18:20h	Ezek 27:7P	*Ezek 32:27W*
Ezek 18:20T	Ezek 27:11t	*Ezek 32:27U*
Ezek 18:22T	*Ezek 27:11W*	Ezek 32:28U
Ezek 18:24T	Ezek 27:12Y	Ezek 32:29U

Ezek 32:30U	Ezek 45:18B	Hos 1:7P
Ezek 32:32U	Ezek 45:19h	Hos 1:2Y
Ezek 33:3B	Ezek 45:21B	*Hos 1:2Y*
Ezek 33:4B	Ezek 46:11W	Hos 1:5B
Ezek 33:6B	Ezek 46:20h	Hos 1:7B
Ezek 33:12T	Ezek 46:22U	Hos 2:4Y
Ezek 33:13T	Ezek 46:23U	Hos 2:6Y
Ezek 33:13T	Ezek 47:11W	Hos 2:20B
Ezek 33:18T	Dan 1:8Y	Hos 4:12Y
Ezek 34:2U	Dan 1:21Y	*Hos 4:12Y*
Ezek 34:4B	Dan 3:15Y	Hos 5:1Y
Ezek 34:16B	Dan 3:17Y	Hos 5:4Y
Ezek 34:19P	Dan 3:20W	Hos 8:8W
Ezek 35:8W	Dan 3:23W	Hos 8:10W
Ezek 35:12N	Dan 4:30N	Hos 9:3B
Ezek 36:4U	Dan 5:2B	Hos 9:10Y
Ezek 36:18W	Dan 5:3B	Hos 9:12B
Ezek 36:19W	Dan 5:12P	Hos 9:17W
Ezek 36:21W	Dan 5:16P	Hos 10:13W
Ezek 36:22W	Dan 5:17Y	Hos 14:9B
Ezek 36:23W	Dan 6:11Y	Joel 1:2Y
Ezek 36:30W	Dan 6:14Y	Joel 2:4P
Ezek 37:8B	Dan 7:7H	Joel 2:7W
Ezek 37:9W	Dan 7:19H	Joel 2:19W
Ezek 37:23W	Dan 8:7B	Joel 2:23B
Ezek 38:4P	Dan 8:22B	Joel 3:1Y
Ezek 39:18W	Dan 9:12B	Joel 3:5B
Ezek 39:21W	Dan 9:16T	*Joel 3:5B*
Ezek 39:28W	Dan 9:18T	Joel 4:2W
Ezek 40:4Y	Dan 9:27W	Joel 4:9W
Ezek 40:1B	Dan 10:3B	Joel 4:11W
Ezek 40:39h	Dan 10:18Y	Amos 1:5B
Ezek 42:13h	Dan 11:2B	Amos 2:15W
Ezek 43:7W	Dan 11:13B	Amos 2:16W
Ezek 43:21h	Dan 11:22B	Amos 3:12B
Ezek 44:5Y	Dan 11:26B	Amos 4:11P
Ezek 44:25t	Dan 11:27U	Amos 8:5B
Ezek 44:29h	Dan 11:28B	Amos 9:8h
Ezek 45:8t	Dan 11:40P	Obad 1:1W
Ezek 45:17h	*Dan 11:40B*	Obad 1:2W

Appendix 1

Obad 1:3W	Hab 3:7Y	*Zech 11:16B*
Obad 1:5W	Hab 3:19W	Zech 12:6B
Obad 1:9W	Zeph 1:10B	Zech 12:11B
Mic 3:3B	Zech 1:17B	Zech 13:4Y
Mic 5:7W	Zech 2:4H	Zech 14:3W
Mic 6:5T	Zech 2:11t	Zech 14:10U
Mic 6:6A	Zech 2:16B	Zech 14:12B
Mic 7:9T	Zech 3:2B	Zech 14:14W
Nah 1:3B	Zech 7:1Y1	*Zech 14:14B*
Nah 2:4W	Zech 8:13W	Zech 14:21B
Nah 2:4B	Zech 8:22B	Mal 1:6Y
Nah 3:3W	Zech 9:14B	Mal 1:11W
Nah 3:4Y	Zech 10:6W	*Mal 1:11W*
Nah 3:4Y	Zech 10:9Y	Mal 1:14W
Hab 1:5W	Zech 10:12W	Mal 2:6B
Hab 1:10Y	Zech 11:2B	Mal 2:11B
Hab 1:13W	Zech 11:16B	

APPENDIX 2

Coded Groups of Authors
in Deuteronomy 5–28

Name	Groups	Chapters	All Chapters Coded Except:
Micaiah	140	24	None (all coded)
Daniel	138	20	10, 18, 21, 27
Huldah	126	20	10, 17, 19–20
Jacob	122	23	20
Asaiah	110	22	17, 23
Azariah	106	21	10, 23, 26
Ezra	95	22	15, 23
Shephatiah	79	18	10, 17–18, 20, 24, 27
Jonathan	74	21	10, 18, 20
Hushim	73	20	10, 17, 22, 27
Jeremiah	73	20	11, 17, 22–23
Adonijah	66	19	13, 15, 17–18, 20
Shemaiah	66	20	5, 17, 22–23
Jesse	65	19	9, 17, 20–22
Shelemiah	62	17	13, 20–24, 27
Abel	60	16	10, 13, 17–19, 21-22, 27
Amminadab	59	19	5, 18, 23, 25, 27
Mattithiah	59	19	10, 18, 20, 23, 27
Mattaniah	56	18	10, 17–18, 23, 25, 27
Ahikam	54	16	5, 10, 13, 17, 19, 21–22, 27
Isaac	53	18	5, 10, 18, 21, 23, 27

Appendix 2

Name	Groups	Chapters	All Chapters Coded Except:
Nethaniah	53	16	5, 10, 18, 20–21, 23, 26–27
Jonadab	52	14	5, 9, 15, 17–18, 20, 22–23, 26–27
Zebadiah	52	16	5–6, 10, 12, 15, 17, 19, 22
Abijah	51	16	5, 15, 18, 20, 22–25
Shaphan	51	18	5, 10, 12, 17, 23, 27
Uzziah	50	16	5, 13, 18, 20, 22–24, 27
Azrikam	50	19	17–21
Pedaiah	50	16	5, 11, 13, 15, 17–18, 22, 24
Eliab	49	21	19, 21, 27
Elijah	49	14	7, 9, 15, 17–18, 20–22, 25, 27
Jerimoth	49	19	6, 13, 18, 21–22
Menahem	49	21	17–18, 21
Shemariah	49	16	5, 12–13, 18, 21–23, 26–27
Gemariah	48	17	10, 17, 21–24, 27
Iddo	48	14	13, 15, 17–18, 20–21, 23–24, 26, 28
Delaiah	47	18	10, 13, 17–19, 22
Josiah	47	17	5, 16–17, 20, 22, 24, 26
Eliphal	46	20	17, 19–21
Nogah	46	16	10, 14, 17–18, 21–23, 27
Hananiah	46	18	5, 6, 11, 13–14, 17
Shallum	46	16	5, 10, 14, 17–18, 23, 26–27
Elishama	45	14	5, 10–11, 13, 17, 19, 21–23, 26
Joram	45	19	10, 17, 23, 25, 27
Mijamin	45	21	5, 21, 24
Shelomoth	45	16	10, 13, 17, 19–20, 23, 25, 27
Seraiah	45	18	5, 11, 17, 19, 24, 26

Bibliography

Ackerman, Susan. *Warrior, Dancer, Seductress, Queen: Women in Judges and Biblical Israel*. Anchor Bible Reference Library. New Haven: Yale University Press, 1998.

Albright, William F. "King Joiachin in Exile." *Biblical Archaeologist* 5 (1942) 50–55.

Althann, Robert. "Gedaliah." In *ABD* 2:923–24.

———. "Zedekiah." In *ABD* 6:1068–71.

Astour, Michael C. "Zoar." In *ABD* 6:1107.

Berlin, Adele, and Marc Zvi Brettler. "Psalms." In Jewish Study Bible, edited by Adele Berlin and Marc Zvi Brettler, 1280–446. New York: Oxford University Press, 1999.

Bird, Phyllis A. *Missing Persons and Mistaken Identities: Women and Gender in Ancient Israel*. Overtures to Biblical Theology. Minneapolis: Fortress, 1997.

———. "Women (Old Testament)." In *ABD* 6:951–57.

Blank, S. H. "Book of Proverbs." In *IDB* 3:936–40.

Boling, Robert G. "Book of Joshua." In *ABD* 3:1002–15.

Brenner, Athalya, et al. *Genesis*. Minneapolis: Fortress, 2010.

Burrows, Millar. *The Dead Sea Scrolls*. New York: Viking, 1955.

Clifford, Richard J. "Isaiah, Book of (Second Isaiah)." In *ABD* 3:490–501.

Collins, John J. "Book of Daniel." In *ABD* 2:29–37.

Cross, Frank Moore. *Canaanite Myth and Hebrew Epic: Essays in the History of the Religion of Israel*. Cambridge: Harvard University Press, 1973.

Davies, S. Hinton. "Elder in the OT." In *IDB* 2:72–73.

Evans, Carl D. "Asa." In *ABD* 1:468–70.

Exum, J. Cheryl. "Feminist Criticism." In *Judges & Method: New Approaches in Biblical Studies*, 65–89. 2nd ed. Minneapolis: Fortress, 2007.

Fiorenza, Elizabeth Schüssler. *But She Said: Feminist Practices of Biblical Interpretation*. Boston: Beacon, 1992.

———. "Feminist Hermeneutics." In *ABD* 2:783–91.

Fontaine, Carole. *Smooth Words: Women, Proverbs, and Performance*. JSOT Supplements 356. London: Sheffield Academic, 2002.

Gafney, Wilda C. *Daughters of Miriam: Women Prophets in Ancient Israel*. Minneapolis: Fortress, 2008.

Ginzberg, Louis. *Legends of the Jews*. Philadelphia: Jewish Publication Society, 1913.

Golletz, Rand. *Consensus Is Not Kumbaya: Lessons in Tough-Minded Leadership*. Garden City, NY: Morgan James, 2011.

Harland, J. P. "Sodom." In *IDB* 4:395–97.

Harvey, D. "Deborah." In *IDB* 1:808–9.

Herion, Gary A. "Second Quarter." In *ABD* 5:1065.

Bibliography

Kam, Rose Sallberg. *Their Stories, Our Stories: Women of the Bible.* New York: Continuum, 1998.

Katzenstein, H. J. "Tyre." In *ABD* 6:686–90.

Kavanagh, Preston. *The Exilic Code: Ciphers, Word Links, and Dating in Exilic and Post-Exilic Biblical Literature.* Eugene, OR: Pickwick Publications, 2009.

———. "The Jehoiachin Code in Scripture's Priestly Benediction." *Bib* 88 (2007) 234–44.

———. *Secrets of the Jewish Exile: The Bible's Codes, Messiah, and Suffering Servant.* Tarentum, PA: Word Association, 2005.

———. *The Shaphan Group: The Fifteen Authors Who Shaped the Hebrew Bible.* Eugene, OR: Pickwick Publications, 2011.

King, Philip J., and Lawrence E. Stager. *Life in Biblical Israel.* Library of Ancient Israel. Louisville: Westminster, 2001.

Klein, Ralph W. "Book of 1–2 Chronicles." In *ABD* 1:992–1002.

———. "Books of Ezra-Nehemiah." In *ABD* 2:731–42.

Kudlek, Manfred, and Erich H. Mickler. *Solar and Lunar Eclipses of the Ancient Near East from 3000 B.C. to 0.* AOAT 1. Kevelaer: Butzon & Bercker, 1971.

LaCocque, André. *Ruth.* Translated by K. C. Hanson. Continental Commentaries Minneapolis: Fortress, 2004.

Levinson, Bernard M. "Deuteronomy: Introduction and Annotation." In *JSB* 356–62.

Lipinski, Edward. "Jeremiah." In *EncJud* 9:1345–59.

Lundbom, Jack R. "Jeremiah." In *ABD* 3:684–98.

Mallowan, Max. "Cyrus the Great (558–529 B.C.)." *Iran* 10 (1972) 1–17.

McKenzie, Steven L. "Deuteronomistic History." In *ABD* 2:160–68.

Meyers, Carol. "Contesting the Notion of Patriarchy." In *A Question of Sex? Gender and Difference in the Hebrew Bible*, edited by Deborah W. Rooke, 84–105. Hebrew Bible Monographs 14. Sheffield: Sheffield Phoenix, 2007.

———. *Discovering Eve: Ancient Israel Women in Context.* New York: Oxford University Press, 1988.

———. "Everyday Life: Women in the Period of the Hebrew Bible." In *Women's Bible Commentary*, edited by Carol A. Newsom and Sharon H. Ringe, 251–59. Expanded ed. Louisville: Westminster, 1998.

———. *Households and Holiness: The Religious Culture of Israelite Women.* Facets. Minneapolis: Fortress, 2005.

Murphy, Roland E. "Wisdom in the OT." In *ABD* 6:920–931.

Neusner, Jacob. *The Babylonian Talmud.* Peabody, MA: Hendrickson, 2005.

Newsom, Carol A., and Sharon H. Ringe. *Women's Bible Commentary.* Expanded ed. Louisville: Westminster, 1998.

Nicholson, Ward. "Longevity & Health in Ancient Paleolithic vs. Neolithic Peoples." No pages. Online: http://www.beyondveg.com/nicholson-w/angel-1984/angel.

North, Robert. "Ezra." In *ABD* 2:726–8.

O'Connor, Kathleen M. "Jeremiah." In *Women's Bible Commentary*, edited by Carol A. Newsom and Sharon H. Ringe, 178–91. Expanded ed. Louisville: Westminster, 1998.

Olmstead, A. T. *History of the Persian Empire.* Chicago: University of Chicago Press, 1948.

Olyan, Saul M. *Asherah and the Cult of Yahweh in Israel.* Society of Biblical Literature Monograph Series 34. Atlanta: Scholars, 1988.

Pomeroy, Sarah B. *Chattel or Person? The Status of Women in the Mishnah.* New York: Oxford University Press, 1988.

Ramsey, George W. "Joshua." In *ABD* 3:999–1000.

Rothkoff, Aaron. "Huldah: In the Aggadah." In *EncJud* 8:1063.

Ruether, Rosemary R. "Prophetic Tradition and the Liberation of Women." *Feminist Theology* (1994) 58–73.

Scott, Robert B. Y. "Book of Proverbs." In *EncJud* 13:1268–73.

Seitz, Christopher R. "Book of Isaiah: First Isaiah." In *ABD* 3:472–88.

Shanks, Hershel. "When Did Ancient Israel Begin?" *BAR* 38/1 (2012) 59–62, 67.

Stager, Lawrence E. "The Archaeology of the Family in Ancient Israel." *BASOR* 260 (1985) 1–29.

Steinberg, Naomi. "Social-Scientific Criticism." In *Judges & Method: New Approaches in Biblical Studies*, edited by Gale A. Yee, 46–64. 2nd ed. Minneapolis: Fortress, 2007.

Trible, Phyllis. *God and the Rhetoric of Sexuality.* Overtures to Biblical Theology. Philadelphia: Fortress, 1978.

———. *Texts of Terror: Literary-Feminist Readings of Biblical Narratives.* Overtures to Biblical Theology. Philadelphia: Fortress, 1984.

Walton, John H. "The Imagery of the Substitute King Ritual in Isaiah's Fourth Servant Song." *JBL* 122 (2003) 734–43.

Ward, J. M. "Elnathan." In *IDB* 2:94.

Wegner, Judith R. "Leviticus." In *Women's Bible Commentary*, edited by Carol A. Newsom and Sharon H. Ringe, 40–48. Expanded ed. Louisville: Westminster, 1998.

Weidner, Ernest F. "Jojachin, Koenig von Juda, in babylonischen Keilschrifttexten." In *Mélanges Syriens offerts à M. René Dussaud*, 2:923–35. 2 vols. Paris: Guethner, 1939.

Williamson, H. G. M. *Chronicles.* NCBC. Grand Rapids: Eerdmans, 1982.

Yee, Gale A, editor. *Judges & Method: New Approaches in Biblical Studies.* 2nd ed. Minneapolis: Fortress, 2007.

Zimmerli, Walther. *Ezekiel 1.* Translated by Ronald E. Clements. Hermeneia. Philadelphia: Fortress, 1979.

Index of Scripture

Index of Modern Authors

Index of Subjects

Index of Subjects